# the UNLIKELY FELON

*A Memoir of Ambition, Elder Care and Jail*

*W.C. YOUNG*

*Although the events in this book are true,*
*the names of some people and places have been changed to protect their privacy.*

ISBN: 9781667819471
Published through W.C. Young (William Young)
and printed by BookBaby Publishing.
*Printed in the United States of America*

**Unlikelyfelon.com**

*This book is dedicated to:*

The love of my life, Kay. Angel from God.

My incredible kids and amazing sister.

The best grandparents I could have ever wished for.

Caregivers throughout the world.

The people who supported us through our journey and transformation.

All those who are hungry for something more, yet who are fearful
of what might be or not be. Let this story move you, whether you see it
as right or wrong. Let it make you think, cry, laugh, and get angry.
But in the end, stand up for who you are and where you're going.
Most of all, know that you can survive anything and that there is
always another day, someone to help you, and a chance to change.
Don't ever give up.

Thank you, God.

# Contents

# Author's Note

This is a true story about three generations of my family. It's a book about love and the law, and in it I share my experience with family issues including adoption, suicide, elder care, dementia, and what it's like to be in the so-called "sandwich generation"—adults who are caring for aging parents (or in my case, grandparents) while also raising young children.

As the real-life events in this book unfolded, I took notes in a planner, and I journaled constantly, especially during the legal process. In the beginning, this was done to help me plan and to track time commitments. As the legal situation evolved, I continued to note events and recorded my thoughts. In the end, the words I wrote proved a lifeline to something meaningful, substantial. Everything in this book is real life—in all its beauty and pain.

I chose to write my story—our family's story—with love as my intention, and with details recorded to the best of my recollection. I didn't want the media's perception of this family saga to define our story because news outlets almost always have an agenda, and they report details accordingly.

The names and identifying details of most individuals and places I wrote about have been changed to protect their privacy. That is the only change. There are some conversations that I do not remember in complete detail. They have been recreated for readability, but they're based on the truth. My memories are individual and personal, and others may recall events and conversations differently than I did, which is an outcome I respect. However, this is my story, my nightmare, and my evolution. It is hard to believe it happened, but it did.

This book contains content about suicide and thoughts of suicide.
If you or someone you know is having suicidal thoughts,
contact the toll-free National Suicide Prevention Lifeline:
1-800-273-TALK, suicidepreventionlifeline.org

# Introduction

I n the early 1990s I was in college, and my good friend moved into my apartment. We'll call him Stu. We shared a small bedroom with two twin beds. His goal was to make the football team, and mine was to make the baseball team.

One day Stu was looking at the bulletin board on the wall above my small desk, which was crammed into a corner, and he asked me, "What's with all the three-by-five cards?" I told him they contained my goals for both the present and the future. He pulled down one of the white cards, looked at me with an odd smirk on his face. "Willy, this one says 'Change the world and become a billionaire—at any cost.'" He stared at me. "Really? At *any* cost? The billionaire thing is great, but..."

I still remember that moment, but now I think I should have written a card that said, "Try to avoid the legal system."

Many memoirs, especially those by a famous person, have little to no connection to your life. This one is different. It's about being in jail—not just figuratively but actually. It's about how I was a successful person living the American dream and then how everything I built for twenty years, including businesses, my reputation, and friendships crumbled in moments. You may have experienced the loss of a loved one, a business, or something incredibly important to you. You remember that sick feeling in the bottom of your stomach. Perhaps you have dreams about it and then wake up and realize it's just a dream. Mine was reality.

As a result, I appreciate the words of Auschwitz survivor Viktor Frankl more than ever before, not because I lived through anything close to the hell he experienced, but because I now understand his thoughts about his evolution. He wrote, "No man should judge unless he asks himself in absolute honesty whether in a similar situation he might not have done the same." Between stimulus and response there is a space. In that space is our power to choose our response. In our response lies our growth and our freedom."

I quote from the movie *The Shawshank Redemption* for three reasons: I love it, I've seen it nine or ten times, and I identify with the characters Andy and Red because they fought to hang on to their dignity, self-worth, and hope, even within a system that wanted to break their spirit and strip them of their humanity.

My grandparents were an invaluable part of my life. They were strong and helpful—until they weren't. Life changes, and we all become old. As I watched mine age, they taught me about taking pride in your life and your situation. They were courageous, elegant, and proud. Yet in the end, they would lose their balance at the drop of a hat, forget what they were trying to say, and often their faces showed how lost they felt. Each time their health deteriorated, I tried to learn more about the aging process. Cancer and heart attacks are usually a death knell for the aged, but the most common health issues for most elderly people are the more minor ones like osteoporosis, obesity, poor oral health, and substance abuse. Then you go up a level to shingles, respiratory disease, and diabetes, although many times these can be controlled with drug therapy or changes in lifestyle. I've learned that the greatest perils of aging are falling, influenza, and pneumonia, followed by Alzheimer's disease and depression. These last two are difficult because they make life so much harder for the elderly person experiencing the disease/s and for the caregiver in more ways than is imaginable.

Have you ever been a caregiver? Are you one right now? If not, give it time—you likely will be. Currently the statistics say you have about an 80 percent chance of becoming a caregiver. One of the heroes of this story is my wife, Kay, the most amazing caregiver the world has ever seen. As you read this book, you'll witness her evolution and how she and I became more and more connected as we faced the deaths of loved ones and then legal problems—though we were both scared out of our minds. How could anyone's marriage survive this tragedy?

By the end of this story, you will understand who Kay is and why she loves the way she does. I'm the closest thing to the villain of this story. Some of you reading this will be angry with me, while others will sympathize. Others might secretly enjoy watching a train wreck—and this is a train wreck. I hope this story makes you think, scares the hell out of some of you, and maybe challenges some of your deeper thoughts. Thank you for reading it. I'm very grateful. Get ready because the knock, knock is coming—the day that you will be called to meet a challenge that requires all your bravery and patience and your best, authentic self during the challenging times ahead.

# Prologue

## February 9, 2011

*"You always do what you want to do. This is true with every act.*
*You may say that you had to do something, or that you*
*were forced to, but, actually, whatever you do, you do by choice."*

— W. CLEMENT STONE

Intense pounding on the front door broke the early-morning silence. My wife, Kay, was already up dressed, and her red hair was pulled back in a ponytail. At five foot five, she's in great physical shape with beautiful facial features—like a combination of Jennifer Aniston and Kelly Preston. When Kay smiles, everybody smiles. Even wearing jeans, she looks more like a professional model than an exhausted mom. She headed toward the front door with our five-year old daughter in tow. I was lying on the couch in my grey hoodie and black athletic shorts trying to catch my breath after my intense morning treadmill run.

By the time Kay got to the door, the knocks were like drum accents. With one hand on the knob, she lifted the blinds on the adjacent window and peeked out. Then, in a calm voice, she turned to me and said, "It looks like the police are here."

I got up and started toward the door, thinking someone was hurt in the front yard or a dog had gone missing. As Kay slowly opened the door, I watched in horror as it burst open, sending her stumbling toward me. Someone's arm and knee popped into view, followed by a shoulder and body. Someone was invading our house! The intruder, a woman in a police jacket, rushed toward me, shouting "Don't move!" A posse of men and women in plain clothes followed her inside.

Instinctively, I grabbed Kay so she wouldn't get knocked over. "What the hell are you doing?" I shouted at the woman. "You have the wrong house!" The words shot out of my mouth at the same time my body surged forward like a firecracker had exploded behind me.

"I'm Detective Paula Starrett, and we have the right house." She glared at me. "Aren't you William?" She snapped her head toward Kay, "And you're Kay?"

We both answered "yes" in sync.

Starrett's dark hair was pulled back with a clip, and her black pants looked like winter jogging gear. She seemed dressed for a workout, not a police search. Her black eyes widened as she began shouting orders to her posse, and one of the three other officers positioned himself at my side and grabbed my arm.

Detective Starrett continued. "This is a search and we have a warrant." More officers entered the house—this time through the back door. To me, everything was moving in slow motion. While Starrett spoke, the officer who held me by my arm yanked it behind my back and guided me toward one of the living room corners. "Keep your hands behind your back and don't turn around!" he said. He and Starrett acted like they'd done this before.

Shocked, I did what he said. I'd seen a few episodes of *Cops* and saw how officers made mincemeat out of shirtless goons who resisted arrest. Just before I turned to face the wall, my eyes locked with Kay's. We exchanged no words, but in some telepathic, nonverbal way we both asked each other, "What did you *do*?"

In movies, we see the lives of people being turned upside down in an instant, but this kind of thing wasn't supposed to happen in real life. I will never forget that exact moment. It was February 9, 2011, at about 7:45 a.m. Most of the life I had built up to that moment died in that instant, but I didn't know it yet.

# CHAPTER 1

# The Judgment

## May 13, 2013

*"You're braver than you believe, stronger than you seem,*
*and smarter than you think."*

— CHRISTOPHER ROBIN TO WINNIE THE POOH

We all have days in our life we remember: the birth of a child, a wedding day, a graduation, the death of a close relative, that big twenty-first birthday. Most of these memories are positive. I'll always remember May 13, 2013, but it was *not* a good day. Kay and I arrived at the courthouse early for an event no one dreams could possibly happen to them: the sentencing phase of a criminal case. On this typical spring day in Colorado—with lots of sun and a slight chill in the air—the legal system would to pass judgment on us.

As we entered the courthouse, it felt like everyone was staring at us. It felt like someone had their hands around my throat and was pressing firmly—not aggressively, but enough to cause discomfort. I had felt this pressure since the day of the police search 25 months earlier.

When the county courthouse elevator opened its doors, we hurried in. With each passing floor, the pressure around my neck intensified. By the time the door opened on the fourth floor, I nearly fell to the ground trying to escape.

When Kay and I made our way around the corner to our assigned courtroom, I couldn't believe my eyes. Friends, family, and business associates were lined up on both sides of the hallway as far as I could see. There must have been 150 to 200 people with their faces showing either concern, sympathy, or love. Some displayed all three. The group included friends from high school and some from the business ventures we had been involved in. More than I could count were from nonprofits Kay and I had helped. Almost seventy were from the children's foundation we'd devoted eleven years of our lives to supporting.

There were numerous tight hugs and handshakes until my defense attorney, Jack, interrupted. He guided Kay and me into a small room near the courtroom entrance. Before court was called into session, he wanted us and Sharon, Kay's defense attorney, to have a quick meeting. "It's just the four of us, so let's make sure one last time that you're sure about your plea," Jack said. He handed each of us two pieces of paper stapled together. "Here are the documents you'll each sign."

I said, "This is it?"

"That's it."

I began to read, and suddenly Kay's lawyer became uncharacteristically emotional. With her eyes watering, Sharon blurted, "Today I celebrate thirty-five years of sobriety. Been a long road."

"Yes, that's great," I said, as if her great personal achievement could somehow make my pain go away. At that moment, I didn't give a shit about her monumental moment. Later I felt bad, but I was scared out of my mind. Just to be a smartass, I wanted to shout, "I've been sober for thirteen hours." But I didn't.

Sharon added, "I'm so sorry about today, but the guilty plea is your best move."

"It is, but it's hard to accept." Asking Sharon to go with us for a drink afterward seemed inappropriate.

The documents detailed the charge—theft—and our plea. By signing them, we were agreeing in writing to the case and the judge's upcoming decision. I held in the tears as best I could, but as usual they started to flow. Kay's tears were coming down too as she looked at me, waiting for me to sign. She so appropriately said, "Its okay Babe. This was for our family. Gram and Gramps know the truth about all of this. Somewhere, someway, somehow they are with us today, and they know we never stole from them." I placed the pen on the paper and signed my name, then Kay signed hers.

"I know."

Jack said and stood up and opened the door. "It's time."

"Wait!" I said. "Do you mind if I say a quick prayer?"

"Of course, go ahead."

I had found my spiritual self during the journey of the previous two years. This would be the second most intense prayer of my life—second only to the words I gave before each of my children were born. I asked—I begged—God to help us and to move the judge to leniency. "Amen."

Jack opened the courtroom door, and we followed him in. We headed down the middle of the room, passing row after row packed on both sides with family, friends, and the media. All the people in the hallway had made their way in. There wasn't an empty place to sit.

Bob Smith and his wife, Mary, sat directly behind the DA, along with their friend Cindy. It was a phone call from the Smiths' lawyer that had started the legal process that now brought us into this courtroom. I glanced their way, but Bob and Mary were looking away at the opposite wall, trying not to make eye contact with me. I'm sure they had mixed feelings. We had vacationed together. We were friends. Once we had been close, and I'd known them since I was a young boy because Mary was Gramps's daughter. Their attorney had called the police.

Kay and I and our lawyers took our places at the defendant's table. With shaky hands, I reached for the black-and-yellow water pitcher and poured the water into a small glass, nearly spilling it all over. Members of the media were in the second row behind the DA, scribbling away in their notepads. A *Denver Post* writer had used the term "stolen," to describe what Kay and I had done. We had not stolen anything. We had taken care of family members who needed care and used money we were told we could use.

It angered me to see the *9News* TV reporter there. When Kay's and my arrest was the lead story on the five o'clock news, the video showed all kinds of different logos flashing on the screen: Netflix, Frontier Airlines, Xcel Energy. They tried to characterize us as Ponzi schemers who jetted all over the country spending millions of dollars on luxury vacations while using my grandparents' money to pay our utility and video-streaming bills. That was never the case. We had barely survived emotionally or financially during awful times when we helped family members who were sick, unable to care for themselves, and dying. One news channel used the word *bilked* to describe my handling of my grandparents' estate. I never cheated or defrauded anyone. As far as I was concerned, I used my inheritance with permission to save our family.

After the judge entered, the district attorney, Kathy Cline, began her presentation. She went over the case, outlining the state's position. She covered the use of my grandparents' funds and which parts of the case she felt were legal and illegal.

When it was Jack's turn on the podium, he highlighted the hours of caregiving Kay and I did, our business achievements, our community service, and the many ways we supported our family. He finished by stating, "We estimate that Mr. and Mrs. Young did more than ten thousand hours of caregiving for their Gram and Gramps." Then he turned to the judge. "Your Honor, we ask for the minimum sentence in this case. You'll agree these are extenuating circumstances."

Next it was time for six people to speak on our behalf. We'd requested more than 150, including my friend Keith from college and Ben and Pat, who were fellow board members from the Denver Active 20-30 Children's Foundation. My sister, Sadie, spoke for both me and Kay.

Keith started by describing our twenty years of friendship and told the judge he trusted me with his life. Then Ben highlighted the way Kay and I had saved a local children's foundation from shutting down. Sadly, Pat decided not to present as he was intimidated by the media presence at the courthouse and the earlier negative media coverage of our story.

Next, Sharon called Toni, Celia, and Sadie to the podium. Toni had gone through a similar caregiving struggle with her mom and dad at the same assisted-living facility where my grandparents lived. Kay had known her for nearly twenty years. Celia was our neighbor and Kay's best friend, who watched in horror when the police searched our home. Celia got our kids out of the house and kept them safe during the chaotic day of the police search.

All three women described Kay's selflessness and emphasized her commitment to taking care of her mother during the last eight years of her life. In addition, Kay spent more than ten years caregiving for Gram and Gramps.

When they were finished, the judge turned to me and asked, "Mr. Young, would you like to make a statement?" I answered "yes."

Up to this moment, our day in court had been an emotional roller coaster, but my statement was mostly my attorney Jack's language. What *I* wanted to say was that this entire drama was bullshit. I wanted to explain that Kay and I had permission as my grandparents' executors to make decisions on their behalf. We had good intentions, but when our business was stolen from us, it started a rockslide with so much momentum that we had few choices. Even though I should have made so many better choices, I wanted to defend what we had done.

Jack knew what I wanted to say and how I wanted to say it—but he knew better. So, with my voice cracking, I read the statement he prepared, becoming more emotional with each word. I told the judge I made decisions to save our family and our business at the time. Some of those decisions were wrong and we were sorry for causing so much confusion and anger. As I look back now, there were at least five times when I could have changed what we were doing and the eventual outcome of those choices.

It was Kay's turn after I sat down. She talked about how much she had given to those around her and about her love for Gram and Gramps. She was authentic and inspiring. She truly loved Gram and Gramps more than words could ever express.

After we finished, the judge didn't say a word. He sat back in his chair and maintained his stoic facial expression while he thumbed through a pile of paperwork. Maybe one minute passed, but it felt like years. Then he cleared his throat and said, "Mr. and Mrs. Young, you have lots of support." He stopped and looked at the pile of documents. As he rubbed his chin, he continued, "I have lots of letters in my hands asking me to give you a reprieve. And I can see our courtroom is filled." He held up a handful of letters saying, "All these letters—over 200—point to your community work and all the people you've helped. You've been a rock in the community for so many. You've been a fixture and example for the local community by providing resources, sacrificing your time, and giving of both your time and money." His tone was soft and filled with empathy. "You could have written 'IOU' on checks and financial paperwork, and we wouldn't be here today. However, the law isn't always about intentions, it's about results. It's about words that define law. And in this case, the results are not good. The community expects more from people like you. I believe you both *intended* to take care of your grandparents. You *did* take exceptionally good care of your grandparents. That is not the issue. Your lack of transparency shows a lack of judgment. You were irresponsible, and you have to pay a price for that part."

I started to panic. The judge continued, "To put you in prison, I would need to take someone out. Our prisons are crowded with lots of bad people who intentionally hurt others and who made bad decisions."

I wasn't sure if the judge was scaring the rest of the people or making me understand what a fragile place I was in. His explanation covered the prison system, overcrowding issues, crime rates, and how bleak things looked for those caught in the system. Guilt or innocence takes a back seat to predication and public perception. Kay and I were now caught in that very system.

Our oldest daughter, Cali, began to sob uncontrollably. She sat directly behind me, and hearing her loud whimpers intensified my anxiety. Part of me wanted to turn around say, "Be quiet!" The other part wanted to stand up, reach over, and hug her. I wanted to tell her how sorry we were for giving her up for adoption as a baby twenty-six years before. I wanted to tell her how sad I was that Kay and I missed all her birthdays, graduations, and sports achievements. God, how do you give up your child? I thought.

My mind also leapt to how Jack was always hesitant about answering questions on prison, jail, and work release. Now I wondered, *Am I going to prison?*

Judge Monarch progressed into the sentencing. He put his glasses back on and looked over them, staring straight at Kay and me. "We have a civil society, and you should be commended. Every person in a helpless situation requires assistance, someone to prop up a pillow, lift them up, and get them necessities. The elderly need help and service. Thank God for people like the two of you who are willing to provide care, to help. You made sacrifices that others didn't."

He understands us, I thought.

Then the judge directed us to stand. My arms shook like someone with a fever as I pushed away from the table. I slid back my chair and stood as straight as I could. The room was so quiet I could hear the blood pumping through my arms, starting at the bottom of my head, flowing down my neck, into my arms, and then pumping back out again. I could hardly breathe, knowing that from this moment forward, nothing would ever be the same.

CHAPTER 2

# What Did You Do?

## 1979

*"I neither know nor think that I know."*

— SOCRATES

You've all met someone like the person I used to be. You might be married to him, have lived with him, partnered with him, raised him, loved him, or beat the crap out of him. If you're being kind you might use the words "overly confident," but if you're honest you'd say he was smug and cocky. For some, the word "intense" might come to mind.

You're probably familiar with the usual hard-knocks story: deadbeat parents, lack of interest in school, poverty. Teens who get sucked into drugs or booze or petty theft. A future full of menial jobs, addiction, jail, prison. I had many of these same challenges growing up, but that's not all of my story. At a young age I could see that the cards were stacked against me, and I decided I would change my destiny. I set my sites on becoming a bil-lionaire. With the help of amazing grandparents, I worked hard in school, launched successful entrepreneurial businesses, was heralded as a fund-raising guru, became educated, married a wonderful woman, and had four children and a great house in a nice, upscale neighborhood. And still I ended up on the wrong side of the law.

I grew up in a suburb north of Denver called Thornton, nicknamed "T" Town. I never was sure whether the "T" stood for "Thornton" or "trash." When I was young it was farmland mixed in with the new 1970s suburbia-development strategy of placing a small subdivision in the middle of vast, open land. The houses were boring, with similar colors and models. Bi-level next to ranch next to bi-level next to … You get the picture.

My mother, father, younger sister, and I lived in a 1,400-square-foot box of a house just south of 100th Avenue off of Detroit Street. Our backyard was a steep hill full of weeds, but luckily we lived next to a nice park. We had a one-car garage that was filled to the ceiling with junk. We moved there when I was seven, in 1978, and it was an upgrade from the 700-square-foot house we had two miles away. However, something went wrong when we moved. That same year my mom's father died of a brain aneuryism, and my dad started to lose interest in the family.

I was the stereotypical, lower middle-class white kid who was attempting to make it out of a low-income neighborhood. I spent most of my youth attempting to climb the success ladder in spite of the mass chaos around me. There were one or two kids in our school with significant financial resources, but most, like me, were trying to use education, sports, a unique talent (juggling for one kid), or some other means to escape. Ironically, despite my young ambitions, I was on a course that led to legal problems decades later.

A huge hurdle was dealing with my dysfunctional parents. My father was disconnected, and my mother suffered with mental illness. (Later in life she was diagnosed with bipolar disorder and mild schizophrenia.) Neither acted like an adult or grasped the fact that they were parents or that parenting required a certain level of maturity. They divorced when I was eleven, which was five years too late.

The years weren't all bad. Up until I was seven, we seemed like a normal family. My parents even gave me a nice train set that circled the Christmas tree in 1979, but most of my memories included one gigantic boondoggle after another. There was always drama in our house. I vividly remember Mom's sister knocking out Mom's tooth and pummeling her face, which required stitches.

My sister, Sadie, did her best to act normal. She was a picky eater, cried at the drop of a hat, fell instantly asleep when any motor vehicle started moving, and played with any kind of toy we had in the house. Like most big brothers, I can remember tormenting her sometimes. I can still hear my grandparents saying, "Now Willy, leave your sister alone," while she screamed at the top of her lungs. But most important, Sadie was my pal for life—loving, giving—and she always had my back.

My childhood taught me all the ways to *not* be a good parent. Our saga included one parent, usually Dad, living with us at the house while the other moved into an apartment—or, in my mother's case, sometimes moving in with another guy. Then our parents would switch places. Mostly they didn't give a crap about us. They would hit me and Sadie, but I guess most of their generation spanked and hit. It was close to abuse, but not violent. It was the emotional negligence that is still raw, even now.

By 1979, when I was eight years old, Sadie and I started spending weekends at the house of my paternal grandparents, Helen and Frank Higgins. In their early sixties, Gram and Gramps were young for their age and could match our juvenile energy. If they were tired, they never showed it.

Gram was tall for a woman born in 1917, and her color-treated auburn hair looked like umber tan had been mixed in with an autumn red, topped by a maroon overlay. Gramps looked like he was cut from a 1950s-era JC Penney advertisement. Well groomed with short hair, he was always clean shaven, and his soft eyes seemed constantly watery.

Most Friday and Saturday nights were spent in my grandparents' basement at a ten-foot round table. Its surface was a radiant red that you don't typically see in today's furniture stores. We played board games like Candy Land and Gramps's favorite, Chinese Checkers. I remember the sound of Gram's giggle as she would try to hit the right Simon Says color button when it flashed, and I can still see Sadie's angry glare when I would win another match of Connect Four.

A TV in the corner next to the wood fireplace was usually showing PBS classics like *The Lawrence Welk Show* or maybe some boring kid's© VHS movie. For obvious reasons I preferred to watch *Private School* starring Phoebe Cates or *The Blue Lagoon* with Brooke Shields, but Gram limited us to wholesome Disney films like *The Apple Dumpling Gang*.

That red table doubled as a game center/psychiatrist's couch. Weekends were filled with deep conversations between the four of us while our parents were off doing God knows what. Gram and Gramps had this incredible way of getting us to open up. We didn't really notice because we were having fun while they asked us questions about all types of subjects. Sadie and I talked. Gram and Gramps listened. I mean *really* listened. They made eye contact and used follow-up questions. This was the opposite of being at home. Our parents spoke *at* us, if they spoke at all, and not with us. They usually ignored us kids.

Gram was always good to us. I'm sure I was difficult to raise, yet she kept pushing me to accomplish big goals, and she loved me unconditionally. "Willy, you're as good as it gets," she would say. I wondered if she had angel wings or a superhero cape. She was also very generous. I didn't know until later in life that she had purchased most of my parents' belongings during my youth: cars, appliances, furniture. She cosigned for my parents' first house. Later in life I learned that the amount of money Gram gave my parents was significant. In addition, she and Gramps provided financial support to me and Sadie in the form of sports equipment, school supplies, and small stipends during college.

Gram ran the show, directing the whole family like a Broadway producer. She was tough on my mom and dad, but they never did much to make her proud. She didn't like my mom and told people that she wasn't good enough for my dad. I'm sure that devasted my mother and helped send the marriage spiraling. Gram also micromanaged Dad, constantly telling him what to do and how to do it. He responded with anger. It was a formula for disaster. He never really grew up, often acting like a rebellious teen, even as a fifty-year-old man.

Always straightforward, Gram offered well-intended words of advice that sometimes came across as hurtful. I'm sure her personal philosophy was "What doesn't kill you—or entirely destroy your self-esteem—makes you stronger."

In the mid-eighties when I was a teenager, Gram seemed like a drill sergeant, and we argued because I thought I knew it all. She would simply look me in the eyes like she was reading my soul and put me in my proper place.

It was obvious if Gram liked you or if she didn't. You knew where you stood, which was important because she had a loud bark. Although I never saw her bite anyone, rumors floated around. She had a way of making me laugh. I would start a conversation with "Hey Gram" and then ask her a question. She'd respond with a grin and ask, "What did you *do*?"

Gram had a great sense of humor and was a good teaser. But her catch phrase, "What did you *do*?" foreshadowed the future. The Will I grew up to be was overly ambitious, and at a young age I stopped bothering to dot the i's and cross the t's. I went to jail, not because I had a criminal mind but because I made poor decisions. I figured my altruism excused my cutting corners, and I assumed everyone would see my motives as selfless. I became like Gram running the show: making unilateral decisions, supporting the family financially, and making my own family my number-one responsibility the way she made Sadie and me number one.

If Gram was the pusher, then Gramps was the embracer. He chose to talk softly rather than yell. My parents liked to yell and, at times, push.

Gramps would smile and you'd smile back. He lowered his voice and spoke to you with respect. Occasionally, he would give you a scary, angry look, but the smile was coming soon after. You knew he meant business, but it was always done with love, not pain or anger. He grabbed your hand softly so you didn't notice that his fingers were calloused from years of hard work.

Gramps often wore a bespoke jacket and a black-banded grey fedora. He could look as natural in a tuxedo as he did in overalls. He was so clean and organized it made you feel like a bum. As a WWII veteran who lived through the Great Depression, Gramps lived by the Golden Rule with a deep empathy for others and unwavering pride in his country. Family was his number-one responsibility.

Gram and Gramps were strong, healthy, and incredible role models. They, not my parents, steered me along a path to becoming a decent human being—although watching my parents put off important decisions or make bad choices must have influenced me. They were careless, and I became careless. I'm sure I overcompensated for their shortcomings as parents by overachieving and trying to be a "superhero" grandson. The end justified the means—no matter what I had to do. I *had* to win. My impoverished childhood started the process of my overvaluing material objects. I wish I'd had a crystal ball back then to help me avoid all the future trauma that was coming my way. Maybe I could have changed.

# CHAPTER 3

# Are You Ready to Become a Teen Parent?

## 1987

*"One's philosophy is not best expressed in words;*
*it is expressed in the choices one makes—and the choices*
*we make are ultimately our responsibility."*

— ELEANOR ROOSEVELT

After great weekends with the grandparents, Mondays were business as usual. By the early eighties, my parents had not filed divorce papers, but the marriage was over. Together they were confrontational and anxious, but apart it seemed to work. They both had so many personal problems, parenting was definitely an afterthought. Though their confrontations were mostly emotionally abusive, the fights got physical from time to time. They would scream at each other, and when a wrestling match broke out, I'd jump in and referee. One of my mother's favorite hobbies was calling the local police so they would come provide her with therapy. The reason for calling the cops could be something as innocent and silly as me coming home fifteen minutes late. The police came. They helped. They pretended like they listened and cared. It didn't cost her a dime. "Bye Willy," they would say to me, smiling like they knew they'd be back.

My parents lacked motivation and desire. They never made much money, and they didn't try to start a business or pursue any worthwhile dream. The idea of obtaining further education was never at top of the list, for my mother in particular. My dad, on the other hand, had more degrees than socks, yet he was unemployed half of his life.

Self-improvement and volunteering in the community were seen as a waste of time. My parents were more interested in partying and watching TV, and they rarely left the house except to go to a bar. My mom loved the CBS Friday-night lineup of *The Dukes of Hazzard* and *Dallas*. On Saturday nights ABC aired *The Love Boat* and *Fantasy Island*, her all-time favorite show, which figures since she was in a state of nonreality most of the time. Her favorite dump-bar hangouts were The Mayflower and Fosters. Both places were bulldozed in the early 2000s.

Neither of them had any interest in developing a better life. My dad, a member of Mensa, was over-the-top smart. After he died, I found a copy of the book *The Power of Positive Thinking* by Norman Vincent Peale in my dad's belongings. I'm not sure how much of it he read because he never seemed motivated. Gram probably gave him the book to try to light a fire under him.

Their parenting skills were greatly lacking. My dad was my scout leader for one year before losing interest, and they made it to a few basketball and baseball games here and there. My mom showed up at my senior after-prom party and created a spectacle. Kay and I walked in and there she was, buzzed and talking to all the kids as if she were a student. She hadn't shown up at any school events in years, so she definitely wasn't on the chaperone list. From the reactions of my friends and the chaperones, I knew they were uncomfortable with a parent who was acting like an immature kid. It was like she was trapped emotionally at fifteen years of age. Maybe she was begging me for forgiveness by showing up at this last passage of youth, but it came off more like a prank than an act of apology. Embarrassed, Kay and I quickly left.

After my Dad's death years later, I found his writings, artwork, and other personal projects, which showed he had incredible talent. I never knew about any of that, and he never shared his interests with me. I just always wondered why the hell my parents were wasting their lives.

When it was Dad's turn at home with us, I remember him in the basement listening to music, pretending to be a Jedi Knight while smoking pot from a homemade pot pipe made from a wine bottle and plastic tubing. He made loud swooshing sounds like he was using a Jedi lightsaber to kill a wampa ice creature.

My mom's idea of a "taking care" of me and my sister was binge-watching TV or talking on the phone for hours to one of her three childhood friends. If she prepared dinner—which was seldom—it was overcooked, unhealthy, and tasted lousy. We often ate hamburgers cooked until they were hard as hocky pucks. Afterward, dirty dishes piled up in the sink.

I'm not sure either Mom or Dad ever had real jobs. They just seemed to exist, and Gram was their only consistent money source. Dad would start looking for a job once the unemployment pay ran out. Mom seemed to be laid off every six to twelve months—at least that's what she told me. Both my parents were so lost in their own bullshit that I doubted they would notice if I left for a few days.

Mom spent most of her free time barhopping. Several times when I was a teenager, I suggested she could have earned several college degrees in the time she spent at local dives. Her usual excuse was, "Your father got to finish college and I didn't because I helped him. That's why we're in bad financial shape." I argued she could have become a doctor or lawyer in the years she wasted, and our financial problems would be solved, but she ignored that logic. Looking back, I think how she could have started a business or helped at a nonprofit.

My mom was famous for financial problems, and when the utilities were shut off, her creative answer was always, "Oh, they're doing work again in the neighborhood." Until I was an adult, I thought utility workers were buffoons because our electricity was off so often.

The funny thing about living through rough, uncertain situations is you learn important life skills. My parents were so lame that Sadie and I were forced to be self-sufficient and independent. In other words, we had to figure shit out on our own. Back then, I cursed Mom and Dad for that. Now, I thank them for the experience.

The main thing I figured out as a result of my nonfunctional parents was that I wasn't going to settle for being poor. I also vowed not to become a broke, deadbeat, absentee parent like Mom and Dad. For me, family would always come first. I'd make sure my eventual wife and kids would have just about anything their hearts desired.

I had big dreams. I wanted people to know I mattered, and I was driven to achieve wealth at any cost. Whether I played professional sports—maybe second base for the Chicago Cubs?—or started the next Microsoft, I was going to have a "real" career that gave me money and power. In his book, *Think and Grow Rich*, self-help author Napoleon Hill called it a "burning desire." I had drive *and* desire, which was way more than a burning desire. It was like pouring gasoline on a fire and then throwing in a dynamite stick. While my parents wanted to get high, I wanted to have more money than I knew what to do with. In addition, I wanted to change the world.

• • •

The bright part of my adolescence was that I met Kay when we were just thirteen. I was shy, thin, small, and awkward. She was gorgeous, and her flowing hair was dark red, like crimson and fire with streaks of strawberry blonde and Havana brown. More mature than most girls her age, she looked closer to twenty-five than thirteen. You don't see beautiful girls like this in real life, especially not in eighth grade. She could have been Molly Ringwald in the eighties© movie *Sixteen Candles*. At that age, the only thing going through my mind—besides Madonna's "Crazy for You"—was thinking it would be great to be six inches taller.

On our first date, as we walked home, I positioned myself on the curb while Kay stood in the street gutter so that we appeared to be closer in height. She leaned in and kissed me. My lips just sat there while she pressed her lips to mine. At that moment I fell in love. No, I fell *madly* in love.

Kay was smart, athletic, and non pretentious—as if she didn't know her own incredible appeal. She would become my cornerstone, my therapist, my angel from heaven, and my soul mate.

In our first year of high school, we spent every free moment together, usually playing sports, babysitting my sister, finishing homework, or having sex. We're talking *lots* of sex, which often happens when latchkey kids are unsupervised after school. Sex is powerful and has consequences, especially unprotected sex. So, during Christmas vacation in 1986, my short-term future was set. It's hard to explain, but within a second after completing our lovemaking, my future life passed in front of me. The vision or feeling was like bits and pieces of images shooting in and out of my mind. It only lasted a few seconds, but it scared the hell out of me. Kay would later say she had the exact same type of vision pass through her mind: seeing the next twenty years in an instant. Neither of us mentioned it at the time nor could we describe what we saw, but we both felt it. Something important and major had taken place, and either we had changed destiny or fulfilled it. Don't get me wrong—I was no helpless victim. What fourteen-year-old boy wouldn't give his left leg to have a drop-dead, gorgeous redhead talk to him, let alone touch him?

As our sophomore year progressed, we were enjoying the success of good grades, participating in sports, and spending time away from our crazy families. Kay excelled at basketball, playing on the varsity girls' team as a freshman. But then a new reality started to set in after the crazy sexual experience: Kay was pregnant, and we had some huge decisions to make.

Instead, we froze and did nothing. By May 1987, Kay's stomach was getting big. Neither her baggy sweatshirt nor her one-size-fits-all combo of a knit skirt and top paired with a thick undershirt could hide the pregnancy any longer. Even the "bitchin'" shoulder-padded shirts paired with stirrup pants—which accentuated a woman's shoulders and made her look broader on top—were no longer getting it done. The wide shoulders could no longer distract from Kay's widening hips. People started asking why she'd gained so much weight, so we decided it was time to go to the doctor after almost four months of denial.

Kay scheduled an appointment and had one of her friends drive her. We knew exactly what was happening—how else do you explain no menstrual period for several months accompanied by horrible nausea and vomiting? The little flutters she felt inside seemed like an alien had crawled into her belly. Although I'd heard of girls hiding entire pregnancies, there was no way we were going to hide this baby for five more months. The goal of the doctor's appointment went beyond confirming several positive home-pregnancy tests; it was to end the pregnancy.

When Kay got home, she called me. Part of me was excited, but the rest of me was in bitter turmoil. "How did it go babe?" I asked.

She was crying. "It didn't go."

My voice raised as I started to hyperventilate. I grabbed each side of my head with my hands and clinched my jaw, saying "What do you mean?"

"I'm too far along for an abortion." Her voice crackled as she started to cry.

"*What?*"

Kay choked up. "The doctor had me on the table and then got upset when he realized how far along the pregnancy was."

"How far along did they think?"

"As I suspected, almost five months." She took a deep breath and continued, "But I'm relieved. I couldn't have done it anyways."

"Yeah, I knew you couldn't."

"Too scary. Oh God …" Her voice trembled. "What will we do?"

I paused for a while, not sure whether to cry, scream, or throw the phone at the wall. The sick feeling that started in my stomach felt like it was going down my legs and then up to my neck. It was like drowning on dry land. "I don't know," I said.

"I can't tell my parents. And you can't tell your mom."

"Oh God, if I tell my mom, you know what a dramatic shit-show that will turn into. She'll have a temper tantrum, play the victim, maybe even threaten to kill herself."

"I know. Let's try to figure this out soon." She sighed. "But I don't know what to do right now."

Later in life, my disappointment at learning the abortion wasn't possible turned to gratitude. In fact, it turns out that day was one of the best of my life. Thank God the doctor couldn't do the procedure. The doctor didn't just save a baby, he saved all of us, and he saved me—at least for a while.

Kay's pregnancy happened during a time when schools didn't have onsite nurseries and few people accepted the reality of teenage pregnancies. Ashamed, we worried we would be ostracized, that we were failures. As the next few weeks passed by, we continued our denial, doing our best to hide Kay's appearance and avoiding conversations about it.

Then one day after school, Kay called me, panicked. "She knows!"

"What?" I quickly went from sitting down to standing. Nervously, I started to pace.

"Mom found the doctor's paperwork in my bag. She and my dad want your mom and dad to come over to our house tonight."

"They want to *meet*? Where? Which house?" I was dumbfounded.

"Your mom, dad, whoever. My parents are acting crazy."

"Oh shit! Oh my God!" I dropped to the floor on my knees as if I were praying. I don't know what Kay said before we hung up, but I hyperventilated and thought about taking my own life. How was I going to become a billionaire if I had to raise a child when I was a teenager? I would have to tell my family that I was going to be a father. I would have to tell my mentally ill mother.

My sister arrived home from school a short time later and walked into the front room. She looked up at me, and I stared down at her. "What's wrong?" she asked.

I couldn't speak. Sadie knew. She knew how I was wired and that something had been wrong with Kay and me for a while. Not many words were required, but I shook as I began to tell her, and I felt my knees buckling. My throat tightened, and the words erupted from my mouth: "Kay is … She's pregnant!"

"Oh God," said Sadie. "Are you sure?" Her eyes filled with tears as she held on to me. This little girl, barely eleven years old, was so strong. We just stood there and held onto each other as tightly as humanly possible.

"I have to tell Mom."

"No! That's *not* good," said Sadie. "Is there anything else we can do?"

"But I have to! Kay's parents, Ed and Lena, want to meet with Mom and Dad tonight. I'm not sure how Mom will react. And I have to call Dad too."

We both knew what was coming. Sadie said, "Mom will act like she does with everything else. She'll be out of control, screaming, crying, and making it all about herself. She'll be in her glory, acting in front of her audience. She loves this drama." She sighed. "What about telling Gram and Gramps?"

"Oh God, I couldn't. They would be so disappointed in me."

I didn't tell my grandparents this one secret of my life until three years before Gramp's death.

• • •

Two days later, the meeting with Kay's parents and my parents was about as comfortable as having surgery without anesthesia. I had not seen my dad in several months, but he showed up. Kay's mom yelled at her, acting more concerned about her maternal reputation than the future of the baby. My mom wanted Kay to get an abortion, which did not go over well with Kay's parents. And, Kay's dad stared me down the entire time. If you could kill someone with your stare, then he would have killed me. It looked like his head was going to explode from the top at any moment. Kay's mom was set on the baby being "their" problem and not my family's. And "they" had a solution: Kay would go to Florida, where they knew a couple that would adopt the baby.

Our baby arrived in early October 1987, thirty-six days past the due date. The separation from the infant girl was awful for Kay, who told me over the phone she felt disgusted and depressed. She suffered from intense postpartum depression, and after a month of moping around, her mother decided the best cure for her emotions was to try to get the baby back.

• • •

"Are you ready to answer our questions?" The voice of the attorney in Florida was harsh as she began my phone deposition, which included Kay; Diane Clayman, the adoptive mother; and the judge in the adoption lawsuit. It was May 15, 1988, and the only phone connections we had in our house were in Mom's bedroom and the kitchen—so I had chosen the bedroom. It was cold, and the sun was almost gone as the early-evening sunset turned the sky pink. I sat on the edge of the bed, moving my head back and forth. I was a basket case—more nervous than any time in my life. I was moving between looking at the ceiling and the floor and then staring at the green, push-button wall phone. Whenever I think back on this day, I realize it was a watershed moment for me. At sixteen years old, how good a parent could I have been? A teenage brain is not mature enough to handle this type of adult situation.

The judge in Florida had issued an emergency hearing regarding custody. The lawyer continued, "When did Kay decide she didn't want to give up the baby?"

I wanted to throw up, but found the strength to answer by saying, "I'm not exactly sure."

"Did she tell you she wanted to keep the baby?"

"Yes."

"When?"

"I'm not remembering exactly."

"Is one of you lying?" she asked.

The next thirty minutes were filled with questions fired at me as if I were the target at a shooting range. I didn't want to hurt Kay, but I wanted the baby issue to go away. I wasn't ready to be a father. I wasn't old enough to drive, let alone take care of a small being. I didn't want my dreams to die. I'm sure the thought of raising a baby at sixteen was filtering my answers. I was scared to death, and I kept praying and closing my eyes in between deep breaths.

The attorneys bickered over legal mumbo-jumbo, which gave me a short break. As the deposition continued, I was becoming nauseous. I kept evaluating whether I was doing well or screwing this up for Kay.

The lawyer began again. "Kay stayed with Diane and Robert Clayman, who are the baby's adoptive parents, in Florida—is that right?"

"Yes."

"For almost five months?"

"That sounds right."

"What did she do there?"

"She stayed at their home and helped with housework and chores. Her and Diane became great friends. She read books, and she said she drove around in an old, beat-up, red Toyota truck Robert let her use."

"Did Kay work or go to school?"

"No."

"Did you see her?"

"I didn't."

"Did you call her?"

"Not as much as I should have."

"What do you mean?"

"I was upset and disappointed about the whole thing."

"Whole thing?"

"The pregnancy, having a child as a teenager. It's embarrassing. I wanted the whole thing to go away."

"Was Kay free to come and go from the house as she pleased?"

"What do you mean?"

"Was she being held there against her will by the Claymans?"

"No."

"So, did she agree to give the baby to the Claymans?"

"Yes, but now she wants her—the baby—back."

"What do you mean *now*?"

"Well, I mean Kay always wanted her."

"Wanted her then or now, Mr. Young? There's a big difference. Which one is it?"

"I'm trying to say …"

"What are you saying? Just say it. Did *you* want to keep the baby?"

I thought, *God no I didn't want the child.* I would have jumped through the window at that moment, if the act would have made this situation go way.

"Mr. Young!" There was a pause "Mr. Young, are you there? Let me say it again because you're not answering the question! Did *you* want her?"

I didn't answer.

"Okay, you're not going to answer. We'll get back to that. What about the financial demands of keeping a child?"

"Oh. I'm sorry. Yes, we can manage. We can take care of a baby."

"Financially you can?"

"Oh, yeah. Uhh, well, I'm not sure. I'll have to get a job."

"Without a high school diploma or college degree? What kind of job can you get?"

"I have always found a way."

"What kind of future will this child have? Where will you live? Will you get married?"

"I'll be finishing high school and I have had a job in the summers working for Adams County Park and Recreation. I'm not sure yet where we will live …"

The lawyer interrupted me, adding insult to injury. "And with your mentally challenged mother and dysfunctional family life, what kind of home will that be for a child?"

"Probably not good."

As we ended the deposition, the judge said, "I'll make my decision by next week. Thank you, Mr. Young."

I sat there holding the phone as the dial tone blared, and I knew I hadn't done a good job for Kay. She wanted to keep the baby, but I wanted to run away as far as I could go.

The next morning the phone rang. When I answered no one was on the line. After the phone rang a second time, I said hello again. This time I heard crying, and Kay said, "Wait."

I asked if she was okay. She kept crying, so I just stood there listening. She calmed down enough to tell me the judge had ruled against us. It was no surprise to me. Our baby was gone.

When Kay returned to school the next week, I continued treating her like a stranger—the way I had since the moment she left for Florida months ago. Dating other girls numbed the pain for a little while, but then the guilt would set in and I'd feel like shit. I felt like I had hijacked the adoption process because in my mind I would have been a shitty parent like my parents.

While Kay was going through hell in Florida, I acted like a jerk. And now, even though she was back, I was still treating her horribly and trying to forget the entire situation ever happened.

Kay was brave and started dating other people. She came to me at the beginning of 1988 and said she had found a guy she really liked but she was giving me one last chance to get back together with her. I actually made a good decision and agreed to have us try to build a new relationship.

# CHAPTER 4

# What Were Your Intentions?

1990

*"Most of the evil in this world is done*
*by and through 'good' intentions."*

— AYN RAND

My early years in Thornton, Colorado, seemed more like a prison term than a childhood. Thornton had lots of good people, but the culture was more about surviving than thriving. I graduated in the top 10 percent of my high school class, was a Hall of Fame inductee (all-conference in three sports), and headed to Colorado State University after passing up on a few Division III offers to play three college sports. At CSU, I was president of my college business fraternity for two years, I attempted to play on the baseball team, and I graduated with a business degree.

None of this would have been possible if Gram and Gramps hadn't given me a foundation that was missing from my parents. During college I started to realize how much my grandparents had been teaching me, especially in terms of values, and I started to listen more. I was growing closer to them, and I was learning who they really were.

Gram grew up in a large Mormon family in Utah. Her upbringing instilled a strong foundation in Christian values, and even though she left the Mormon Church at age nineteen to become a Methodist, she maintained her Mormon ties and friendships throughout her life. She held on to her childhood faith and demonstrated her commitment to God and others.

In 1936 she married a mining engineer named William Young, my namesake. They spent the next five years in mining camps throughout the western US. Later, she nursed returning WWII veterans, helped injured miners in the Utah mining camps, and led almost every church organization she joined. If you were brought up by parents or grandparents who lived through the Depression, you understand the impact of those difficult times on their dispositions. Like many of that generation, Gram put up a tough front, projecting a positive, simple, loving philosophy. Where others saw irritability and impatience in her, I started to see sweetness and strength. She helped her family make ends meet when she was a teenager by working odd jobs, and she wore the same clothes day after day because she couldn't afford a closet full of dresses. She watched her baby sister die in a tragic accident. She never would tell me what exactly happened or what type of accident it was, but I could tell the feelings were still raw. None of these hardships got to her, and she was a pro at compartmentalizing her emotions.

Gram raised my dad by herself after her first husband, William Young, died. Dad was fifteen. Her center was the church, regardless of denomination. "Will, all of us are God's people," she would tell me. "We all need a shoulder to cry on from time to time and a positive word to uplift us at our moments of weakness. Never turn your back on God. Keep him close and know, listen, and believe."

Later, during my journey through the hell of the trial, remembering Gram's honest and direct words connected me to my faith in my darkest hours. I recalled conversations that meant nothing when I was a kid, but they were my lifeline when I was an adult.

Gram's strong personality helped make her exceptional in an era when women didn't speak out. She could be harsh and critical, yet she provided unconditional support and prayed for everyone. She taught me that helping others was more important than anything else.

Gram always made me feel like Superman. I was the shortest player on the basketball court and the littlest guy on the baseball field. In school I was known as the odd kid with challenging parents. But Gram encouraged me. She'd tell me, "Willy, you're the best, and there's nothing you can't do. Don't ever let anyone tell you that you can't do something." I say these same words to my kids every night when I put them to bed.

Gram made an incredible difference in the lives of those close to her and in her local community. She championed those who needed defending; she sobbed and offered condolences for other people's tragedies. And she was very generous. She made sure you never left her house empty handed, even if all she had to give you was a handful of stale candy corn, a discolored vase with a small crack, or—my personal favorite—moldy banana bread. She often gifted me with an out-of-date calendar, which I'd hang in my bedroom to remind me of the importance of giving.

Gram was an example to my sister and me, showing us the importance of intentions. She taught us intent is not only nine-tenths of the law but nine-tenths of your actions. When things went wrong, she would ask the simple question, "What were your intentions?" I always took her words to heart and strived to live my life with good intentions.

While Gram emphasized personal values, Gramps was all about hard work and discipline. Even though he was Gram's third husband, he acted like her first. He'd worked for a nickel an hour as a youth, so when adversity struck, he believed in picking yourself up by the bootstraps and moving forward. His advice was short and often unorthodox, but spot on. Before my first job he advised, "If you have nothing else to do at work, grab a broom and start sweeping." He wanted me to keep moving, stay busy, and not goof around. He continued, "If all you can do is hold the broom, then just stand there holding onto it. If you've already swept one area, then do it again. If you have to go to the bathroom, take the broom with you." I chuckled at this. He didn't.

Growing up on a farm in Wiggins, Colorado, Gramps learned to do a lot with a little. He helped raise his little brother and didn't stop watching over him until his brother's death at age ninety. I remember many stories about his farm life, and in old age, growing things in the garden was Gramps's passion. He had learned the physical skills, but the stories and lessons were his legacy.

One memorable experience with him made a big impact on me. It was his explanation of a compost pit and then taking me out back to finish building one. We placed one red brick on top of another and then put one shovel of manure inside the rectangular formation. As the bricks mounted, we ended up with a strange-looking structure. The walls were about four feet high and fifteen-by-fifteen feet square. It smelled like nasty shit when we were done, but later in life I realized the underlying message he was getting across. His lesson wasn't about engineering, but rather about your own feeling of personal self-worth and how to treat the earth and your fellow man the same: with kindness. He was showing me the importance of finishing a job and fulfilling your commitment. This was his chance to stress simple principles like always recycle, appreciate the environment, live within your means, and remember that material things aren't as important as the earth. I may not have gotten all his messages, but I never forgot the compost pit.

Though our politics, religious beliefs, and life expectations often weren't the same, Gramps's soul rubbed off on me. He had a saying that could make Sadie and me laugh even when we were crying or pouting:

"Those who love you love to see you smile.

Smiling comes so easy that frowning's not worthwhile.

So smile, Smile, Smile, SMILE!"

He repeated the word "smile" until we not only smiled but laughed. I never knew where this saying came from or why it had such a profound effect, but the way Gramps said it worked every time. It was the best medicine a child could ever receive.

Gramps's generation stopped the Nazis, founded the suburbs, and created real prosperity. He demonstrated amazing strength and a special faith in God. He lived by example rather than just words. He was trustworthy, caring, helpful, and chivalrous. He was a throwback to an era when men opened car doors for women, were mannerly, and respected authority and elders. He had set the bar so high I felt there was no coming close, but I wanted to try.

The way Gramps treated Gram was a great example of love for me. He always let Gram do and say whatever she wanted. Even when she was harsh, he knew she was looking out for his health and best interest. But he also knew she needed to feel in control. Her intent was always good, even if her delivery was awful. And seeing his soft smile and partial grin seemed to calm her and make the world right again for that split second.

Even though Gram drove Gramps nuts with her directives—"Dad get this," "Dad do that," "Dad, where *are* you?" "Dad, what are you *doing*?"—he never snapped back, not even when these barked commands came while his hands were full of tools or he had a pitchfork buried deep into the garden soil. I swear you could hear Gram's loud "Dad" call from miles away. Dogs in nearby counties must have covered their ears. Gramps's knee-jerk reaction of a grimace and a frown would shift as he walked into the house, grabbed the glass of lemonade or iced tea out of Gram's hand, gave her a soft kiss, and said "Thank you, my dear." I'm sure he wasn't thirsty, because no more than fifteen to thirty minutes had gone by since the last glass. But he acted like that beverage was the perfect thing. "That's the best drink, honey," he would say. He knew what real love was and how to show it.

There were also the moments when Gram assumed Gramps could read her mind or that he did something her way because it was the "correct/right way." Her comments usually went something like this: "Dad, why aren't you at the park with the kids? The weather is fantastic!" Or "Dad, when are you going to take the kids to the store?" I still remember the indescribable look he gave her as she dictated directions. If it were me, I would have said, "What the hell, dipshit? I should have read your god-damn mind!" Or, when he was already on his way to the store with us, I would have said, "No shit, Sherlock. Where do you think I was going?" But Gramps never said a mean word; he simply gave a quiet growl and a half-grin.

He loved Gram in a special way and allowed her to micromanage him. She acted like a five-star general, and he played the pleasant lieutenant who cleaned up after she dropped psychological bombs or offered support to an unlucky person she insulted. He showed respect and restraint in sit-uations when another man might have used swear words or a fist. And Gramps did all this while carrying her purse! It was large and filled with useless junk, and it got bigger as she got older. His back probably ached from carrying that huge purse; I know mine hurt from watching him. But still he adored her.

Gram was his second wife, and he was her third husband, but it was as if they'd been together forever. They met in church. As Gram described it: "I waited a few days until the body was cold to take action," referring to the death of Gramps's first wife. Apparently, Gram had her eye on him long before his first wife's passing. She always said this in a joking spirit, but knowing Gram, it was true.

My grandparents' relationship was built on a mutual love of God. The Lord was always first in their household, and their church commit-ments took up most of their time. They saw their faith in God as a foun-dation for supporting the community, and they modeled good behavior for their families and friends, proving their faith in action rather than just words. Their view of God came from their individual perspectives, over time. When they made a promise, they kept it, and when you made one to them, you were expected to keep yours.

Years later, when Gram's and Gramps's health was deteriorating, I didn't forget my allegiance to them or the debt I owed them for raising me to become a strong and decent person, a caring man, and a loving husband and father. I was committed to keeping the promises I had made to them, and I made that commitment a priority. I had every intention of fulfilling my role as a compassionate grandson and executor of their estate. The trouble was that I made silly assumptions, didn't pay attention to details, and let some important stuff fall between the cracks. I was sometimes reckless, and other times my head was caught in the clouds, dreaming about becoming successful and rich.

# CHAPTER 5

# Do You Want to Get Filthy Rich?

**1995**

*"We grow spiritually much more
by doing it wrong than doing it right."*

— RICHARD ROHR

A fter graduating from college in 1995, I started to think more about my future. Gram and Gramps had helped mold me into something. I didn't know what yet, but something. Although I copied Jason Priestley's *Beverly Hills, 90210* TV-show hairstyle—with classic sideburns and curly hairline—before mine started to recede—I wanted to be more and achieve more. I wanted to be wealthy. Rich. Make that filthy rich. My motto was always fake it until you eventually make it. And I did. Well, I did for a little while. No Oscars, Emmys, or Super Bowl rings yet, but you get the picture.

By August of 1995, Kay and I had completed an eight-year journey that started with giving up a child for adoption and ended with us becoming husband and wife. We bought a townhome and started our life together. My mom was on her third marriage; the second one to a great guy had fallen apart. While Mom was on the marriage carousel, Dad married a women ten years his junior. They ended up having two boys, but later their marriage was a disaster.

Kay had a great job managing a local men's formalwear store while I did business development for a temporary-personnel agency. We were doing what every young couple strives to do: build a successful life. But three months after taking our vows, an event made a significant impact on me in ways I never dreamed could happen.

Kay and I were at the MGM Grand in Las Vegas for a two-day workshop called "Journey Beyond Perception." It was a super-hyped 1990s training session for Equinox International's multilevel-marketing business format—otherwise known as a "pyramid scheme." It was created to help us attendees develop our visions and goals and to let our dreams run crazy and loose. Unfortunately, I had a miserable cold the entire time.

Spotlights hit the stage, and music burst out of the sound system. "Journey Beyond Perception" was starting, and Bill Gouldd—the lead circus trainer for the event—appeared at center stage. I use the word "circus" because it was an over-the-top, strobe-lights-everywhere, music-blasting, mega-size stage event. It was multilevel marketing on steroids. Bill played the part more like the lead singer of a rock group than a trainer for a network-marketing business. I'd heard a rumor that Bill added an extra "d" to Gouldd to make it appear different and bigger. Another story claimed he added the extra letter because a spiritual advisor suggested he was out of balance.

Bill was a very good motivational speaker: captivating and larger than life, despite an odd lisp when he tried to pronounce words starting with the letter "g" or "f." His trainings were part motivational, part military shakedown. Kay and I left feeling both inspired and scared to death. Some of our family and friends knew we were involved in this new Equinox International company. I hadn't told Gram or Gramps, probably because I was scared of what they would think of the get-rich-quick concept.

We hoped the two-day event would change our financial lives, our business, and make our future brighter. Kay and I had returned almost all of our wedding presents to pay for the training fees and travel costs for this once-in-a-lifetime opportunity. To save money, we shared a small hotel room with six other people. The combination of my horrible head cold and the lack of privacy made our stay uncomfortable, but we were committed.

During the weekend, Gouldd performed weird skits, and one titled "Death" was particularly crazy. They turned off all the lights, banged on drums or metal, and then shot fire as Bill leapt to the front of the stage, wearing black garb and a dark mask. He held a Grim Reaper scythe and spoke about death and how quickly it comes. Without warning, he fired off questions to the audience like, "Are you giving life everything you have? Are you living with any regrets? Are you going to get rich before you die? Are you shorting yourself?" These questions and threats went on for about fifteen minutes, ending with him reminding us that the next time The Reaper showed up, it would be your death. Gouldd was famous for using skits like this to help you "improve" your personality and take more risks.

It was a genius piece of theater, both shocking and deep. It worked, though most of the audience, like Kay and me, went deep into debt to participate. Part of Bill's process was teaching us the power of greed. It was a world view that prioritized winning and becoming rich at any cost. I remember thinking to myself I'd rather die than not be rich.

Bill's content helped people discover the negative "scripts" they learned about money as a child. He also helped people uncover dreams they might have buried. Many of these lessons defined Kay and me for many years to come, but most of these "motivations" became bad habits later on. Gouldd's seminar set the tone for our future, the type of marriage we would have, and the dreams we would follow. Our journey was just beginning.

Our marriage was all about taking risks, supporting each other's crazy dreams, and helping each other walk through fire. We loved each other, but the dream and vision of grandeur was taking center stage in our marriage. We were living John Mellencamp's, "Jack and Diane" song. We were two

Americans kids "doing the best they can"—which for us meant we were trying to get rich as fast as we could. We were trying to escape childhoods marked by lack. When you ask for things and always hear "no," it pushes you one of two ways. One is to stop asking; the other is to never stop asking. Kay and I never stopped asking.

The Equinox International Vegas seminar was a way of growing my ego. Everything I did was starting to center around wealth and getting rich at any cost. That weekend with Bill Gouldd was the seed that would later grow into a tree of distraction and dishonesty. The training seemed to give us a license to change the rules or bend them once in a while if—and only if—bending was your last option. But at the time, I kept following my billionaire dream.

On the positive side, Gouldd taught me never to give up, no matter the cost. Kay and I opened an office for our Equinox company, went into debt, and started filling our garage with Equinox products we couldn't sell. But there was always a bigger vision. More around the corner. I was always just one win away from The Big Win.

Of course there was a negative side: I learned to cut corners and adopted the philosophy of "the end justifies the means." On one hand, some of my money habits were good, such as visioning, inspiring, drive, and commitment. I improved my discipline and understood what the word *commitment* really meant. I could now make sacrifices—or at least I *told* myself I was sacrificing—for something better or more important. All the time I'd say to myself: "You have to give up what you have in order to get what you want."

On the other hand, when you're pushing for "more," you don't always notice negative behaviors as they develop, such as looking the other way with regard to unethical practices or creating an environment of hero worship. This was the point when I started crossing the line and bending the rules—a lot. I was caught between that "poor kid from Thornton" mentality and a self-actualizing adult.

In the end, it turned out that Gouldd had broken numerous laws and was sued for false advertising and deceptive earnings claims. Four years after starting Equinox International, Gouldd was shut down by the Federal Trade Commission for running an illegal pyramid scheme and other illegal activities. The company had grown at an exponential pace that redefined the multilevel marketing industry. However, in the end Gouldd's tactics proved to be fear based, and he settled the lawsuits in the courts.

I always said I would *bend* the rules but not break them. Sometimes that line gets blurry. Gram and Gramps had taught me history, values, and appreciation for what you have, yet there I was, a young man who believed money was the solution to all my past and present problems. I had so many mixed feelings. My grandparents' positive-minded, value-based ideology pushed on me, yet I hungered for more—to always try to attain "bigger" and "better." In my mind, a billionaire lifestyle was the answer, even though my grandparents had taught me that love and gratitude go deeper.

As 1995 ended, Kay and I were desperate for a new opportunity. Gram and Gramps were doing well. They were in their early eighties but seemed like they were in their sixties. They were active, and we thought they would live forever. When I would ask Gram if she needed anything, she always said, "Oh honey! Dad and I are fine—better than fine. You worry about you and your beautiful bride."

Our time in the Equinox multilevel-marketing company ended up draining our finances instead of advancing our dreams. Our next business venture was another multilevel marketing group: selling Startronics laptops that included internet access.

During this time, an incredible opportunity took shape. After each sales presentation, a client would say, "I don't want the laptop, but how do I get the internet access?" One question kept popping in my mind: What if Kay and I sold internet access *with* the computer?

# CHAPTER 6

# Where's My Jet?

## 1998

*"When we are no longer able to change a situation,*
*we are challenged to change ourselves."*

— VIKTOR FRANKEL

In early 1996, Kay and I finally freed ourselves of the Equinox cult, then dipped our toes in a few other multilevel programs selling laptops and calling cards. In 1998 we thought we'd found the answer to our billion-aire dreams: we started XploreNet, one of the first 56K Internet Service Providers (ISPs) in Colorado—with our friend Trent Hamilton. As I look back now, I wonder if our motivation was post-eighties yuppie greed or the nineties' new get-rich culture. Either way, we kept up the pursuit.

These were the days before AOL (America Online) had 56K speed or high-speed access. At the time, small mom-and-pop ISPs were spring-ing up everywhere, so we joined the race to connect as many people to the internet as our US Robotics chassis (an internet server–connecting device) could handle. Trent, Kay, and I often spent evenings and weekends tech-supporting customers, teaching folks to use email, and addressing questions about this new thing called the World Wide Web. Our big dream was that XploreNet would make us millionaires, which was one step closer to a billion.

I met Trent during the Equinox days. He'd been through personal dramas, including a divorce and losing a business. Like us, he followed Gouldd's formula and encountered the same debt issues at the end of the gold-digging tunnel. He too held on to the get-wealthy dream, and his introverted personality counterbalanced my extroverted salesman approach. He was a good person and, like me, he was willing to take the necessary risks to reach his dreams. That was the key: Trent wanted to get filthy rich too. We were ready to make it—and make it big.

In late 1995, my grandparents invested $5,000 in our company. They also encouraged Kay to get an additional bachelor's degree or a masters if she wanted, and they offered to pay for tuition. They loved Kay so much and were willing to do anything to help us.

Using my grandparents' investment, Trent's home line of credit, and by maxing out the one credit card we had left, we pushed forward. We opened our minds to methods for additional funding, new product opportunities, and the dream of becoming Billionaires with a capital "B"! However, we were still barely surviving. I would walk to Burger King with three dollars in change in my pocket. A Whopper Value Meal was $2.89, and I would count out the change on the counter next to the cash register, just to make sure I had enough. It was embarrassing, but I knew it was short term.

One day, Trent and I were tucking flyers under windshield wipers in local parking lots when a man with a foreign accent and an obvious limp stopped Trent and asked if our firm needed money. Although it was an odd question, Trent played along. Our financial condition was so bad that this guy could have asked if we needed food. Without hesitating, Trent said, "Yes, yes we do. Why are you asking?" The man gave us his card and said,

"I'll be in touch." His name was Mathis Arquette, and he was an old-school investment broker.

A few weeks later, Trent, Kay, and I were seated at a boardroom table in a downtown Denver Kinko's preparing for a conference call with investors from Germany. Mathis was French, in his early seventies, and had a limp from contracting polio as a child. His favorite saying was, "You cannot put the toothpaste back in the tube," which cracked me up every time. He had lived in the States for thirty years but still had a chopping accent when he spoke English. He also talked very close to your face like a real Frenchman.

Mathis had worked with our potential investors for many years. We could hardly see them when the video call began. This was before high-resolution and high-speed video conferencing. We were lucky we could even hear them. We later learned they were billionaires from Germany.

We started our dog-and-pony show with terribly prepared PowerPoint slides and finished with a clichéd "hockey stick" line chart, illustrated by a long, horizontal line of almost no growth that swooshes upward to depict rapid growth, like the angle of a hockey stick. The investors began speaking in German. I had no idea what they were saying and then realized that *Hallo* must be "Hello," and *sonnigar Tag* must mean "sunny day."

We rambled on for about twenty minutes. When we finished there was no response. After a minute or so, a female voice said in broken English, "You expect growth. This you show us?"

I looked at Mathis, and he nodded passionately, his head going up and down.

I blurted out, "Yes! Yes, we do."

The woman began to address Mathis in German. After she was done, he turned to me and said, "She is asking, 'How much money do you need?'"

I wanted so badly to ask, "How much do you have to give us?" But Mathis had coached us to ask for $250,000. So I stayed on script: "We need $250,000."

The female investor spoke to Mathis again in German and ended in broken English asking if he thought the plan would work. He answered, "I do."

Then she continued the conversation, asking questions in German with a few English words mixed in. I looked at Mathis and said, "What is she saying?"

"She's says okay. You get the money."

Trent, Kay, and I just stared at each other, not sure what to do. We were finally on our way to reaching our big dream. We didn't know what the money would really do for us, but it was something. Three years later, we were voted a top technology company in the local newspaper for both service and revenue growth. Between 1998 and 2004 we opened XploreNet offices in Chicago, London, and Denver, and our staff grew to nearly thirty people. We also donated thousands of dollars in technology work to several nonprofits throughout Colorado.

In 2001, I was blessed to be voted a 40 Under 40 Award winner in the *Denver Business Journal*, where the editors picked the top forty up-and-coming young professionals in Colorado. This, of course, fed my ego even more. I could see the gold mine now.

I was receiving all kinds of accolades, on the fast track to big time success, accomplishing goals, winning awards, meeting all the right people, creating a powerful Rolodex, and pushing the envelope. We even survived the 2001 dot-com collapse by closing the offices in 2002, laying off most of our staff, and ultimately moving the operations back into Kay's and my townhome as a last-ditch effort to stay in business. During the roller-coaster ride, we helped key brands like Imagine Entertainment, Quiznos, Pak Mail, and many other large brands build their first web footprint and/or online stores and launch their initial digital brands. We weren't the greatest online software company ever created, but we never gave up. Mathis never let me forget that our firm was in good company and that our start-up date was around the same time some great brands started. He reminded me that a company named Google incorporated four days before us. Netflix started three days after us. He also wrote me a check for $3,000 when we couldn't make the rent payment after the 2001 dot-com meltdown.

By 2005, my ego was completely out of control. Nothing was good enough, big enough, or special enough. Author Roger J. Corless wrote: "Trying to be happy by accumulating possessions is like trying to satisfy hunger by taping sandwiches all over your body." In my case, this applied to accumulating accolades too. And I preferred peanut butter and jelly.

I wasn't the smartest guy in the room, but I didn't back away from anything. I could sell, had a drive to win, and was a solution finder. Make that a solution *creator*, never mind reality. While I was chasing dreams, my parents were settling for the minimum. They hadn't changed much in the last ten years. My mom and dad were still nonexistent in my life. It wasn't just their fault. I had no desire to connect with them, and I had given up. We talked on the phone once in a while, and Kay and I had the entire family over for a Christmas dinner at our loft. But the time with them was more shallow than deep.

I still wanted to do anything I could to be different from them and to be better. Why would I bother when I was wearing $1,500 suits, $300 shoes, and $175 custom shirts? Even my belt cost $80, which I loved to point out each time I got the chance. One professional ensemble cost around $2,800. I was trying to be Gordon Gekko, Michael Douglas's character in *Wall Street*, except I didn't have the billions, and I thought I was better looking.

Kay and I were living in our hip downtown pad called Palace Lofts, sandwiched about three blocks away from the Pepsi Center to the north and Coors Field about ten blocks to the south. The word "loft" was becoming popular to attach to these renovated old buildings. My office was a two-block walk away, located in restaurant-laden Larimer Square. The area, nicknamed LoDo, was the ideal place to continue my rich look and feeling.

While I played Gordon Gekko, Kay continued in her role as a committed executive director of a unique, all-volunteer foundation and multi-million-dollar nonprofit called Denver Active 20-30, which operated one of the largest charity fundraising polo events in the US. She left XploreNet in 2002 and stepped in when the 20-30's polo event was thirty days from shuttering after a fourteen-year run. A spat with a dysfunctional management company had forced the 20-30 president at the time to look for a new administrator and a lifeline. Instead, he found a miracle named Kay.

She took over as executive director of the foundation on a Tuesday night at eight o'clock, and we headed over to the old management company's office to pick up the boxes—some new, some old and dusty. We loaded both cars with as many as we could fit, but it took two trips. Kay turned our townhome into a war room, put together a battle plan, and pulled it off. The polo event went off as planned, and although it didn't raise the funds it previously did, the process showcased Kay's ability to work under pressure, her resolve to complete key tasks, and her commitment to finishing projects. She had never let anyone down before, and this time was no different.

Kay saved the foundation from bankruptcy and rescued the main event. She was a finalist for the *Denver Business Journal's* Outstanding Women in Business award. And now she was doing double duty running the foundation while also taking care of her mom, Lena, who suffered from COPD, a disease that obstructs airflow to the lungs. For nearly eight years Kay was Lena's caregiver. The boundaries between career and family life were nonexistent, and the work was endless. The list of tasks required for both of Kay's parents consumed many hours daily, including running errands, driving to doctors' appointments, cleaning their house, buying them clothes, doing their legal work, paying bills, picking up groceries and prescriptions, and doing laundry. Kay had also been paying her parents' $645 monthly rent, thousands in medical bills, and most of their other monthly expenses. This went on for years. Time spent helping her mom caused Kay to miss personal appointments, forced vacations to be rescheduled, and required that Kay spend hours at the office on weekends. She turned down invitations to special events and dates with friends.

Kay spent many nights with her mom in a hospital room, attempting to sleep in an uncomfortable combination chair/bed next to Lena's hospital bed. Throughout those nights, she would guide her mom to and from the bathroom. The next day would bring yet another conversation with a doctor, hoping and praying the news would be good, or at least different this time. We always thought there would be a turning point: Lena would feel better, regain her strength, become more self-sufficient. That never happened.

The phone calls Kay received from her sister, her dad, or the hospital at all hours of the day or night never ended. She dropped everything to come help or go to the hospital. These calls and the pressure to help took a toll on Kay and weighed on both of us. The process of watching her mom deteriorate as her quality of life slowly disappeared crushed us.

To keep up with my fast-paced networking lifestyle, I had to push all this out of my mind. There were years that I attended more than 200 events in a year. I knew a lot of people, but I had to admit I didn't really *know* anybody. And no one knew the real me. I was starting to lose myself, although I didn't see it yet. I saw people as opportunities rather than real, breathing souls. One person could lead to another, who could lead to another. The next person might lead me to the promised land of new opportunity and wealth. People often described me as "buttoned up," which is a real nice way to say I was a smug asshole.

Even though I strived to say and hear positive thoughts and messages, I wasn't acting like my true self. I led like a general, but inside I was weak and full of anxiety. I didn't let anyone in. I kept conversations shallow, which I figured out later was a protection mechanism developed from my childhood. If I let others know my weaknesses, they could be used against me. I could be ridiculed or devastated by opening up. The person I confided in today might know my competitor, tell them how to get me, or become my competitor down the road. It was ego driven and stupid.

In the fall, we found out Kay was pregnant—our first child since we were teenagers. We were excited about a future child coming into our life, but I was also worried. My mom's and dad's poor attempts at parenting left a sour taste in my mouth, and I didn't want to make the same mistakes.

When we got pregnant, however, part of me believed fatherhood might be a bridge to some kind of relationship with my parents.

At this point in my life, my parents were still lost. They continued to struggle with day-to-day life, losing jobs, falling down financially, and demonstrating careless attitudes. The last thing they could understand were my "big dreams." When my mom bragged that she had kept a job for one full year, I thought, *They should give you the fucking Nobel Prize for Economics.*

I could tolerate my parents for brief times during the holidays—inviting one or the other to our house for a family get-together. They could never be in the same room together, which was fine with me. They never asked about my businesses. They never were interested in the details of my life. I would feel guilty when I watched friends having close relationships with their parents. That feeling would pass, though, and I'd go about my normal life. If we talked once every three or four months, I was fulfilled. If we didn't talk for six months I didn't think much of it.

Although I wrote down my blessings daily in a gratitude journal, they were just words. I was faking it to make it. I was going through the mental exercise, but I didn't feel anything. Along the way my appreciation became more checklist driven than earnest. There were great times and fantastic events, yet all I could see were the shortcomings. I'd think *I should have made more money and won more awards by now. I should be flying around in my fucking jet already.*

I compared myself with others' performances and evaluated success as material accumulation. I was good, but not as good as or as rich as this guy or that guy, etc. My high level of confidence (cockiness) was about to get me in trouble.

Ironically, Kay's and my concerns about caring for Lena and a newborn at the same time were about to vanish. However, our caregiving days were just beginning. If you said we were unprepared and overmatched, it would be an understatement.

# CHAPTER 7

# Is She Breathing?

## 2005

*"Of all the titles I've been privileged to have,*
*'Dad' has always been the best."*

— KEN NORTON

Walmart is usually a place for people-watching, deep discounts, below-average service, and cheap stuff made in China. It's not the best place for an emotional breakdown, but that was about to change because on February 27, 2005, Kay answered her phone while we were at Walmart shopping for yet another get-well card for her mother. As we made our way through the greeting-card aisle, her phone rang.

Kay answered, and within seconds she fell to her knees while tears streamed down her face. I tried to grab her, concerned because she was pregnant, but she was like a wet noodle and slowly slid through my arms and down to the floor. She sobbed uncontrollably while desperately screaming into the phone, "What do you mean? Is she breathing? Call 911! Dad, *do* something! You haven't called? "Call NOW!"

"What's going on?" I asked. She didn't need to answer; my gut knew.

I could barely understand Kay through the compulsive gasps. "It's my mom. She's ... she's ... not breathing. My Dad says she's ... she's not breathing." She dropped the card, left the cart in the middle of the aisle and started running toward the exit."Let's go! We have to go. Go now! Let's go!"

We ran out of the store as quickly as we could move. Kay was sobbing and confused, so I grabbed her arm and helped her through the doors to the parking lot.

We arrived at her parent's apartment about twenty minutes later. When her Dad opened the door, Kay said, "Dad, where is she?" He pointed toward the bedroom. Kay flew past him like an Oklahoma tornado, almost tripping down the hallway and rushing straight to the back bedroom. Her mom was slumped over, pale. Not breathing. The oxygen mask she needed to breathe after a lifetime of heavy smoking was still barely hanging on. Kay broke the peacefulness of the room and uttered in sorrow, "Oh Mom, you're gone."

My heart pounded as I leaned against the bedroom doorframe to keep my knees from buckling under me. I was ten feet away as Kay embraced Lena. I just stared, watching as Kay leaned over and kissed her mom's forehead. It was a soft, prolonged kiss. I could see so much emotion flowing through Kay. The room was silent. I haven't seen many dead bodies in my life, but Lena looked at peace.

As Kay gently put her mom's head down she said, "What did you do to yourself?

The tragedy was that Lena stopped smoking, but it was many years too late.

"You could have been around for so much longer without cigarettes," Kay moaned. "What about your grandbaby on the way?" I wanted to go to Kay and hold her, but this was their moment. It was raw and painful, but spiritual.

I felt the tears welling up, and I thought how ironic it was that Kay and I started dating exactly twenty years ago from the day that chronic obstructive pulmonary disease and a lifetime of smoking caught up with Lena. Her heart had finally stopped.

Kay continued whispering. "You fought hard. I'm so proud of you. I'm angry too, Mom, but I know it was your time. I love you."

I remembered one of our last conversations at the hospital before Lena died. While Kay went to see the doctor, Lena shared her special feelings for Kay. She told me, "An angel from God, that's what she is. Even though I adopted her, she was always mine. God knew. She will always be part of me." Lena ended with, "I'll miss her most of anything on this earth."

Even though my heart was dying for Kay, in some strange way I felt apathetic, watching her hold her mother's dead body. Seeing the pain from her loss was concurrent with a feeling of unforeseen relief. I almost grinned, feeling giddy as I pondered the freedom we would now have as our caregiving days were done. I was sad for Kay, but it was finally over.

Kay stood up from the bed, and when I held her, she had a death grip on me. As she cried, neither of us said a word. It was an incredible release. As I put my hand on her belly to feel our unborn baby, I remembered the emotional, physical, and mental toll taking care of her mother had been on Kay. It had been a second job that she did without complaining and for no pay.

• • •

In April, Kay was in the last stages of pregnancy, showing both the hormonal glow and the pure exhaustion of sleep deprivation. She and Gram had been getting together for lunch or coffee regularly, usually planned around Gram's doctor appointments. The visits inspired, motivated, and calmed Kay. They were an escape from daily work challenges and a way to connect to a mother figure. The pain of Lena's two-month absence was lessened by Gram's presence.

Kay enjoyed Gram's "fireside" chats. She had been spending more and more time with Gram and Gramps, helping them with all kinds of activities and chores. It was no surprise that they were acting more like old friends than family-in-law. Kay seemed to be filling in for the sister Gram had recently lost.

One day, Kay came home after the two of them had had coffee and told me that Gram asked her to be her executor. Kay was stunned, and she argued that my sister, Sadie, should be the executor because she was a closer relative. Gram, like a good car salesperson, had ignored the objections, kept smiling, and didn't relent. Gram had a way of stating things so that you felt the decision was yours, not hers, so you felt like you were in control of the process. Andrew Carnegie would be proud.

Gram told Kay she was like a daughter to her and her only close female friend left in the world. She confided that her mind was going and that time was not on her side. How could Kay say no?

Unlike most of her female relationships, Gram connected at a deep level with Kay. Other women were often a challenge. Even her relationship with her sister had been strained for a significant portion of her life, and my father's two wives and girlfriends were roadkill for her. She chewed them up and spit them out.

Gram didn't like the type of female drama that often accompanied her generation. Her conversations and friendships with men were more natural and smooth, while most female relationships ended because she treated them like second-class citizens or dismissed them because of some perceived girly silliness. It wasn't sexual with men, but rather a mutual respect. She loved men's tough exteriors, macho drive, and serious attitudes. Men considered Gram's positive demeanor and ability to follow through and honor her commitments as male friendly. Back in her day, the man led the family, was strong, and showed guts. She connected with the stereotypical image of John Wayne—and no woman was ever going to be like John.

Kay was the exception. She and Gram could talk, open up to each other, and be authentic. Not that they never disagreed, but they could come to an agreement on common ground.

As they finished their coffee in the café, Gram had told Kay, "Besides, the house is mine and the money is mine, and I'll do with it what I damn well please. I want you to manage the estate, and you and Will can use the money as you see fit."

Then Kay told me that Gram said, "I don't want any other family members involved." Gram had always said, "I don't want anyone from either side of the family to cause problems." She hadn't always seen eye to eye with the extended family—especially some of Gramps's relatives, and the relationship was somewhat bitter with a few of them.

So Kay said yes to being the executor, and from that day on, she began managing Gram's finances and became her primary decision-maker and caregiver. On paper, I would be listed as Power of Attorney, but Kay was always the right choice to lead. Gram knew Sadie and I would get emotionally charged when the time came to provide day-to-day care or make funeral arrangements and finalize key decisions while dividing the assets. She knew Kay would fulfill the role perfectly with no bias, completing the tasks precisely as Gram had wished. I'm sure Kay had no idea of what her commitment would entail over the coming years—or the impact it would have on her life.

This seemed like an easy proposition at the outset. Kay would watch over Gram's account, make sure she didn't bounce checks, and help manage paperwork like insurance forms. We would be able to organize prescriptions and paper files, and still stay connected at arm's length. It would be easy, no big deal. Kay was running the 20-30 Foundation, so we assumed handling a few more tasks each day to help Gram would be of no concern. Wonder Woman would simply become Super Woman.

It wasn't long before the bigger challenges of helping Gram began to appear. We were on a family vacation in Florida during the late summer. Gram called Kay and was furious because the bank had contacted her. Her words stopped us in our tracks. Gram had bounced a few checks but was accusing Kay of doing it.

Kay fielded Gram's questions and told her no one else was writing checks; she was the only one. I became angry and yelled at Kay, telling her we should have had my sister take care of Gram's personal affairs. Kay put her hand over the phone, "I told her to have Sadie be the executor. You know how Gram gets. She won't take no for an answer." I knew that. When Gram had her mind set on something, it was pretty much set in concrete. Kay added, "Plus, she needs my help." Kay was too much of a giver, helper, and lover to not be there for Gram.

I had heard a little bit about the process of elderly people beginning to succumb to Alzheimer's or dementia and had a murky memory of my other grandmother going through it when I was a young teenager. One of my last memories of my mom's mother was looking on in disbelief and clutching Sadie as our grandmother screamed random names and words at the top of her lungs from a medical bed. She was flinging herself left and right while the nursing staff held her down like an injured animal. Her eyes looked as if no one was there. She died soon afterward.

That awful memory was the basis for me to make decisions about my grandparents' caregiving needs. I didn't know how many details someone— either Mom or her sister—had to figure out for their mother. I remember Mom did very little, so I assumed her sister must have done all the caregiving.

By now Kay was also managing Gramps's affairs. I had underestimated what we were really getting into by agreeing to manage my grandparents' estate. I thought we'd eventually update the will at some point to reflect Gram's and Gramps's emerging health conditions, to record any new decisions, to confirm old testaments, and to rewrite specific directives. But for now, it seemed like verbal agreements would work fine, as they had always in both my personal and professional life. Even for business agreements, I relied on emails and handshakes—what I called E&H. It was probably a dumb philosophy, but I believed people when they gave me their word. And I thought they knew my word was set in concrete.

Unfortunately, I was about to get P&K (punched and kicked). I was underestimating how quickly my grandparents' health was deteriorating and how soon the rise in complexity of all aspects of their lives would complicate ours. I don't think anyone is ever prepared to be a full-time caregiver or to help manage another adult's existence for twenty-four hours every day. Even a trained professional has moments of fear, doubt, and anger. I struggle to manage *myself* at times, and I consider myself fairly healthy and mentally lucid. I've heard it said that twenty-four-hour caregiving can be compared to combat duty or surviving a natural disaster. A person can feel all the emotions, from progressive depression to full-on PTSD.

Life marched on, and Kay and I kept moving forward, optimistic as our little Helen Young made her appearance in the world in early May. She was named after Gram, and the twinkle in her eye when she first smiled at me as a newborn reminded me of Gram's twinkle.

It was emotionally difficult for Kay to deliver our seven-pound, six-ounce bundle of joy without her mom physically present. However, we knew Lena's spirit was present in the hospital room because Helen wasn't breathing when she was born. When Kay asked me why the baby wasn't crying, I kept reassuring her that everything was fine. Then three neonatal intensive-care-unit workers rushed into the delivery room. They went to work, and within a few minutes, Helen's lungs were working—at full volume!

As the months rolled by, we tried to relax and enjoy the baby. We were doing very well financially and thought we were managing Gram's and Gramps's health, but an October vacation in Mexico quickly changed our opinion. They were declining rapidly, and we were about to be faced with the daunting task of caring for them and our own child at the same time.

# CHAPTER 8

# The Hurricane

## October 2005

*"Nearly all men can stand adversity, but if you want
to test a man's character, give him power."*

— ABRAHAM LINCOLN

The loud speaker blared in Spanish and English: "Move into the hallway!" Kay and I huddled with five-month-old baby Helen in the hallway of the Playa del Carmen Convention Center as Hurricane Wilma battered the beaches of Mexico's Riviera Maya. Our nice, seven-day vacation to a little resort south of Cancún was quickly turning into a nightmare. There were no more airline seats back to the States, so the three of us plus my brother-in-law, sister-in-law, niece, and her husband were stranded in a monster of a storm.

Early October offers great prices on trips to the Caribbean—along with potentially hazardous weather—so even though Helen was very tiny, we jumped at the chance for a getaway with Kay's sister and her family.

Back in Denver, Sadie was keeping an eye on Gram and Gramps, and we got some down time. Well, almost.

The winds and rain began to hit really hard at around five o'clock Thursday afternoon. At first, the staff at our resort began encouraging guests to gather in the lobby and board a bus to the convention center. Soon they demanded we evacuate. We were allowed to bring just one small bag per person.

A five-minute bus ride took us to the Playa del Carmen convention center, where we were all herded into the main room of the center. The first few hours were like a social cocktail hour with lots of food, water, conversations, and even alcoholic drinks. The staff was intent on continuing our vacation experience even as we awaited the arrival of the hurricane.

Some kind of sixth sense must have kicked in because I moved my family from the large center room and into the hallway, where people were gathering in groups. Our group of eleven included my immediate family of three, Kay's sister (whom everybody calls "Sis") and her husband Don, my niece and her husband, and two couples from Detroit that we'd just met minutes before. We all started to work together.

The first step was to grab as many chairs as we could get our hands on. The chairs had wool padding and no arm rests. We arranged them side by side—much like a wagon train circled up at night, with five-month-old baby Helen in the middle. Bringing her on the trip seemed like a good idea, but now we were worried. We all settled in, trying to get comfortable. As the storm grew stronger, we heard loud bangs against the outside walls, made by flying debris and crashing waves. It sounded like a combination rock concert/NASCAR race. Around eleven o'clock that night, there was a loud boom from the main convention space as a large portion of the ceiling collapsed, crashing water and roofing material onto the floor and people below. Fortunately, most of the injuries were minor. We didn't see it happen, but the sound was terrifying. Moving into the hallway when we did was a blessing.

Everyone who had been sitting in the main space rushed into the hallway where we were set up. Our custom "fort" area was now cramped. I started to get nervous. A narrow brick-and-concrete hallway was our only defense against the elements.

"Helen doesn't look right," said Kay in a scared-mother tone. I was at a loss. What had I been thinking when I put our child's life in danger by taking her to Mexico? I agreed that Helen looked flushed and assumed she must be overheated from a slight fever or because the air conditioning was off and there was no fresh air circulating through the narrow hall. We couldn't stroll across the street to a pharmacy to pick up some infant Advil, so we put out a message to other groups, hoping to find a fan. Twenty minutes later, a kind lady walked up and handed us a small, battery-powered fan. Helen had become a mini-celebrity among the other evacuees.

By now the brick walls were vibrating, causing an eerie sound like in the movie *Titanic*, when the boat started to creak before it broke into two large chunks. Otherwise, it was silent outside. I thought that meant it was over, but it wasn't. We were centered in Wilma's eye for almost eighteen hours, which was unheard of, since an average one lasts two to three hours.

As morning turned into afternoon, the faucets quit working, so we had no drinking water. It was difficult to breathe with no fresh air. Our food rations decreased by the minute, and meals were reduced to a slice of thin lunchmeat crammed between two small slices of bread. The staff must have seen that tempers were beginning to fray because they began taking small groups to the back door, which opened to the docking/shipping area. We were allowed to stand outside for fifteen-minute periods. The warm breeze felt so good that I smiled and stretched. The ocean—about a football field's length away—resembled a mountain lake on a still day. I thought we'd just be fine.

After midnight, we tried to sleep. We used a watch system with each of us taking a turn keeping an eye on Helen and our belongings while the others slept, grabbed a few minutes of fresh air, or went to the restroom.

Three hours of sleep got me through the night; I was focused only on Kay's and Helen's well-being.

Thursday became Friday, and the staff warned us that the hurricane was moving again with one final burst of wind. This last tango turned out to be worse than the initial hit. We heard the center room, which was mostly roofless, filling with water. Outside, it sounded like thousands of people were simultaneously throwing rocks at the building.

When the hurricane finally passed, we felt like we'd survived a plane crash. We had endured more than twenty-four hours of punishing winds and one of the highest-rated hurricanes in Central/North American history.

After a few hours, we boarded a bus and were dropped off at our resort. Most of our room was intact, though the sliding-glass door had torn apart and there was water damage to the floor. The manager offered to move us to another room, but we stayed, requesting only that they cover the door and sweep out the glass. Kay and I slept on top of the bed with Helen safe between us.

The next day was Monday, and when I woke up I was panicked, realizing we hadn't been in touch with Gram and Gramps for three days. In the last year, a day never passed without us knowing where they were or talking at least once a day. I started stressing. *Are they taking their meds? Is the house locked at night? Are there any water problems or leaks in their basement?* Playa del Carmen was without cell service, and we hadn't yet learned the fate of the airport, roads, or town. That first morning after the storm, I began a new ritual: arriving at the front desk immediately after breakfast. Several of us guests would circle the area, waiting for our contact, Norberto Sanchez, who had a goatee and wore colorful, button-up shirts. I never saw where he came from, but he would suddenly appear and let us know if we were on "the list" to leave, but he didn't know when we would actually depart. Then he disappeared again. Only one airplane could land at the airport at a time because of all the damage, so the airlines provided Norberto with a list of guests who had a confirmed seat on each plane.

One day after another passed, and each day Norberto had the same reaction: he would shake his head in disgust while saying in a mixture of English and Spanish, "Oh, Mr. Jung, so sorry, but you not on the *lista*. Me *lo siento*. "Later, I figured out he was saying Mr. "Joven," which means "Young" in Spanish.

Six days after our scheduled departure date, we had a new problem; Helen was running out of diapers and, more important, infant formula. She had a digestive problem that only a special, high-priced formula helped. I had to figure out how to find this formula. I wasn't sure what to do, so I headed outside to clear my head. As I came around the corner, I spotted a lone taxi in the hotel drop-off area. I went toward it in a full-tilt sprint, but my flip-flops gave out and I slid through a large puddle of water and crashed into the taxi door. With my adrenaline pumping, I didn't notice the nasty cut on my butt and thigh until later.

"Can you take me into the town?" I shouted to the driver. "My baby needs formula!"

"*Sí*," the taxi driver replied.

As I started to get in, I looked back to see about twenty people running toward the car, probably wondering if more taxis would be arriving soon. Then it hit me: I didn't know where I was going or if I had enough money for the taxi and formula.

"I have cash," I said, handing the driver a twenty-dollar bill. "Lots more for you. Please don't leave. I pay you the rest."

"Yes, *sí*."

I ran back in the lobby, grabbed my brother-in-law, Don Leverson, and pulled him aside." You *have* to come with me. I don't know where the hell I'm going or what mess I'll find when I arrive."

I'd known Don, Kay's brother-in-law, since shortly after meeting Kay, when he had a groovy seventies© mustache. He's a big teddy bear who's always willing to go above and beyond for his friends and family. He agreed to go with me, so we hopped in the cab, hoping the driver was legitimate.

The taxi headed to the downtown area. I could see damaged roads, buildings, and ripped-apart vegetation. It reminded me of the Vietnam movies I watched in college showing decimation after a napalm bomb blast. The scene nearer the town was chaos: debris everywhere and people walking through it. All the power was out, and I could smell rotting trash and something like burning wood.

The taxi driver knew of a pharmacy and stopped in an alley. He pointed toward a half-open garage door and said, "*Allí,*" which meant "there" in Spanish). I got out and headed over. I couldn't see into the garage because it was completely dark inside. Suddenly a man poked his head out, nearly banging into mine. I handed him the formula-can wrapper and asked, "Do you have this special type of baby formula?" He examined the label, then looked me at me in surprise and back at the label. He was probably wondering why I was asking for baby formula rather than liquor, water, or cigarettes. "*Bebé?*" he asked.

"Yes, yes! That's it. Formula for a Bee-be."

"I be right back."

The man disappeared into the dark building. I crossed my fingers and prayed. Within a few minutes, to my disbelief, the man presented a formula can to me like he was a waiter presenting a bottle of fine wine for approval. I looked at it and smiled. "Thank you!" I said in high-pitched appreciation. "*Gracias!* Yes, *sí.* That's the one!" I wanted to kiss him, but I jumped back into the taxi to return to the resort as soon as possible. My baby daughter was going to be okay.

The next day, taxi service became regular, so I headed back into town to call my sister. Sadie was relieved to hear from me—and she was overwhelmed. She'd been filling in as a contact person for our grandparents, and she was surprised that they called her for some kind of help several times every day. It was the first time she realized their needs were expanding exponentially.

By the end of the week, which was seven days past our original departure date, I mentioned to Uncle Don that I wondered whom we needed to bribe to get on "the list." If they were evacuating the country in alphabetical order, it would be a long winter for us Youngs.

Finally, after fifteen days, Norberto made his normal morning appearance and said the magical words: "Mr. Jung, I have good news for you!" He announced it like we'd won an award. "Mr. Jung, you are on the list for tomorrow morning. Your family be going to *su casa*."

The morning couldn't come fast enough. We were excited to be going home but nervous about the pre-WWII method they were using to land planes. The airport was without radar or air traffic control.

Our bus pulled up to the airport, and we could see that the terminal was partially destroyed with just one runway remaining. There was a simple security check where a TSA worker looked in our bags, patted us down, gave us the father-son-holy ghost sign, and sent us out the door. Before boarding, I watched another United plane land, make a U-turn, and take off as soon as all the people were loaded.

As we walked down the stairs to the tarmac, a fear of death gripped me. I was falling forward from the weight of one bag strapped around my neck while I had a tight grip on Helen that forced her little head to pop out from under my arm. My other hand was holding Kay's tight enough to turn it blue.

Our plane touched down on the single runway. Boarding was a strange feeling because there were no tickets. We just had to find an open seat, stow our bags, fasten our seat belts, and pray. Shouts of joy erupted as the plane headed down the runaway. Most people were clapping, some were crying, and others smiled from ear to ear. We really weren't sure where the plane was headed; some people said Chicago, others said Houston, while some in the back rows muttered about San Diego. I didn't care. When we arrived at Chicago's Midway Airport, I was thrilled to be on US soil.

Once home, we found ourselves in a new phase. The nine extra days we were gone had been difficult for Sadie and our grandparents' neighbors, who struggled to keep up with all of Gram's and Gramps's needs. Concerns about them living alone were growing daily.

Like a lot of people, Kay had hidden our grandparents' initial major decline, partly because admitting that loved ones need extensive help is tough to acknowledge. It's hard on kids, and it's insulting to the elders, who are unlikely to admit they're struggling. So out of both fear and love, everyone in the family pretends nothing's wrong. Unfortunately, Sadie was in the dark about many of Gram and Gramps's issues, and our trip was the first time she had to change her schedule to stop by after work. She was getting an earful of Gram's newly developing wrath and both grandparents' mood swings. Witnessing Gramps's weakened physical health was unsettling for her. Sadie watched him nearly trip or fall with almost each step. I could see the fear in her face as she explained what we'd missed.

I'd been in denial, constantly suggesting to the family that the grandparents were fine—that they were strong and would work through any obstacles. Gram was the toughest lady I've ever known, and I was sure she'd bounce back. When we returned from Mexico, however, we were all forced to stop denying that they needed help—more help than we could give them, honestly. Unbeknownst to me at the time, Hurricane Wilma was just an early warning of the tumultuous storm ahead for our family.

# CHAPTER 9

# The Revealing of PeakView Senior Living

## 2006

*"My grandfather always said that living is like licking honey off a thorn."*

— LOUIS ADAMIC

The fiasco surrounding our grandparents while Kay and I were stranded in Mexico was eye opening, and by early spring of 2006, the whole family was convinced that Gram and Gramps needed skilled care sooner than expected. On several occasions we'd asked them about visiting assisted-living facilities, but the answer was always "no" or "not yet." Finally, our persistence paid off, and they agreed to visit a retirement community for a tour.

"Welcome to PeakView Senior Living!" said the marketing director with a greasy smile. "Let's take a look at your future home." He wore an Italian suit, and his brown hair was slicked back. I wasn't sure if we were visiting an elder-care facility or were being sold a car, but for sure the guy was in ramped-up sales mode.

Gram glanced at me and offered an awkward wink; she knew his sales pitch was in high gear. She herself had sold everything from Bibles to real estate to makeup, so she knew the drill, but she smiled gently back at the salesman and said, "It's great to meet you. What a lovely place you have." Though she was starting to forget a lot of things, Gram could still converse politely with a stranger.

We started the tour by going into the tall, newly renovated Senior Living building with a beautiful Rocky Mountain view. Residents aged fifty-five and older who were still independent lived here. Most residents were self-sufficient, in overall good health, and their minds were still intact. It was a nice place, but the sales pitch felt similar to one at a Sandals Resort. The slick salesman promised active, "mature" (their word) women and men who were enjoying the sunset years of their life.

Next, we headed to the much smaller Assisted Living building, which was located about two hundred yards away. Sandwiched between two back roads and a car wash, it seemed purposely hidden from the main area. As I learned later it was smaller because most people lived only nine to eighteen months after their poor health landed them there.

As we walked in we were greeted by vacant stares and a horrible smell: a combination of body odor, rotten water, sweat, feces, and urine. It was as if someone took all these odors, put them in a sock, and hid them for a month. The hint of strong chemicals only made the bad smell worse.

The elderly residents looked completely lost as they sat in wheelchairs parked against the outside wall and stared straight ahead. Some had what looked like slobber on their cheeks. A cold jacket of imminent death wrapped around me. It felt like the Grim Reaper was coming around the corner at any moment.

*God bless the staff for doing a thankless job*, I thought. No doubt they were underpaid and overworked, yet they had to deal with adults filling their pants, vomiting on themselves, and talking incessantly. As I watched them doing their job, I thought it was similar to taking care of babies and toddlers. I wouldn't blame the caregivers if they wanted to yell or scream at the residents when they asked repetitive questions, shouted with anger out of the blue, or experienced wild mood swings. The workers performed their duties with great patience only to have misdirected rage come their way—often accompanied by feces.

We finished the tour at the Alzheimer's special unit, which I'm sure they saved for last because it was like walking into a Stephen King novel. If there is such a place as Hell, my bet is it resembles the mental/memory-care unit of an assisted-living facility. We noticed old pictures on the wall, old carpet, and the smell of death—or near death. The gruesome place was filled with lost souls who have no past, present, or future. Their faces registered either total confusion or a wide smile that showed their complete disconnection from reality.

As we started to exit, Gramps asked about the food. A little grin appeared on his face, which made me laugh. Though struggling physically, he was still mentally in good shape. He'd always had an odd sense of humor about food, probably because he loved to eat. He liked to eat slowly, as if he had all the time in the world. When I say he was a slow eater, I mean *really* slow. He could have been inducted into the *Guinness Book of World Records* for slowest chewer. And like me, he had that hard-to-cure problem of too much hand to mouth. (Many of us have this eating-too-much disorder.). If PeakView would eventually be Gramps's last stop, by God he was making sure the cuisine was top notch.

The marketing director blurted, "The food is to die for!" As the words exited his mouth, his horrified smile told me he realized too late his unfortunate choice of words. We continued walking back to the main building for the dramatic, big closing event.

The sales guy looked at Gram and addressed her by first name: "Helen, how about some lunch? Doesn't this place feel like home?"

Before he could finish, she corrected him. "You can call me Mrs. Higgins. And let's talk cost." Even though Gram sometimes repeated herself, she still acted proud and strong.

"Cost" was an ugly word, and I knew that Mr. Marketing's answer would either put us on the right foot or kill our attempt of gently easing my grandparents into the downward-spiraling process of assisted living. He started to go through each level of care, covering the buy-in cost options versus monthly fees. Like any good salesman, he showed us average numbers and return on investment. He delivered the bad news by bookending it with good news. It was similar to a time-share presentation, only you would be sharing with death.

Gramps acted like he was listening, but with his diminished hearing, he was probably trying to read lips. Gram smiled, paid close attention, and waited for her chance to end the session. When it came she cut him off abruptly. "That will be all, dear. We're good, and we have another appointment down the road. We need to go."

As we drove away, Gram let us know that PeakView was a lovely place but there would be no need to worry about assisted living for a while. For a very *long* while. Once again she was in denial. I smiled back at her—part relieved, part worried—without saying a word.

Little did I know that less than two-and-a-half years later, I would be dealing with the tragedy of moving these two wonderful and beloved people into this hellhole.

• • •

A few months later, during the summer of 2006, we started to see our future when a Sunday-afternoon conversation with Gram and Gramps turned serious. Selling their house had always been a touchy subject that could trigger Gram's defensiveness. Usually she stated, "We're still fine in our home" or "Mind your own damn business." But after the visit to

PeakView, Kay figured she would gently saunter into the topic by asking, "What current house projects can we help with, Gramps?"

Gram responded, assuming we had another meaning. "Yes, dear, the time will come when we can't take care of this house," she said. "And there's a lot of stuff to deal with, I know." With a firm look on her face, she glanced up at Gramps and Kay, and then addressed me. "Will, I want *you* to sell it when the time comes for us to leave it."

I was caught off guard. I argued that I was not a realtor, but she interrupted me. "I've always told you that you could do anything you put your mind to, haven't I?" she said. "Look what you've done in your business. Just promise me that when the time comes you'll sell this house. This is your family duty. You're the leader of this family, and we're depending on you."

I didn't know which way the conversation was going this time. Gram still had moments of clarity in between lost looks or repeating herself. As she continued, her hands moved gently across the kitchen table. She started explaining the possible scenarios like a backyard quarterback draws his next offensive play in the dirt: "Pay yourself the commission and take fees for whatever is necessary: the costs for taking care of us, for cleaning up this mess, for fixing things. Our money is yours. You take care of *you* guys—and you do that first." Little did I know how abiding by her wishes would later cause so much pain.

As I stared out the sliding-glass door contemplating having to fix, clean, and organize fifty years of stuff and trying to figure out when I'd have the time, energy, or motivation to do it. I went back in time. I remembered the smell of apple pie. Gram's kitchen always smelled like baked goodies, from cookies to banana bread. I could see Gramps's garden beyond the patio. Though it wasn't as big and lavish as in past years, it was still full of beautiful, award-winning dahlias bursting with purple, green, and blue. They shot up like a Fourth of July fireworks show.

I turned back toward Gram and was hit by the memory of sitting at this same table as a small child and eating a bowl of bread and milk that our grandparents sometimes fed us for dinner. I hated bread and milk, but Sadie liked it.

How could I deny any request from these people who shaped my life and made sure Sadie and I were cared for? Finally, I replied in a hesitant voice, "Okay … I guess." I looked from Gramps's face to Kay's, then back to Gramps. His head nodded up and down as he almost leaned into the conversation. I wasn't sure if his nod was an agreement with Gram or if he was falling asleep—it was too close to call.

I was one of the few people in the world who could even dare to argue or stand up to Gram. My answer must have sounded insipid as I expressed my doubt about pulling it off. I told her a better idea might be to use a realtor. I was probably in denial that they would ever become incapacitated and have to leave this great home. Also, I didn't want to have to deal with an old house that would need lots of work.

Gram changed her stance, looked in my eyes, and said with a raised voice, "*No!* I'm serious, Will. You promise me. And you promise *now!*"

Gram didn't want to hear "no." She was convincing. I knew right away this was not the time to make any great stand, so I d promised her that, yes, I would fix up the house and sell it.

This wasn't the first time this conversation about someday selling the house had taken place, but this time I felt a sense of urgency more than ever before. Even so, we never updated my grandparents' will to reflect my promise to sell the house or Gram's intentions that the money from the sale should go to me and Kay. It was a colossal mistake. I was denying they would ever really need to leave their house, and even though I was a grown man, I still felt like a little kid with them. It would have been better for everybody if I had accepted that the roles had been reversed. Instead of remaining as authority figures, Gram and Gramps were already in the process of being reduced to childlike status with occasional flashes of adult coherency. It was a painful time for me—having to think about the house and their situation. And so I let the hustle and bustle of life take over and didn't update their wills as planned. It was the last time we would discuss the matter, which I would later regret deeply.

• • •

For the rest of the summer and fall of 2006, I didn't have time to worry about my grandparents because I was struggling with my own mental health. My journey was about becoming a billionaire and being the best at everything. And that pressure to excel was mounting.

Two of my close friends called me "Billion" instead of William, and I was beginning to wonder if my priorities were ridiculous and whether I was delusional. I looked down my nose at other people and their paltry ambitions. I was pursuing *real* goals. *My* dreams were significant—far more important than those of the people around me.

During that summer, a breakfast meeting in Broomfield changed the direction of my life and caused some future challenges. I became involved with a new venture called Talus. I and four other cofounders created the company to solve one major issue in health care: price transparency. Through indices and futures contacts, we thought we had something special. Our business concept was to help reduce the cost of health care by showing more data details and eventually having an open market to trade health care. Together we dreamed we could save the country. Later, my time and commitment to this venture helped doom me.

In October, Kay and I moved with Helen, now a toddler, into a beautiful, 5,000-square-foot, semi-custom home. It had a "water feature"—a pond—in the backyard, just thirty feet from the tee box of one of the holes on a gorgeous golf course. We were moving up, and I was making all the right moves. Or at least it appeared that way.

I cultivated just the right image for myself with wide-ranging roles: I was a leader as CEO of XploreNet; I was a philanthropist as event chair for the 20-30 Foundation Polo Classic; I was an investor in a number of small startups. These got me noticed. I was a Type A personality—important and impressive—or at least *I* thought so. Others were noticing me too. I was meeting with local community leaders and often had lunch with owners, managers, and coaches of local professional sports teams. I was interviewed on TV news from time to time about the 20-30 polo event or because I was a member of many nonprofit boards.

I was also tossing around the idea of entering politics. One investor in a political-advisory/PR and marketing firm that I'd helped start was preparing me to run for mayor of Denver. He helped me create a game plan that connected my private life to the life of a potential public servant, which meant image mattered if I were going to become a high-profile person. Image would matter a *lot*. We started lining up donors for funding, planned the next steps for raising campaign money, and threw around ideas for logo designs. I felt invincible. Looking back, however, I believe that if I had completed the mayoral run, I would have proved inept at holding public office.

I had few escapes from myself at this point, but helping nonprofit youth organizations raise money fit the need. When I was young, nonprofits in the sports sector saved my life, gave me direction, and provided goals for me to work toward. My involvement with nonprofits was a way to pay back. Also, I could use my skills to raise money, becoming the top fundraiser for the Denver Active 20-30 Children's Foundation, which supported marginalized and at-risk youth.

Because of that work, I had won more awards than I could count: Rookie of the Year, Member of the Year (twice), two-time chair of our main polo event, and the organization's top fundraiser for nine of my eleven years in it. I would go on to be voted a lifetime member, an honor few receive. My fundraising work with 20-30 enabled me to sit on the board of other children's charity nonprofits. I was even on four boards at once, and I served twelve organizations over the years. Each year, I helped 20-30 raise around a million dollars, which the nonprofit gave away to thirty to sixty charities.

I could do anything, get anyone on the phone, make good on any promise, win any game, become anything, and find a solution for any adversarial situation. Instead of relishing the now, however, I was worried about tomorrow, focused on what wasn't working and then pushing for bigger, better, and faster. I found out that as your ego grows, you can lose control. For me, the present was never comfortable, and the future always looked bigger than I could imagine.

My life vision was getting blurred as the reasons for winning overshadowed the facts and emotions. I had been all about the impressive bio—perception over reality. I was selfish, all while telling myself my "path" was about making a difference and helping others. I was a narcissist, although not as bad as my mother. I'd take credit for miracles that were out of my control like marrying an incredible lady, having great health for most of my life, and raising my sister in spite of our mentally ill mother. I even taught vision-board classes for contacts and friends, helping them achieve their vision like I'd accomplished mine.

As 2006 drew to a close, I held on strong, although my breakdown was imminent. Kay and I had made it through a few bumps like her mom's health issues, the dot-com bust of 2001, and the financial sacrifices we had made while growing our business. But little did I know the next few years would place enormous stress on ourselves and our marriage.

*The Shawshank Redemption* is my favorite movie in the world, and in it the Andy Dufresne character tells his prison pal, Red, about his wife. Andy says, "She was beautiful. I loved her. But I guess I couldn't show it enough. I killed her, Red. I didn't pull the trigger. But I drove her away. That's why she died. Because of me, the way I am."

I had no idea that I would put Kay in a horrible position through seemingly innocuous actions and everyday choices. But I learned the hard way that every bad result starts with a few bad decisions.

# CHAPTER 10

# Do Your Job!

## 2008

*"A nation of sheep will beget a government of wolves."*

— EDWARD R. MURROW

In 2008, Kay was running her eighth 20-30 annual polo event as the organization's executive director. It was an intense job: she quarterbacked the auction, ran the day-to-day operations, managed the financials, and assisted all the volunteer members with their tasks. And she loved every bit of it.

Unfortunately, taking care of Gram and Gramps had also become a full-time job. Gram wasn't reliable about paying bills, and she and continued to bounce checks. Neither she nor Gramps had any business driving a car. To add to the responsibility load, Kay was pregnant again.

One day as I passed Kay's desk—we both worked from home—I said, "I think it's time to make a change."

She looked up at me with a worried expression.

"We have businesses and another little one on the way," I said to her in an agonizing tone. "Plus, we have to take care of both Gram and Gramps. We need to figure out something soon because their needs are growing with each passing day."

We'd been delaying the conversation about moving my grandparents to assisted living or finding some kind of in-house nurse/caregiver. If those solutions didn't fit, Kay would have to start planning to help them every day. I hadn't committed to any certain direction yet, but I was good at providing challenging questions.

Kay sighed. "You think now is the time?"

"If we don't figure this out now, when *will* we figure it out?" I shrugged. "How do we take care of the grandparents and still run our life? And if we're not taking care of them, then who will?"

"I love my role as executive director," she said. "And I'm not sure I want to give it up. It seems like we're victims of this situation. Gram and Gramps need us, but that means sacrificing our current lives to help them. I love them dearly, but providing care has become a fulltime deal. I'm spending more and more hours with them now."

As we talked, we realized that for more than a year and a half, we'd spent every other weekend at Gram and Gramps's house or meeting them at a restaurant or joining them at their church function or chauffeuring them to family events. The crazy thing was that even though the caretaking workload was increasing, we were enjoying it.

Gram and Gramps were in their early nineties, and Kay and I were in our mid-thirties. Yet we were like best friends at a bar talking about the good old days. Gram still exuded self-confidence even though time had taken away her beautiful, young-girl looks. Overall she was aging gracefully, even though her mind was starting to go. She always attempted to stand tall and erect, but it was a struggle as her back and shoulders fell forward from the inevitable pull of gravity. She could be abrupt, demanding, and abrasive one minute; the next moment she could be quite a pussycat, which always made weekends with them an adventure.

There was a special toughness in Gram, like a survivalist. If I could pick only a few people to be with in a military foxhole, she would be near the top of my list. When the shooting stopped, I could envision two scenarios: putting my hands around her throat squeezing in frustration or hugging her tightly with gratitude because she saved my life. Gram would never give up on someone she loved, and I was never going to give up on her.

A long life of dealing with adversity and pain had grooved Gram's personality. She survived the Great Depression at age fifteen, got married at nineteen, lost her first husband to lung cancer, lived through several major wars, raised children by herself, and beat breast cancer during her eighties. From witnessing lots of death and wading through life's dramas, she had earned her stripes.

Gram outlived husbands, a sister, and a son. A family member once joked that she alone would decide when it was time to die, and she would veto God, if necessary. *And* she would decide if she went to Hell rather than Heaven. If she chose Hell, I have no doubt that the Devil himself would take notice as she organized "No More Pitchfork" groups and led protest rallies to lower the temperature. Gram's demanding, impatient, irritable side was always counterbalanced by kindness, courage, commitment, discipline, responsibility, and respectability.

Gram got angry when the people around her lacked the awareness to do as she did and help, support, and give to other people. She was stunned when family members or friends didn't pick up a check or pay their share of a restaurant bill. It was never about money; it was about principle and mutual respect. There was lots of laughter and tears, but always mutual respect.

Up until now, we could have been college friends buying shots at Fort Ram (a bar in Fort Collins in the early 1990s) with Gram singing karaoke. It was awesome. Most people Kay's and my age simply dealt with their elders by hiding them away or avoiding them. For most people, spending Saturday night with the grandparents doesn't usually include the words "fun" or "exciting," but for us it meant having a great time. We loved being with Gram and Gramps, but those good times were fast becoming memories.

Even as a grown man, I fell asleep on their couch during our many discussions. It was old and smelled odd, but something about the comfort put me to sleep. Even when I was wide awake, as soon as I hit that couch, I started to snooze as we talked about the Depression, Gramps's time in World War II, their first jobs, Gram's days in Utah or selling real estate, living through the death of their spouses, working jobs that paid a nickel an hour, and living in a house with no indoor plumbing.

Kay and I usually heard our grandparents' stories more than once, but they were interesting, entertaining, and laden with lessons. I never fully appreciated those moments until many years later when our conversations consisted of repeating the same answer to the same question over and over and over.

We loved these special moments with them, but the demands for caregiving were only growing, and the two of us were falling behind. It was like we could see the tsunami coming but kept trying to enjoy the sunny beach. We were in denial and delusional, and we continued doing whatever we could to care for them. But we were caught in a trap and were quickly running out of options. Helping the grandparents had blown up into a ten- to thirty-hour-per-week job. It was like the old frog-in-the-frying-pan story. Once the frog realizes he's hot, it's too late.

So Kay and I went from spending quiet weekend nights together to switching our plans at the drop of the hat to assist Gram and Gramps. It might be an emergency errand, a quick drive to the hospital, or to go fix something at their house.

Ultimately, we decided the only choice was for Kay to give up her contract managing the Foundation and take care of the grandparents full time. That way they could stay in their home, and Kay would help out daily by phone or in person. Looking back, I now realize we had other choices, but at the time it wasn't clear. We could have met with all the family members and asked others to contribute time and resources to the effort. Or we could have searched for professional consultants or other in-home care providers. We didn't.

"Honey, we really can do this," I assured Kay, who was not willing to say no. Her entire life she'd helped people—any time, any way possible. Now was no different. I thought she could stay home with Helen and the second baby and manage Gram's and Gramps's lives at the same time. I'm sure the thought of this new commitment overwhelmed her, but she never mentioned fear or anxiety. She kept up the solider front. My grinning optimism exemplified my idealism. Kay was unrattled, and she acted like we could pull this off. If I'd said, "We can run a marathon today and climb Mount Everest tomorrow," she probably wouldn't have blinked either. Kay might have been playing a good game of poker, but she went with the plan.

Over the following months, however, another gigantic problem emerged, which neither of us dreamed possible: our single-income family became a zero-income family when one of my former employees decided that professional ethics were optional.

On April 29, 2008, XploreNet's lead software developer, Tayson Mitchell, sat down in my office after a key business meeting. Tayson's thin, black-framed glasses made him look part Clark Kent, part nerdy IT guy. He was smart and stand-offish, especially if he didn't like you.

My gut told me something wasn't right, partly because it wasn't like Tayson to get social after business meetings. He was more of a meet-and-run kind of guy. I always joked that Tayson probably left his car idling during meetings so he could make a quick escape afterward.

The prospective, web-development customer we'd just met with had agreed to work with us to implement a project. It would be complicated, but I thanked God as I walked back to my office. It was a six-figure account, and with the economy plummeting into a nationwide "Great" Recession and with fraudulent mortgage-backed securities about to take center stage, a new client with significant revenue was definitely welcomed.

I was surprised at Tayson's uncharacteristic request to hold a meeting in person because he emphasized privacy. He was also the kind of guy who was unfiltered and would blurt out politically incorrect words and didn't care who heard. As I sat down, my concern was rising like a thermometer in the Arizona dessert. My gut screamed that something was very wrong. Tayson sat across from me with a stony look. He'd been a great employee since 1996, helping the business grow and overcome many challenges.

Tayson joined us as lead developer one year after we started the business. He was the driving force for us to develop web and database service offerings. Now, as he sat in my office, his silence and odd look scared the hell out of me. He had always been direct.

He moved to the edge of his seat, stared straight at me, and took a big, deep breath. "Today is my last day with the company," he said, "and I'm taking all the clients with me."

I don't remember my first words. I could hear my heart pounding in my chest, and I'm not sure if my pause lasted just a few seconds or half an hour. "What the fuck are you talking about?" I said. "That's real funny." I wondered if Bryan, a former employee who loved playing practical jokes on me, was going to jump out from behind the door and say, "We got you good on this one, you S.O.B!"

Instead, Tayson continued with a cocky monologue that I could tell was rehearsed, though the delivery was choppy: "I helped bring in many of our clients, so I'm taking them with me—and my attorney says I can do that." The agony continued when he added, "I've already spoken to many of the clients, and they've agreed to come with me."

When no candid camera appeared, I realized this was no joke. My mind was reeling, and all I could think was *We should have had written agreements with all of our clients!*

At this point, I was going back and forth between wanting to punch Tayson or throw something. "Is this a joke?" I said. "You can't be serious."

Tayson said, "I'm serious. I'm dead serious."

My first instinct was to half-chastise him and then throw in a motivational speech, so I started, "Tayson, we built this company together and for ten years you've been well taken care of. Both you and your attorney."

I stopped to catch my breath. Then I continued, "Does your attorney have a real law degree? Apparently he didn't go to law school because those clients belong to the firm, and you've lost your fucking mind. You got some bad advice." Then I played up the positive. "You've worked from home on your own schedule, and you've been well compensated. I gave you everything I could."

Tayson challenged me. "But you haven't paid me my commission correctly in six months," he said. "And payments have been short or delayed."

"I know, but you're aware of our struggle; we've been through this many times before. I've always come through haven't I? We've been having cash-flow issues."

"We *always* have cash-flow problems."

"So this isn't anything new to you," I reasoned. "We always figure it out."

"I'm tired of this cash-flow shit. You always have one excuse after another."

I leaned in. "You know we'll make it. We *always* make it through. Clients always pay us late. The economy has been a little rough."

"I've been thinking about this for a long time and I'm done," said Tayson. "No more. I'm moving on. I'm burned out. I helped bring on the clients, so I'm taking them with me."

Tayson's final words that day were the beginning of more challenges than I could ever have fathomed. Although I didn't know it yet, I was starting to reap what I had sown. I hadn't been paying attention to details. I was letting little things go, and not making the people around me accountable. I was caught in the sad lie: the one you tell yourself when your life feels like a train coming off the tracks, but you refuse to change course and just keep moving at the same speed, hell-bent on that same destination: the train wreck. I had already convinced myself that the end justified the means.

As the eighteen-month legal battle with Tayson over the business, rights to clients, and damages took shape, I brought suit against Tayson for $2 million in losses. My personal income had plummeted from more than mid six figures to almost zero. He and I ended up coming to a nondisclosure settlement, which was short of the damages I had asked for. His actions caused my income to drop significantly. I was devastated and angry, but the conflict was minor in comparison with what lay ahead.

• • •

"Please come right away, dear. Gramps has fallen." Gram's voice was tear-filled and despondent.

"Again?" I tried to cloak my frustration. This had happened before.

"He's on the driveway, and I think he's really hurt this time."

"Call the ambulance, I'll be right there!"

It was early May, 2008, and Gramps's falls were becoming a regular occurrence. When I arrived some twenty-five minutes after Gram's call, the paramedics had already loaded him into the ambulance. They told me that when they arrived my grandfather was lying on his side, having trouble breathing. They mentioned they thought he'd been lying there for a long time, which seemed reasonable since Gram often forgot if he was outside or in the neighborhood. Later on, Gramps's explanation for this fall was the driveway jumped up and got him. He noted the apparent one-inch difference where the sidewalk and gutter meet.

The situation was becoming tragic. This was the third fall in a few short months, and this time he'd broken two ribs. I stepped into the back of the ambulance and we headed to the emergency room.

Kay had hired two nurses in sixty days. One quit, and Kay fired the other one for not arriving to work on time. The nurses helped Gram with laundry, grocery shopping, and cooking. The first could work only two days a week, so Kay filled in on the other days. Gram had become more depressed and was putting plastic containers in the toaster oven. Gramps let the water run in the backyard all night.

Gram made it hard on each nurse, saying they were stealing things. In one case, she thought the nurse was coming on to Gramps. We let them go before they had the chance to quit. The nurses were supposed to cover day care while Kay and I filled in on evenings and weekends. We were desperately trying to keep the grandparents in their home, but our options were diminishing between Gramps falling and Gram giving the nurses hell.

• • •

Even though Gramps was deteriorating physically, he still went with the flow. Ever since I could remember that was his way. And over the last ten years, his relationship with Kay had grown stronger. When he said Kay's name, the words "jewel of the family" often followed. And when Gramps looked at Kay his eyes had a special glow, like a sparkling lake when the sunrise first hits it. Not a romantic look, but similar to a new parent looking at their newborn for the first time. He saw through her exterior to her heart. And she to his. Similar values and characteristics made a comfortable connection. They related to each other as kindred souls who found their way to Earth to perform miracles and act like angels. When she smiled, he melted; when he laughed, she giggled. The feelings were mutual and heartfelt. Although Kay was not his biological daughter or granddaughter, he introduced her as "my daughter, Kay."

The two of them could talk. I mean *really* talk—for hours about real stuff, long-ago memories, and pivotal life moments. Kay was one of the few people in the world Gramps would ask for help. Most of the time he didn't need to ask, she just knew. She helped without giving him the chance to say no. He didn't need to say anything. He knew. She knew. We all knew. She was his guardian angel.

Kay had lost her grandparents before she was old enough to know them, and Gramps fit the part, a spot-on match for the role. Even though she was a grown woman she acted like a little girl when she was in his presence. Not immature—just protected, safe, secure.

Gramps and Kay were always excited to see each other, and they could talk for hours. But sometimes their long conversations got him in trouble. One time, while Gram was in the operating room having minor surgery, Kay kept Gramps company in the hospital cafeteria. They got lost in conversation, talking about everything from too-small, inappropriately sized farmer's overalls to what it felt like sitting in a real Model T automobile.

Two-and-a-half hours flew by when suddenly Kay heard an announcement over the hospital intercom. "Gramps, is that your name coming over the sound system?" she asked.

"What, honey?"

"Gramps, I think they just said your name over the loudspeaker."

"Oh geez! Oh no!" Gramps looked like he was getting pulled over by the police. Gram's procedure had ended an hour before. They hurried to her room as fast as a ninety-year-old man could move. They turned the corner to see Gram sitting in her hospital bed, arms crossed and a pissed-off look on her face. "Dad! Where have you *been*?"

Kay and Gramps looked at each other, both trying to hide their chuckles.

Gram yelled, "This isn't funny! Where the hell have you been, Dad?"

The only woman in the world that Gram would let Gramps hang out with was Kay. Gram's extreme level of jealously was something I'd never seen before. It included nurses, lawyers, doctors, police, grocery clerks, cleaning people, insurance agents, ministers, and flight attendants. Even Jesus would have been a threat. But she knew Kay's and Gramps's connection was different, and she never complained about it. In fact, Gram felt at peace knowing Kay was there to help even if Gram physically couldn't or soon would be passing on. Nobody questioned that connection, which only grew stronger as the summer of 2008 moved forward.

• • •

Although Gram and Gramps could manage some personal affairs, communicate with friends, and interact with neighbors, their decline was speeding up. They were well past retirement age but still enjoyed their freedom, free time, and each other. However, the problem with elderly mental demise is that there's no definite point when the reality of one's circumstance becomes obvious. Anyone who's been through it with a loved one knows the last phase of an elderly person losing their independence and ability to function on their own doesn't start on a Monday and end on Tuesday. It is a gradual occurrence, like a thief in the night stealing bits of memory, personality, and ability. The days pass, the symptoms worsen, the denial grows, and the options disappear. Before you know it, time is up and either you have planned well and lucked out or you're in a desperate situation to find alternative caregivers. We were the latter, playing a game I like to call "Help, Leave, and Pray." You show up to help, then afterward you leave your loved one's home and pray as you're driving away that they'll be safe for the night. It's not a fun game, and there is no winner.

Gram and Gramps were diminishing both physically and mentally, reverting back to their childhood. They were acting like infants who needed constant supervision and, yes, an occasional diaper change. We didn't need elder care, we needed an onsite therapist and babysitter.

"He's sleeping in the garage again," said one of the kind neighbors who called at nine o'clock one night. This neighbor kept an eye on my grandparents when Kay or I weren't on site. During that summer, Gramps was falling asleep somewhere besides bed at least once a week. If there wasn't a car-related issue like driving and getting lost or forgetting where the car was parked, my grandparents were leaving on the house lights all night long.

It became routine to head over to find Gramps peacefully snoring inside the car with the key still in the ignition and a bag of groceries in the passenger seat. One leg was usually hanging out the open car door while the other leg was still engaging the brake. Luckily, he put the car in park before snoozing off. He looked like he'd had a stroke, but he was okay. Once again, we would gently guide him into the house and lock everything up behind us. We left thanking God nothing had caught fire, that the car had not gone through the back of the garage, that no one was hurt.

All the worries and the night rescues were killing me and Kay. It was time to admit the truth: Gram and Gramps could no longer stay alone in their house. Like many people in our country, we were getting in way over our heads with the demands of caregiving. We had become part of the "sandwich generation," jammed between taking care of kids while watching over parents or, in our case, taking care of grandparents. We were beginning the initial phase of caregiver emotions: guilt, sadness, and loneliness. We felt alone because caregiving for adults has become one of the largest secret problems in our country. It is silent and hidden, yet according to Caregiver.org, more than forty million people provide in-home elder care. There are estimates that another seventy-two million people will require it in the next fifteen years. (Caregiver.org is the website of the Family Caregiver Alliance, dedicated to improving quality of life for family caregivers and the people who receive their care.)

Gram's and Gramps's growing needs were changing Kay and me as much or more than it was changing them. Even with Sadie helping out when she could, it wasn't enough. Tragically, every time we arrived at their house a new surprise awaited. On one occasion in August, I rang the doorbell several times, and after some hard, unanswered knocks on the door I headed around back. I came through the side gate only to find Gram sitting on the patio lost in her own thoughts. She looked great with her hair beautifully styled. Her shampoo, cut, and styling was a weekly tradition as far back as I could remember. The weather was mild; I could see why the gentle breeze made her feel good. She noticed me, smiled while tilting her head, and said, "Why hello, Will." I could see in her eyes that it was getting harder for her to remember my name. Her smile told me she still knew my face, but the names were starting to fade.

"Gram, I knocked on the front door, but you didn't hear me."

"Well, dear, I'm enjoying the nice afternoon." She seemed completely unconcerned.

"Where is Gramps?"

"I don't know. Did you see him out front?"

"No. When was the last time *you* saw him?" I was getting a little nervous about his whereabouts, so I walked into the kitchen from the back door to find messy counters with dishes piled up and a growing mountain of mail. We had only been away for two days. It reminded me of the meth houses you see on TV when the police bust the addicted renters. Items were on the floor and under the kitchen table; bags were stacked side by side between the garage and basement doors. Somehow, in less than thirty-six hours, they had destroyed the house. I'd never seen it this messy in my life. They always had everything organized, clean, and proper.

I felt bad. To me it was an unspoken rule that you take care of your family but you don't talk about it. And, God forbid, don't ask for help. Besides, there *was* no one else to help. My dad was nonexistent in my life and had a very shallow relationship with the grandparents. At this point, he was divorced for a second time and was searching for yet another job. When he did see Gram, he blew up at her, yelling and acting like a small child having a temper tantrum. He treated her with so much disrespect, and he was mean to her. Unfortunately, Gramps's daughter lived on the other side of the country. They spoke by phone and had a good relationship, but she couldn't be there to help.

Hiring a full-time nurse for both of Gram and Gramps didn't seem to make sense. If you've dealt with this situation, then you know. If not, let me describe it for you. Imagine a family member managing your entire life including all your day-to-day activities, answering all your emails and phone calls, opening and organizing all your mail. (Thank God my grandparents didn't use a computer or email!) Your growing task list would include tracking all the financial accounts, insurance of all kinds, multiple vendors for home, car, job/business, and any other critical issues a person deals with on a daily, weekly, or monthly basis. Every financial transaction. Every needed correspondence. For God's sake, you practically need an act of Congress to change a mailing address with Social Security. And because of HIPPA, the Health Insurance Portability and Accountability Act law that was established to protect our medical histories, it's nearly impossible to receive or update medical-insurance information.

Now add to the scenario your own physical health issues and unstable mental and emotional situation, and you have an impending disaster. This was now us. Kay and I were stuck in a mental tub. Each day more water was rushing in, filling the bathtub to the top and leaving us gasping for air with no escape. We should have said something to our friends or family. We should have asked for help. We didn't.

We kept pushing onward, not wanting anyone to know the truth. We kept telling ourselves we could figure everything out. By this point, we were way beyond receiving legal advice. I continued to *not* meet with an estate attorney because an estate lawyer I met at a networking function told me wills are purposely left loose on the front end because estate lawyers make their biggest money on the back end when all hell breaks loose. I thought we could do everything through trust. Besides, I was *me*, and I never let anyone down. I always figured out the situation, and everybody around me just followed my lead. I would make sure everyone was taken care of—as I always had. It didn't need to be detailed out. That was pretty dumb thinking.

Kay and I were proud, and we had promised Gram and Gramps we would take care of them. My grandparents had basically raised me. They had helped me during every major step in my life. Now it was our turn to help them. I had to suck it up and figure it out. *We're family*, I told myself. *This is a private issue. Don't let everyone down. Do your job.*

Kay and I didn't want to let Gram and Gramps down, so we kept taking care of everyone as we had always done. What we lacked in choices we made up in courage. However, sooner or later the house of cards would fall—and fall hard.

CHAPTER 11

# The Big Meeting

## September 16, 2008

*"If there were no bad people,
there would be no good lawyers."*

— CHARLES DICKENS

N ew York City in the fall is something to see. The rain comes down sideways in a mist with the smell of ocean, gas fumes, hot dogs, and condescension all mixed together. Seeing NYC on TV or in a movie just doesn't give you a real appreciation for the place. If you've been there, then you know Frank Sinatra was right when he sang, "I want to be a part of it, New York, New York."

My two business partners and I hurtled in a taxi toward the financial district for a meeting at Standard & Poor's to discuss our innovative startup business, Talus. Though I have met some incredibly nice people from this part of the country, this taxi driver was not one of them. He drove with an angry look on his face and at a speed that made it seem like he was

93

trying out for the Indianapolis 500. His repeated pushing on the horn and screaming at the top of his lungs at every driver who passed him made me think he had some kind of mental illness.

Laird Bolden, Talus's idea guy, suddenly shouted, "I forgot my passport," so loudly it reminded me of a Tourette's outburst.

"You need it to get in!" said Steve Murphy. "S&P's office is tighter than Fort Knox. It's got more security then the airport." Steve was our business development person. "You wondered about cold-calling businesses by walking into their Financial District buildings. You're about to see why I laughed at you."

Laird rooted in his briefcase and then shouted, "My passport! I *do* have it."

We were on our way to the most important meeting in the history of Talus. We cofounded Talus to solve one major issue in health care: price transparency. Through indices and futures contacts, we were onto something special. Our business concept was to help reduce the cost of health care by showing more data details and eventually having an open market to trade health care. The idea behind our startup was to help reduce the cost of health care and save the country. Many friends had given me their "angel" investment because they cared about our potential solution to the health-care crisis and thought they could receive a big payday when their investment was returned upon our success.

Laird, Steve, and I were about to present in front of Standard & Poor's, one of the most successful financial research and indexing companies in the world. We believed some average guys from Denver were about to explode onto the business scene like five dynamite sticks going off.

If today's meeting with Paul Scalia and Nick Joseph at the S&P index firm went well, I finally would get rewarded for all the years of hard work since Talus launched in 2006. With XploreNet struggling due to the recession, Talus might be all I would have left. Our persistence with the business plan had paid off, and in a few minutes we would be in front of this renowned index firm. One of the firm's tracking tools is a foundational piece of economic indexing in the United States—you hear and see the Standard & Poor's brand and index (S&P 500) every morning and night when the markets open and close each day.

As we waited in the lobby, we watched stressed-out employees come and go, looking like they hadn't slept in weeks. Our timing couldn't have been worse because it was September 16, 2008, the morning after Lehman Brothers had failed. This day would later be remembered as a pivotal moment in the Great Recession, which started in March. There already was Black Tuesday and Black Monday. Now, as I sat in the lobby sweating, I dubbed the day "Barf in a Bag While Throwing Yourself into the Hudson River Tuesday."

When Nick Joseph came out to meet us, his handshake was weak and his skin pale. Paul Scalia soon joined us, and as we walked down the hallway he rattled off a crazy monologue about how bad the market was this morning. It felt like Armageddon. After a year of conference calls, emails, business summaries, back-and-forth business plans, strategy documents, and heartfelt wishful thinking, our key meeting was being interrupted by one of the largest financial collapses in US history since the Great Depression.

We sat at a conference table and, without any small talk, Gene plunged in. "You mentioned in our last phone call that you had an entry point. So what is it?" He sounded like we'd just run over his dog. "You realize Lehman, AIG, and God knows who else are done," he continued. "Add these to the Bear Sterns list. Fucking finished."

"Yes," the three of us said together, like army recruits at boot camp.

Paul jumped in. "How do we get this to market and do it fast?"

I said the only thing I could think of: "We have a new index product." For effect I added, "And it's the solution to the health-care crisis in America. Laird is going to diagram it for you." Not exactly the best-prepared intro, but we were pretty damn far down the gold mine. I was determined to keep things moving even if nuclear bombs were exploding around us.

In a tone more like a demand than invitation, Paul asked Laird to go ahead with the presentation.

Laird stood up and gave me a blank look as he moved to the front. I smiled and winked at him. I suspect my gesture appeared more like a nervous tic than confident posturing. At the white board, Laird slowly picked up the marker.

My heart pounded. I wasn't feeling well because I'd only slept a couple of hours.

Laird peeled around and nervously grabbed the bottle of Fiji Water on the edge of the table. He loosened the cap and drank from it like he'd been in the desert all night. I wondered if he was having stage fright. The room was dead silent, and with each gulp he took I wondered when, and if, he was going to start.

Laird Bolden was normally a cool customer. Steve introduced us three years before at a breakfast meeting in Broomfield. What made us click was his understanding of health care from both the medical and financial sides. Laird's daughter, Brianna, had special medical needs and was in a vegetative state. Her brain had stopped developing *in utero* several months into the pregnancy. I really appreciated his relationship with her. Though Brianna passed away during her teenage years, in 2007, I remember seeing her smile for the first time and it lit up the room. As I watched Laird's presentation, I remembered Brianna's bright smile and was reminded of a time our families had dinner together. Helen had asked, "Daddy, can I go in with Brianna and play?"

"I'm not sure if you should go into Brianna's room with her," I told her. "You know she can't talk or play or move very well."

Helen replied, "That's okay."

Later, when I peeked around the corner to check on them, Helen was in Brianna's hospital bed. They were smiling and watching a movie. Just seeing their joy reminded me of the importance of life at any level. It was a spiritual moment I've never forgotten.

On the drive home, Helen had asked, "Why can't Brianna speak?"

I said, "I don't know. It's some type of birth defect, honey."

Without missing a beat she said, "Daddy, I think she talks with her eyes."

"Yes, I think you're right." I wiped back tears. A few years later, Brianna died.

Now, in the conference room, Laird cleared his throat to begin. My future—all of our futures—was in his hands. No sweat was showing on his forehead ... yet. He turned back to the whiteboard and began diagramming our Talus Healthcare Index and Trading Platform. Laird mumbled and stuttered, "It is difficult to overstate the threat that health-care costs ..." He trailed off, then started again, louder and clearer this time. "Currently health-care costs pose a threat to the strength of our economy, and attempted solutions to the problem have been ineffective. No— check that. They've actually exacerbated the problem. We at Talus believe the problem is a function of health-care costs and not lack of coverage."

Laird continued for almost half an hour, explaining our business plan in detail. Then he took a deep breath and continued, "Without a public index to measure the market, pricing information is almost completely absent because most health-care tools measure health care on a macro level by making an estimate, or held in confidence. Health-care data is expensive, difficult to filter, and even harder to organize into meaningful pricing points. Yet it's how doctors and hospitals get paid."

Paul Scalia interrupted, "So Talus has developed an index that measures the actual cost of medical procedures done in the health-care industry? And this type of index has never been available to the industry before?" We nodded.

We spent the next two hours covering the size of the market and all the other details with our index partner's colleagues, who seemed to be on the same page. They were getting it: Talus could make health-care costs transparent so health care could potentially be traded on the market just like other commodities like oil or wheat

Laird summed it all up: "There would be lots of buyers for this index."

It was obvious Paul had other things on his mind than three guys from Colorado with a great idea, but Nick Joseph seemed determined to see what we had or didn't have. He asked the nuts-and-bolts questions, and we answered each in detail until Nick was on the same page. The momentum of the meeting had shifted from confusion to excitement. It had also exceeded our ninety-minute window and lasted more than three hours.

After some quick handshakes, the magic words came from Nick's mouth: "We'll send over the letter of intent."

I looked at him, "What? Did you say 'LOI'?"

"Yes, I think it's a good next step."

"Yes, I agree." I couldn't stop smiling. "Thank you! We're excited to move forward." A letter of intent meant we were going to work together.

The cab shot out of the parking lot like a hyper-speed jet, and I said a few prayers. As we careened around a corner, I gripped the seatbelt and door handle, and my knuckles turned white. I was pushing myself back into the seat as if I were on a roller coaster plummeting over a steep hill. While I prayed we wouldn't die in a car wreck, Steve and Laird were high-fiving and pretending to order Porsches online.

*Man, that was a great meeting*, I thought. I'd show my friends who ribbed me because our website was talusexchange.com ("tal u sex change")— which unfortunately my partners hadn't noticed. My friends joked about us promoting gender transformation when our dream was revolutionizing health care.

I grabbed my phone and called Kay. "We're going to be billionaires!" I shouted, "We're getting the letter of intent. Standard & Poor's loved it! The Index Firm is on board!"

When Kay didn't react, I continued. "Well, they kind of loved it," I added. "Okay, I think they like it a lot."

Kay's silence told me something wasn't right, "Good job babe, I'm so proud of you!" Her response sounded contrived and completely exhausted.

"Are you okay?" I asked.

"I'm getting more concerned about Gramps," she replied.

"What's going on now?"

Kay told me the director of the New Day Rehabilitation Center—where Gramps had been placed while he recuperated after another fall—had called to say Gramps was getting worse both physically and mentally.

"He'll need to go to a permanent facility," Kay said. I could hear the grief in her voice.

"It's okay!" Nothing could bring me down. "Talus is going to take off, and we can help Gram and Gramps. We'll be able to take care of the entire family."

"I know, but we have another meeting scheduled tomorrow to review a care plan for Gramps. We'll need to make some decisions soon."

Kay told me she had called Gramps's daughter, Mary Smith, who lived in the Midwest to let her know that we would be moving him to a nursing home sooner than expected. As Mary always did, she told Kay that whatever we thought was best, we should do. Plus, Mary and her husband, Bob, were both traveling in different parts of the country.

As our Talus team headed to the airport, Kay continued, "Gramps needs somewhere to go for rehab. He's exhausted and needs a break from Gram." The weight of taking care of Gram while trying to manage his own changes and limitations was causing Gramps to deteriorate by the day. He could no longer do both. Either his health would worsen, or her independence would have to go.

"The only place he should go right now is to *our* house," Kay stated. "I don't want him to go to a facility yet."

I quickly objected. "But you're pregnant! And I have another trip coming up."

Kay sighed, but she sounded brighter. "It's okay. We'll love having him with us. We can make it work."

When we arrived at the airport, Steve and Laird raced off to a restaurant while I stayed by the windows, facing our assigned gate. Instead of celebrating our success, I stood there feeling nervous about Gram and Gramps and wondering what might become of them.

Two days later, Kay and I hatched a plan for Gramps's escape from Gram, who was waiting for him to get out of the rehab center. We had to be tricky and delicate because Gram could smell deception a mile away. We picked up Gramps the next afternoon from the New Day Center, which was more of a rundown hellhole than a rehab center. We made a few pee stops for him on the way home—at least he *thought* he was going home. When we arrived at our house, he was in his element. Even though it wasn't his house, walking into ours seemed to set him free. It was like a weight lifted off his shoulders.

Although Gramps didn't sleep well at night, during the day he enjoyed the warm sunrays as they cut across the backyard. I observed from the window as he watched water trickle down rocks and form bubbles as it splashed into the pond and met up with the water lilies. Our backyard faced the west, so though the sun was harsh in the afternoon, the yard was a cool oasis in the morning. It was the perfect backdrop for Gramps as he leaned on his walker with one hand and used the other to point and describe plants. Although beautiful and well-manicured, our yard didn't compare to Gramps's own spacious garden—a luscious, green, holy place filled with every type of vegetable and flower imaginable. His garden was proof of Ralph Waldo Emerson's famous line of poetry, "Earth laughs in flowers." Gramps would pause, take a deep breath to gather his thoughts, wipe the sweat from his brow, and then start again like a professor facilitating a class discussion. He couldn't wait to work with Kay in the yard.

Gramps started every morning with a newspaper, oatmeal that had to include salt, and a freshly brewed cup of coffee. As Kay smiled and handed him the mug, acting as both caregiver and student, she asked if he would show her today the right way to plant flowers. And, sure enough, he smiled, and his eyes sparkled. Unconstrained enthusiasm took over, and his feet started moving slowly to the back door. When he finally made it outside, he was back in his happy place.

Kay would take it all in as he covered the finer points of proper soil spread, water allocation, and seed depth. His main points connected the entire plant's lifecycle to unique life lessons like faith, integrity, and spirit. Kay and Gramps had done these sessions many times before, but now it was in *our* yard. And now we knew times like these were limited.

As he spoke, a twinkle came to his eye and his wide smile left no secrets. His gardening passion only magnified his reputation as an award-winning dahlia grower. He knew everything about planting flowers and high-altitude gardening. At ninety-one years old, his wisdom, confidence, and gentle approach made others feel great. Over the years, he had spent many summers as a volunteer for the Colorado State gardening department. He even answered phone calls regarding flower cultivation.

A trip to our backyard gave Gramps something to do in the moment, and it was something meaningful and fulfilling for him. To give him easier access to the garden, we set up a small bed for him in the front living room, which was just ten feet to the bathroom. There were no stairs to climb, no furniture to dodge, and natural light streamed in.

The backyard quickly became his sanctuary, the place he craved to be. At the end of each teaching session, he would say, "Can we do it again tomorrow?" And Kay would reply, "Yes, of course, Gramps." The days were magical, with Kay and Gramps enjoying each other's company and strengthening their friendship with their daily talks as they moved between the kitchen table and backyard. He'd tell her all about growing up on the plains, farm life, picking the fresh vegetables, and the excitement of accompanying his father into town to sell or trade what they'd patiently grown. She'd tell him about her dad and mom's off-again, on-again marriage or family road trips all over the country.

As the second week went on, however, nights became more difficult to get through. While I was traveling for meetings about Talus, Kay was waking up several times a night to lift Gramps on and off the toilet. She was almost eight months pregnant, so maneuvering Gramps in the bathroom wasn't just tough, it was dangerous. She was losing her balance and nearly falling each time, which was often. He was up every thirty minutes trying to go. Inevitably, he would fall asleep on the toilet. Sometimes two hours passed and then he either finished or gave up. Kay would guide him back to bed. Neither one of them ever complained, although sometimes he would cry, embarrassed about it. Kay would work with him until they both were laughing.

When each work trip was over, I could relieve her during the nightly circus. My shift usually started with Kay nudging me at one in the morning to go check on him. I would stumble out of bed and head downstairs to find him struggling to get to the bathroom on his own. I'm sure he was relieved to see my face instead of Kay's—less embarrassing having another male to help. His expression said it all. He would gently turn, look at me, and say, "Will, this is ridiculous! I used to change your diaper, and now you're helping me with mine."

"Yeah, I know, Gramps. Ironic isn't it? But nothing to worry about." I helped him get off the toilet and pulled up his pants. It broke my heart *and* inspired me—both at the same time, just as his positive attitude and reluctance to become depressed moved me. He was accepting the last stage of his life's journey with a constant smile on his face. This amazing man, who as a certified electrician once climbed thirty-foot ladders and descended into large holes to install wiring, was now unable to lift himself off the toilet. His decline would only get worse, and we had no idea what new storm was coming our way.

# CHAPTER 12

# The Big Escape

## 2008

*"A-B-C. A-Always, B-Be, C-Closing. Always be closing.*
*ALWAYS BE CLOSING.*
*A-I-D-A. Attention, Interest, Decision, Action. I made $970,000 last year.*
*How much'd you make? You see, pal, that's who I am, and you're nothing.*
*Nice guy? I don't give a shit. Good father? Go home and play with your kids.*
*You wanna work here—close! Fuck you."*

— ALEC BALDWIN AS BLAKE, *GLENGARRY GLEN ROSS*

Having Gramps stay with us in late September 2008 was wishful thinking on my part, *not* a real solution. It lasted only nine days. As each day passed, Kay and I were realizing that with our little daughter and another baby arriving soon, our house was not the answer for full-time elder care. I knew Kay would keep trying, but it was clear to both of us that Gramps's next stop would need to be PeakView Senior Living. By October, we had to get him over to the facility.

My grandparents could no longer express their opinion about where to place them, so I had to rely on feedback from our earlier tours of assisted living. We had toured several places back in the day, but Gram abruptly walked out if she didn't connect with the feel and environment. Gram's lukewarm feeling about PeakView Senior Living and Gramps's positive perception of the food was all we had to go on. PeakView was the place they disliked the least.

Kay and I agreed that getting Gramps settled first made the most sense. Later we could bring Gram over to be with him. We anticipated she would give us the fight of her life, so we had to be at the top of our game. Every time we showed up to check on Gram, who was still living at the house, her first words were, "Where is Grampa?" She looked like smoke could come out of her ears at any moment when she realized we'd arrived without him. "Will, Where. Is. He?"

I did the best thing I could in the situation: I lied. "He's still at the rehabilitation facility," I said soothingly.

"When will he be home?"

"Not positive on that. Soon, I'm sure."

"I can rehabilitate him. Hell, where is he?"

Kay chimed in, "Gram, you'll be joining him soon."

"If he's dead I don't want to join him! And why would I go to some place like that? I don't need rehabilitation. Where the hell is he? What is going on? Tell me *now!*"

I put on the best poker face I had. "It's a facility that helps with all levels of needs. He won't be there long."

She wasn't going down that easy. "I want to be with him, so tell me where he is!"

That Saturday, we moved Gramps to the facility, bringing only his clothes and a few necessities. Moving furniture out of the house would be a dead giveaway of our plan. It turned into a long three weeks with Gram away from him, as she constantly questioned his whereabouts. Though he missed her too, he seemed calm in his own thoughts. The quiet without her must have been a nice treat. I am sure he told himself it was just a short break and soon they would be back at the house together, taking on the world in their own unique way.

Once Gramps got settled in at PeakView, Kay and I visited him almost daily during those three weeks. His calm expression always made it seem like he'd just received a nice massage or spent fifteen minutes in a hot tub. The anxiety of Gram's constant yelling at him the last few weeks they were together was now gone. She would yell at him to fix the fence, prune the trees, water the grass more, or take out the trash—all ironic directives since he could barely lift himself out of a chair. Gram's fear of her own mind going had caused her to lash out at him.

Now Gramps sat by himself on a crimson, leather couch in the main visiting room, lost in thought as he looked out the window. I remember his face looked lighter, and the color in his cheeks was starting to come back, as if the stress had dissipated. He was himself again.

Gram, however, struggled being on her own. It seemed like she called Kay every fifteen minutes to ask where Gramps was or when Kay was stopping by. The question, "Where is Gramps?" came so often that the words were etched in my mind, and she wasn't satisfied no matter how we answered her. I didn't know whether her dementia was advancing due to the natural process of the disease or if the stress had accelerated it. It was clear it was now or never to get her over to PeakView to be with him.

For the second time in less than four weeks I lied to Gram. I told her she'd go for a visit to spend a few days with Gramps—like a childhood sleepover or a hotel stay. She was excited and helped Kay prepare her two suitcases, one with clothes and the other with makeup, hair dryers. and any other female equipment she could get her hands on. She thought PeakView was a hotel. Within a few days, as we had hoped, she was having a good time just being with him. She had forgotten about the house, or so I thought until she asked, "Will, when will we be going home?"

"When Gramps is done with rehab," I said. I felt a pang of guilt.

"How long will that be?"

"Not sure." I tried a few times to say this was her new home, but that went over like a dud. Instead I asked innocently, "How do you like your new home?"

"My house is at 2590 Bauer Drive," she snapped. Ironically, Gram couldn't remember I had been sitting with her for an hour, but she still could rattle off her address. "And what's wrong with the house?"

"The house is fine. Everything's great." I'm not sure she bought it.

While Gram acted like she was at a resort, Gramps was adapting nicely. In his first few weeks, he had made new friends and spent mornings talking about the old days with them and the staff. On more than one occasion, he delved into a one-sided conversation with a kind stranger.

On one Thursday afternoon, as we sat on the crimson couch, I asked him about his week. He was reading the paper and pointed me to the classified section. "Will, somehow we've come here without a car, so I'm going to buy this one." He was pointing to a red 1995 Dodge station wagon similar to the white one he and Gram used to own.

"Gramps, you don't need a car. You don't drive anymore."

"Oh yes I do. I can."

"You can drive?"

"Absolutely, and now I need to get transportation. I found a few cars yesterday that might work well."

Poor Gramps had no idea they still had a house and a car. I probed a little more, curious to hear his version of the story. His actions hadn't stopped with reading the local classifieds; he also attempted to go make the deal.

The assisted living staff had called Kay earlier in the week to say Gramps had dressed in his nicest garb and made his way out the front door and then down the street, his walker in tow. He made it across one street at the traffic light and headed to the next corner. Luckily, an employee leaving her shift was turning right at the main intersection and saw him pressing the crosswalk button. She was kind enough to intervene. His round trip was about 200 yards. I laughed as Kay told me the story, thinking how amazing it was to make it even that far at his age.

When asked where he was going, his response was, "I was grabbing a bus to go to the car dealer to buy a car." That was his first version of the story; the second version was that he needed to get downtown to an electrical project. Now he was back on the car idea, showing me the classifieds.

Other than this occasional search for a new vehicle or an attempt to get back to his garden, Gramps was doing well, but Gram was not. She became impatient, wanting to leave. She was as difficult as we had anticipated, perhaps even more so. Was she playing us? I wondered. Or was her mental state really deteriorating that fast? PeakView wasn't her cup of tea, and by damn she wasn't going to stay. She was constantly causing havoc, showing up at the front desk at all hours of the day and night asking, "Can we have a new set of towels for our room?" or "Honey will you either have a cab come get us or show us to our car?"

The staff thought it was cute and they played along, telling her they would have the towels sent right away.

"Thank you!" she said. "And remember we're in Room 725." The staff acted like they noted it.

One day Gram escalated her recent attitude to an entirely new level. I'm sure her picture would still be in PeakView's Hall of Fame if they had one. She developed a daily habit of asking the front-desk attendant, "Can we get the bill please? We'd like to check out now." God bless the ladies at the front desk. They just kept smiling day after day, but everyone has a breaking point.

Eventually the staff became weary of her behavior and started calling Kay a few times a week to urge her to help them by talking with Gram. It was crazy. There was one day Gram came to the front desk once every hour. I felt guilty that we hadn't told her the whole truth. Kay was visiting every other day, and I made it over whenever I could.

Now when I saw Gram, her eyes had a different look. They were becoming blanker and disengaged, as if she'd seen a ghost. And she was showing more than short-term memory impairment. There was a deeper loss, like a little bit of her soul was dying each day. One minute it broke my heart to see her like this, but then the next, I was filled with a warm feeling watching her and Gramps cuddle on that red couch like two high-school kids stealing a moment together while hiding from their parents. The staff also caught them doing a lot more than hugging, which, quite frankly, at Gramps's age should have been celebrated, not halted. Kay would tell Gram she was sharing too much information when Gram described their love-making. Once she even told Kay how much Gramps like her "racy" outfit. As embarrassing as these conversations were, it showed us what true, life-long love and commitment was about. And by the way, real life-long love *does* exist.

We finally seemed to be making headway as Gram and Gramps adjusted to their new life. A few months had passed, and we were feeling better because Kay was initially spending less time on their care with them living at the facility. But as we soon discovered, the move that was intended to reduce Kay's caregiving time actually *increased* it. We weren't the only ones dealing with these issues. At this same time, our close friends, Ricardo and Toni, were up to their eyeballs in challenges with her parents. It was giving us a scary look at our near future.

"I've been here since 7:30 this morning," Toni told Kay. Her parents were living at the same retirement community, PeakView Senior Living, and she and Kay compared notes all the time.

"Isn't that three days this week?" Kay asked.

Toni's parents had given her power of attorney, and she was now handling all the duties. "Kay, I don't know how I'm going to keep up with this," Toni confided. "See what you have to look forward to?"

Toni's parents had lived on their own until 2007, so she had been dealing with the increased demands for a while. "When we moved my folks to PeakView Senior Living, I thought it would get easier," she said. "It's not. I'm spending twenty-five to thirty hours a week—sometimes more—dealing with their affairs, and I visit at least three times per week, and sometimes every day."

Toni explained that her round-trip drive to and from PeakView was an hour, which contributed to her stress, and because her parents lived in separate rooms, Toni's visits took three to four hours each time.

In addition to the emotional support she provided, Toni also recited to Kay the litany of her power-of-attorney duties. "I've spent hours on the phone providing necessary documentation to establish me as the power of attorney with banks, doctors, nurses, insurance companies, brokerage firms, the IRS, the Veterans Administration, Social Security, and Medicare," Toni said. She also paid all her parents' bills and went to all doctor appointments with both parents because she had to keep clear, accurate financial records for their Trust. Toni also gathered the necessary documents and met with an accountant to file their income taxes each year.

Talking with Toni helped Kay realize our climb was just beginning. At least we knew someone else who was dealing with similar issues and tasks, but it didn't seem to make our situation any better.

Toni had also disposed of her parent's car, searched for and ordered online various personal sundries that her mother and father needed, and had them delivered to the facility. She shopped for and purchased all their clothing and other material needs, and she shopped for gifts so her parents could give them to other family members for holidays and birthdays. She had washed and ironed all of their clothing until her father died.

There were also many logistical details. Toni and Ricardo had moved her parents out of their initial patio home at PeakView and into separate quarters at the facility when they required different levels of medical care. They personally moved her Dad in and out of three apartments while in the assisted living. Her Mom had also been in three different rooms in the skilled-care wing.

Kay and Toni had become great friends not just because they were both kind and caring but because they were living a similar existence. Toni almost groaned as she described the quarterly Care Conference meetings held for each resident. At the meetings, the resident's overall condition was discussed, and care methods suggested (a family plan). There were the frequent phone calls and meetings with pharmacies, outside doctors, and internal caregivers, in addition to the "exciting" calls. Toni got emotional when she talked about all the many ER trips and hospitalizations for each of her parents during those four years. She would pick them up and drive them to all of their doctor appointments while her Dad was alive and until she could no longer move her mother alone from the car to wheelchair. After that, her mom was transported via van, but Toni always met her at each of the appointments. On average, there were eight doctor appointments a month. As Toni finished, Kay chimed in, "And what about the holidays? How have you been handling those?"

"As long as Mom was mobile, we would pick them up and bring them to our home," said Toni. "We returned them to the facility when they were tired." Once her mom was immobile, the family would go to PeakView for Thanksgiving, Christmas, Easter and their birthdays to celebrate with her parents either before or after the usual family gathering. They would try to attend the Mother's Day Brunch, Christmas Party, and Grandparents' Day event at the facility. Toni continued, "It was fun at first to pick them up and take them out for lunch or dinner or get takeout and have a picnic with them at the facility, but as their health deteriorated those became a lot of work. "We tried to get the grandchildren over to visit with them as much as we could, and while Dad was alive, we often picked them up and took them to church on Sunday mornings or for special church events."

All of this was taxing on Toni's brother too, who flew to Denver once a month for a long weekend to see their parents. And the biggest kicker of all is that Toni would later say that after her father passed, the weekly care load was reduced by less than 25 percent.

Kay and I experienced everything Toni and Ricardo went through, but since our grandparents lived longer, our workload—including calls, bills, and laundry—was everything she said and more. There were so many more tasks, projects, emergencies, necessities, and frustrations for us. Some were expected; others were a surprise. And as time passed the situation and accompanying stress only got worse, especially with a baby on the way.

Kay and I hosted a reveal party for this pregnancy. The nurse had written on a small card the word, "Boy," but when we pulled the card out of the envelope, I couldn't read her handwriting. I thought it said "Bay," so I yelled, "It's a Bay!" Everyone stared at me before they started laughing.

In October 2008, our little man was born, and his appearance gave us a short break from taking care of the grandparents. I never did handle my kids' births very well. I always imagined an epic bloodbath with all hell breaking loose during the last part of delivery. However, when it was all over, I experienced a feeling similar to winning the Super Bowl when the little one finally appeared. Our boy/bay Eddie arrived healthy, and after his birth everything seemed to be falling into place. At least we were pretending it was.

By winter, I had my hands full trying to keep both XploreNet and Talus going. Kay and I were making ends meet, but the future was starting to look bleak. My dad sometimes came for Christmas dinner—Kay was always kind to invite him. Most years he didn't make it over, but in 2008 he showed up. He told us his back was in a lot of pain from riding his bike. Kay urged him to go to the doctor, but he never did.

Kay was tackling the caregiving of our two little ones plus both grandparents—essentially babysitting for four. However, I continued my denial process, and my business behavior became more risky and hard headed. My weak plan was to stay in denial, fooling myself that we could take care of the grandparents while growing our businesses and raising children. It was foolproof.

Aren't all plans foolproof?

# CHAPTER 13

# The Slow Fade

## 2009

*"Nine men in ten are would-be suicides."*

— BENJAMIN FRANKLIN

I wished my father would have helped more with my grandparents, but with his perpetually off-track life, a terrible smoking habit, and poor health, he himself needed help. So even though I was overextended, and even though we had nothing in common, I tried to help him when the opportunity arose, as it did one January day in 2009.

When the door to his apartment opened, the smell hit me like a freight train. I would describe it as rotting corpse meets backed-up sewer line, combined with rotten cheese and vomit. The place was a disaster.

"Dad, you okay?" I called out. I was thinking I might find his dead body.

He appeared from around the corner. "Oh hi. Come on in." As I entered, he said, "The doctor says I'm still not doing well. I feel like I'm getting worse."

He said this so matter-of-factly, it was like he was talking about the weather, when the bitter truth was that prostate cancer had taken center stage in his life.

"Well, maybe the injections the doctors recommended will help. You can't just give up."

He shrugged. "So how much are those shots?" A few weeks back we had talked on the phone about him taking experimental injections to reduce the size of the tumor and halt the spread. Up until this time, my dad stayed in his own world. I had no idea what he was up to or what new job he was doing.

"They're $2,500 to $3,000."

"Each shot?" He was shocked.

"Yes."

These shots provided patients with late-stage prostate cancer a glimmer of hope for halting the disease. Dad had waited too late to go to the doctor, and now he was paying for it.

"I don't have that kind of money," he said.

I remembered the promise I'd made to Gram about taking care of the family, no matter what. "What if you could pay for the shots by reducing your expenses?"

"What do you mean?" He looked suspicious.

"Why don't you move into Gram's house?"

Before I could explain, he jumped in: "Oh, I don't know about that."

I informed him that the house was empty and it needed some work. He could live rent free and watch over things while doing some light cleaning and fix-it-up projects—or so I dreamed.

Dad's apartment was unlivable. He hadn't worked in three or four months, so he was running out of money and his health was deteriorating fast. Metastatic cancer leaves little time for life. The cancer was in his bones, moving up his back, and quickly gaining on his liver. The doctor said he had somewhere between six and nine months left.

The idea of having Dad spend some time in his boyhood home reliving happy memories seemed like a great idea and some cheap therapy. Maybe the environment would take him back to his youth when he was healthy and strong.

Dad sat down and picked up his cigarette, which was still lit. He tapped it on the edge of an ashtray in front of him, knocking off the burned-up ashes. Then, turning toward me, he said, "Okay let's do it. Will you help me move my stuff?"

I reluctantly moved him over the next week. I talked myself into it, reasoning an empty house tends to decay faster than an occupied one. However, the dad I grew up with had never been clean or organized. I remembered now that house projects were always last on his to-do list, even when I was a little kid. But I stuck with my optimistic thinking. In return for no rent, the least he could do was keep the place clean.

When I walked into my grandparents' home a week later for a quick check-in, I was greeted by the same raunchy smell that had sickened me at Dad's apartment. I've never been an obsessive-compulsive cleaning freak, but as I made my way toward the kitchen, I passed several small holes in the carpet and found a three-foot-high pile of dishes on the counter. Gram's wonderful house, which had always smelled like baked treats, now reeked of cigarette smoke. Apparently Dad was so weak that throwing things in the trash had become optional. He did, however, have the strength to rearrange the furniture.

As I glared at the place, he looked at me like a small child caught lying. "What are you doing here?" he demanded. "You didn't call to say you were coming,"

"You promised you wouldn't smoke in the house!" I yelled.

He didn't answer—just gave me a look that told me what I could do with my question. I couldn't speak again for a few minutes. Looking around, I was unsure how to say what needed to be said. Similar to dealing with my grandparents, I had switched positions with my father. Now I was the authoritarian, and he was the guilty kid.

"Look at the place," I demanded. "What's going on?" It was hard to cross-examine my own father. He had grown up in this house and spent his teenage years in the bedroom at the end of the hallway. Maybe it was nostalgia, but his attitude said this was *his* house and he could do what he damn well pleased.

I'm sure many memories flooded back to him as he sat in the beat-up white chair in the dining room. I imagined he sat in the chair as it faced into the backyard and pondered all the changes since he was a boy in this house, his life choices over the last forty years, and how he was battling a terminal illness. I didn't know all the details of his journey or the depth of his anger, but I felt sad for him. Not much had changed. He was angry when I was a kid, and he was still pissed off. I wanted to help, but it was looking like our relationship would continue to be a one-way street.

The next week I moved Dad out of Gram's house to a nice, clean, one-bedroom apartment in Aurora. He could smoke, and the small porch would be good for his stargazing/telescope-viewing hobby.

Now I needed to figure out how to start fixing up Gram and Gramps's house and prepping it for sale. As I drove away from my dad's new apartment, seeing the mountains reminded me of a family discussion six months earlier during an annual, extended-family trip to Glenwood Springs, a resort town three hours west of Denver.

• • •

Glenwood Springs is a beautiful place, nestled at the foot of the western slope of the Rockies. The sun sets over the mountains like a flashlight going off in a dark cave. It was late July in 2008, and the summer weather was hot but manageable. With its natural hot-spring pools, Glenwood Springs was a great backdrop for a Young family meeting, which included a number of relatives, including those from Gramps's side of the family.

From the hotel meeting room, we could look out at people in the pool. Some were sitting in chairs on the edge while others soaked in the hot springs' water for as long as they could take the heat. The end of the pool with cooler water was packed with kids and adults. As always, the hot springs' sulfur smell was strong.

Bob and Mary Smith were there with their son Kyle, Gramps's grandson, who was about the age of our oldest daughter, Cali, whom we gave up for adoption. Kay and I had brought along Helen and Eddie. I'd known Bob and Mary, who were about ten years younger than my parents, since I was a kid, but we weren't close until Kay and I got married. Since that time we'd become good friends. They visited Gramps and Gram once a year, when they would go to dinner with us. And like this trip to Glenwood, we sometimes traveled together. We had done a nice seven-day tour through New England a few years back when Helen was little. Bob and Mary trusted us to help Gram and Gramps and to manage the estate. They also had invested in one of our companies.

We talked about the future now that Gram and Gramps couldn't manage their own day-to-day care or finances. "I'll be the one to sell the house," I announced. "I promised Gram I would. She made me give her my word."

"Yes, I agree we need to sell the house," said Bob. He had a good sense of humor and made sure you knew how smart he was. "You would be perfect for doing that, Will. I like this idea, and I believe you when you say Gram insists you should be the one to do it."

"I've never sold a house before, though," I pointed out.

Bob smirked, looked at me with one eye open and one closed and said, "Well you're the 'messiah,' Will. You can do anything." Everyone laughed, but I was thinking, *Man, I wouldn't want to cross Bob. If he likes you, everything is good. If not, look out!*

Bob was referring to a running family joke between my sister and me because Gram treated me differently than her. Sadie often suggested that Gram thought the sun rose and set with me, and that I was "the Chosen

One." The joke was extended—overextended—to my baby boy. The family dubbed Eddie "the Son of God" after he was born.

By the end of that Glenwood Springs trip, everyone was in agreement that I would fix up the house and sell it, at which point I would pay myself a management fee and commission from the sale.

• • •

After the idea of having my dad take care of the house blew up on me, I knew it was time to focus on cleaning up and selling the house. It was located in the beautiful community of Heartwood, nuzzled into the foothills about fifteen miles west of Denver. This "mature community" was now a combination of retired people, those on the verge of retirement, and young families with small children, dogs, and big dreams. My grandparents' corner lot had large blue spruces in the front yard as well as cottonwoods near the fence lines. Their branches hung over the fence like a forest scene on a postcard.

In January of 2009, I made my way along the front walkway, which once had been lined by beautiful rosebushes. As I grabbed the front-door handle, I was overcome by sadness knowing my Gram and Gramps wouldn't be there to greet me. This was a day I had dreaded for many years, and the thought of cleaning up fifty years of stuff and fixing long-over-due maintenance problems made me cringe. Could I pull this off, and how many months would the process take?

As I headed down the stairs to the basement, I passed family pictures and antique items mounted on both sides. Most of the photos were black and white. One showed my Dad's big smile on the day of his graduation from Army boot camp. He looked sharp and proud in his uniform. I wondered if losing two close high school friends in Vietnam while he was stationed in Germany caused some PTSD. Did he feel guilty that he didn't serve in that hellhole? I also wondered whether the trauma of that loss took away his ability to be emotionally close to Sadie and me. Maybe the whole military experience contributed to the disconnect between him and my mom. I knew, however, that wasn't the only reason for her troubled life. Mom was still up to her usual shenanigans: having property foreclosed on or cars repossessed. Sadie and I tried to avoid the drama as much as we could.

I continued down the stairs. The next picture was one of Gram's first husband, Bill, my namesake. Positioned right below Bill was a picture of Gramps's daughter Mary from a previous marriage. And near the bottom step was a picture of Gram with her sister Hazel—two beautiful girls growing up in Utah.

At the bottom of the stairs, I turned into the laundry room. Toward the end of Gram's life she called it the "junk room." It was cold, musty, and dark. I could almost picture a vintage Ivory Flakes soap box sitting on the top of the washer. The laundry room, finished in true 1960s style, once had a Whirlpool Calypso washer next to an energy-gobbling Eaton Viking clothes dryer. A quarter-inch thick clothesline still ran above Gram's more modern appliances, crisscrossing the entire room. As children, we were never allowed in here. Even now I felt like I was breaking a rule. I caught myself looking over my shoulder, worried that Gram was going to dart in with a stern warning about trespassing.

Now there were piles of clothes, towels, and other items falling out of cabinets and piled two feet high on counters. Many of the clothes were new, price tags still attached. Even the storage area at the end of the narrow room under the stairs, about ten by twenty feet, was packed with junk from floor to ceiling. I started moving things around, nervous I'd find a long-lost relative's body. I wasn't starting to clean, but I just needed to start grasping the true scope of this project.

Overwhelmed, I quickly headed across fifteen feet of grimy, 1970s tile to Gram's room. To the right was a four-by-four-foot liquor rack. Some of the bottles had been there since the '70s. I imagined Gram making her guests a Harvey Wallbanger as she held a bottle of Galliano in one hand and the crystal highball glass in the other. Although she'd never admit it,

I'm sure she knew how to make all the popular drinks back in the day: Tequila Sunrise, Grasshopper, Screwdriver, Manhattan.

The old green rotary phone was there beside the liquor rack. I started to reach for it and recalled Gram answering it, yelling loud enough to wake the dead as she tried to get Gramps's attention. Those were the days when you handed someone the phone through the opening in the hallway rather than walk the additional ten feet to come around the corner.

In Gram's bedroom, the nightstand was slightly open, and items were falling out. The top drawer was packed with medication bottles—empty and full. A Tylenol bottle from 1973 fell out, as did a 1965 Bayer bottle. Most of the drugs had expired at least ten years ago, with a few dating back to the Kennedy presidency.

A funny thing happens when you start going through someone else's stuff: you wonder if you'll find a love letter from a secret affair or that rookie Babe Ruth baseball card worth a tidy fortune. Or maybe the names of my father's birth parents.

Next I headed into Gramps's den, which was a little larger than a modern-day walk-in closet but was considered a small bedroom in 1960. He had used it for the last twenty years as part office and part storage room. There were old bills stashed in the bottom of a green file cabinet, which looked like one you'd see in a 1950s documentary about surviving a nuclear blast. I sat at his desk for a moment and looked at pictures of him in his military uniform, at his first job, and winning ribbons from dahlia-growing contests. The ribbons themselves were pinned next to Masonic awards and plaques.

Even though the basement room was dark and gloomy, it had this positive feel from all the hours Gramps spent organizing his life, praying, or reading the Bible. I made a few notes in my organizer and headed back upstairs to check out Gram's small room on the first floor, another closet-sized space she used as her personal area/storage unit. It had always been junky and cramped. As I came through the door, I was overwhelmed by the floor-to-ceiling shelves of books. Perusing the titles, I giggled, wondering

Whether Gram really read a book on all the different types of dog leashes. Her collection ranged from odd titles to spiritual and self-development books. Some were from before self-development was hip. One particular book caught my eye, *The Science of the Mind*.

I had been subscribing to *Science of Mind Magazine* for a few years. Science of Mind is a spiritual movement started in the early 1920s by Ernest Holmes, who wrote the book about it. It's nondenominational and combines science with spirituality. It has no connection to Scientology, and it honors all paths to God. I had heard about the book but never looked at it.

I took the 500-word book in my hands, opened it, and read the inscription on the inside cover, "For Dad, with all my love." Gram had written in it. I moved several items off the small couch so I could sit down. I started to thumb through and read a few sections. As I did, it struck me that my grandmother had been a member of the Mile Hi Church in Lakewood. Mile Hi used *The Science of the Mind* like a college textbook. I remembered attending church with Gram when I was maybe seven or eight. I could still see the white, bubblelike roof on the building that looked like a large mushroom cloud near Wadsworth and Alameda. I wondered if the building was still there. Little did I know that finding this book would later help save my life. I tossed it in my bag with a few other books to add to my reading list.

By now it was time to go, but after assessing most of the house, I felt I could begin to tackle the job of cleaning out and organizing it. Over the next eight weeks, Kay and I spent twenty to thirty hours a week preparing for the estate sale. More than 500 people showed up, buying all kinds of old stuff, including everything from crap and trinkets to some nice vintage objects. After the sale, we threw away more junk than anyone could imagine: two large, thirty-foot-long dumpsters. With most of the interior belongings gone, we started remodeling and repairing in March 2009.

Chuck, a close family friend, helped us with the remodeling work. I was never much of a handyman or weekend-project warrior, so his expertise was greatly appreciated.

"How's it going Chuck?" I yelled down the hall as I turned the corner one day. When I looked at the floor, I was shocked to see what looked like gorgeous, recently polished hardwood. It had been protected by shag carpeting for as long as I could remember.

Chuck had a mask over his face, a bottle of chemical stripper in one hand, and a putty knife in the other. "It's coming along, but this bathroom needs a lot of work. There's some weird material back there—I'm not even sure what it is—and the tub looks like it's from the early 1900s." Then he looked at me and said ominously, "Did you look at the attic yet?"

"Yeah, I glanced at it."

"Oh, you'll need to do more than that."

I didn't like the sound of that. "What do you mean?"

"You're going to lose your shit. I don't know if I've ever seen that much crap in an attic before."

"Gram joked about how bad it was, and she only asked me to go up there a few times to grab something she really wanted. She was embarrassed about it."

Chuck nodded. "No wonder, it's nuts."

The next week, I arrived to tackle the attic. Chuck was right. I had to hire a man to help me with both carrying down the large items and getting rid of all the junk. We spent five full days clearing all the crap out of it.

With the attic done, the yard was next. I hired the same landscaper I used for my own yard. Marcos was kind in his evaluation, but he let me know it would be a significant job to get it ready. Unfortunately, with Gramps gone for the last six months, the weeds had run amuck. I had tried to keep up with it, but I could never match Gramps's attention to detail and certifiable green thumb.

By May, I was pleasantly surprised to be ahead of schedule. My goal was to have the house sold by the first of August, which I initially thought was a pipe dream. Yet here we were in late spring and it looked like the finish line was less than thirty days away.

My intention of honoring Gram by selling her house and fulfilling my promise would come to fruition. The Great Recession continued to implode the markets, and as May became June, the unemployment rate hit a peak of 10 percent. Our business revenue was still down significantly so the commission and fees I would receive from the sale of the house would help our family.

The closing was on June 9, 2009. It had been on the market only one day when we had a full-priced offer. It was an amazing deal when you factored in the state of the real estate market. Gram must have been helping as a clairvoyant because the process was smooth and too easy. A fantastic young couple with kids purchased it. As we shook hands on the deal, I said, "You'll have lots of great memories in that back yard. I did. I'm sure you'll need to update the inside, but other than that this house is in great shape." Then I added, "Please enjoy every minute, and take great care of the backyard as my Gramps did."

The sale was bittersweet. I knew I'd never see that wonderful little home in Heartwood again. I met Kay for coffee after the closing and told her our life was about to get easier with the house sold. Everyone told us with the house sold and the grandparents living safely at the retirement home, we could get back to normal.

• • •

"Remember what Toni told me? We are there," Kay said soberly one day. I had forgotten that Toni warned Kay about how when her parents went into PeakView Senior Living the work actually *increased*.

Kay added, "Toni says she is still spending tons of time on her mom even though her father passed away." I laughed, thinking there were a million workers in assisted living places to help give each resident with a one-to-one worker/resident ratio. Then I noticed how loud the coffee shop was getting as we continued our conversation. It was packed, and the people next to us seemed to be eavesdropping. The lady quipped, "Oh, yeah, my friend spends half her days at a facility as her mom's memory continues to fade."

Kay turned back to me. "She's right babe. We'll have to figure out how to help Gram and Gramps more."

"*More*? With what?" I was clueless because Kay did most of the caretaking. I helped whenever I could with all my ongoing business ventures, but it wasn't the same as being on call every day like Kay was. Recently, she'd added doing the grandparents' taxes to her ongoing list. We tried not to think about all the work she was doing for them because it made both of us anxious, and it upset me. I felt so guilty that so many responsibilities were falling to her. I was failing as a husband.

Kay said, "I just found out Gramps needs to go to a sleep expert." Her typical weekly tasks included scheduling the grandparents' appointments—most of which were health-care related. She would pick up either Gram or Gramps (sometimes both), and drive to the appointment, listen to the doctor, and implement the doc's recommendations.

One particular visit to a hearing specialist was hard to forget. When Kay told me about it, I couldn't stop laughing. The hearing specialist said the words, "Baseball. Hotdog," then Gramps would respond, "Baseball. Hotdog." She kept repeating the words, and he would repeat what she said. Kay was becoming frustrated because he said the words as if he were deaf or had suddenly taken on a Boston accent. Since he had spent most of his life in Colorado, speaking with a Boston accent was odd. The specialist continued—"Water. Apple."—while looking curiously at Kay. Gramps would repeat, "Water. Apple," still with the odd accent. The audiologist finally looked over to Kay and said, "Why is he talking like me?"

Kay burst out laughing, realizing that Gramps was simply mimicking her every nuance and sound, including the woman's Boston accent and tone. He was old and hard of hearing, but definitely not deaf. After the audiologist determined that he needed stronger hearing aids, he no longer talked like a Bostonian.

Hearing problems, combined with poor sleep at night, were a constant struggle for Gramps. Lying in bed half the day and falling down almost weekly were becoming the norm. One Friday morning, my phone rang. "He's pulled the sink away from the wall!" the voice on the other end was saying.

"What? Who is this? He did what?"

"I'm calling from PeakView Senior Living," said the woman, and your grandfather tried to pull himself up to the sink from the toilet, and it didn't go well. We think he's okay, but it's another bad fall."

I stopped her halfway through the explanation, hung up, and headed over to see this for myself. I arrived to find the cabinet completely detached from the wall. The top of the toilet was damaged, the soap dispenser was gone, and parts of the drywall were missing where the bolts had been pulled out. It looked like someone fell through and implanted themselves in the wall. I surmised Gramps must have reached for something he could grab when he started to fall. He probably had caught the edge of the sink with both hands, and with all his weight going one direction, the entire cabinet must have disintegrated. As I walked out of the facility, reality was sinking in: putting Gram and Gramps in PeakView wasn't reducing the workload, it was merely expanding and changing it.

# CHAPTER 14

# Did Your Dad Kill Himself?

### 2009

*"A father is neither an anchor to hold us back*
*nor a sail to take us there, but a guiding light*
*whose love shows us the way."*

— ANONYMOUS

One day, Sadie called me, sounding worried. "I've tried calling Dad several times, and there's still no answer," she said. "He *always* answers. Do you think he's okay? I was thinking of heading down there."

"No need for you to go over," I told her with a confident tone. It was June 1, 2009, about ten in the morning, and something inside of me knew something was wrong, like maternal instinct when a woman senses her child has been hurt, or like a dog uses his paws to sense thunder or an earthquake coming. I just knew something was wrong. "Don't worry," I told Sadie. "I'm fairly close, and I'll swing by shortly." This was a lie. I was far away but kept insisting she stay put. "I'm sure Dad's okay. I'll let you know."

The universe or God or spirit or whatever higher power one believes in has a way of protecting us. I wanted to head over to Dad's apartment right away, but instead spirit redirected me. I can't remember to this day what task needed to be completed at the office, but I stopped there first. I finished a few irrelevant issues and then drove to Dad's place. The delay was just enough time for Dad's hospice nurse to arrive before me.

As I drove up to the complex and opened my car door, I saw that Sadie had gone anyway. My sister was barely standing. She was hysterical and made a howling cry I will never get out of my head. It's the type of cry that comes out when a person's soul is overflowing. Her sobs were loud, uncontrollable. She had gone against my wishes and come to check on him. My dad's nurse caught Sadie as she was falling to her knees. The nurse looked at me and said, "He's gone."

"He's what?"

"Will, your dad is gone," the nurse said.

"What did he do? What happened? Where is he?" I looked down at the ground, not sure how to react. She was calm. "He decided it was his time. He shot himself." This wasn't the first time one of her patients with stage IV cancer committed suicide.

My first thought was how much fear Dad must have felt. He was alone, probably desperate, angry, and sad. My second thought was *How did he find the guts to do it?*

The police were investigating inside the apartment and wouldn't let anyone enter. My sister's sobs had slowed, and she asked if she could see him, but his nurse quickly responded that it was not a good idea.

Sadie continued begging, "Please! I just want to see him. Please, one more time. Please let me."

"You'll want to remember him as he was, not the way he is today. Trust me." The hospice nurse was right.

I turned around, grabbed my sister, and just held her. I had a feeling this day would eventually come. Once my dad had told me, off the cuff, "I'm going down with my boots on—going out in a flash." Now I knew what he meant. He had told Sadie goodbye two days before. She mentioned it had been a great moment—a nice strong hug, eyes connected, and she had a warm feeling in her heart. I felt good knowing the last moments they'd experienced and the last months of time they spent together would outweigh today and the many earlier years of strain. I felt horrible not getting to say goodbye or to fix thirty-seven years of challenges. I should have tried harder, and I think he wanted to try harder too. I wasn't the kind of boy he wanted. He was into rocks, rough camping, and astronomy. I only wanted to throw baseballs, run with footballs, or shoot basketballs. We just never connected.

The coroner approached me and my sister. "It appears that your father took his own life," she said. "That's the way it appears at this time, but we have to check to make sure the scene is not staged or that no one else was involved. This is standard procedure. I've seen several situations like this, and it does appear to be a suicide. I'm so very sorry for your loss." The coroner tried to tell us with empathy, but we couldn't hear it. Instead, the words just danced in the air like a cold, harsh, December wind. My emotions were raw, cold. I didn't move—just stood there.

I could only imagine what the scene looked like inside his apartment. Dad had been obsessed with guns. Two weeks earlier, he'd made a passionate plea: "I have to get this last project done before I go to any hospice place. Just make sure I get the last project done." The mystery of the last project was solved. It was death by his own hand.

Dad had no intention of ever going to a hospice facility. I would later find out he'd had a friend running him all over town to fix a gun and buy other needed materials. He used a gun with a silencer, while creating the least gruesome aftermath. He had even gone to a Home Depot for an orange bucket and a bag of brown sand to make sure the bullet wouldn't make it to a neighbor's house if it exited his head.

Sadie later joked that the week before his death he told her he wanted to rob a bank and get shot in the process. He seriously wrote out plans and tried to talk her into driving the getaway car. He'd been more detailed and creative about his ending than the rest of his life. Ironically, I would walk the same line a few years later, trying to decide whether to live or die.

After the police left, I opened the door to Dad's apartment. I didn't know what I would find. Blood, brains, yucky stuff? But it had been all cleaned up by the hospice people. I walked through the small living room and into the bedroom to find eighteen loaded guns on the bed. Like the cowboys of yesteryear, Dad had made sure all weapons were loaded and ready for a gunfight or a platoon movement. I thought his last gesture had two meanings: first, it called out his Army days when he ended up serving in Germany while several of his friends died in Vietnam. Second, it was as if he prepared for the final ride, pretending to be a twentieth-century cowboy. The movie *Tombstone* was stuck in the VCR. The VHS tape would not budge. We had to throw it out with the movie still inside. Dad's final act was his own Wild West story. One bullet and a blaze of glory.

I felt like I lost all those years with him. I should have worked harder to find a bridge in our relationship. If I was the family "messiah," I should have been able to fix it. Now he was dead, and I could not go back and do it over.

After my father's passing and the sale of our grandparents' house, I immersed myself in our Talus venture. This had been my trick since I was a young boy. I would focus on goals, on whom I wanted to be, so I could avoid the pain of the situation. Or how I could avoid even talking about what was going wrong or not working out. I could close it out and pretend like everything was good.

I was still hurting from my Dad's loss, my grandparents' home was gone, and I needed revenue. It had been a year since the Talus's famous New York trip, and many of our partner conversations were stalling. Although we had a letter of intent from Standard & Poor's, the large index brand, it remained unsigned. I had brought us this far, so I felt compelled to continue. We were holding on but needed additional funding along with a major index partner.

By the end of 2009, I was running out of time and money. The world economy was still imploding. Where would I find the money that all the generations of our family desperately needed?

# CHAPTER 15

# What Is a Medicare Look-Back Penalty?

## 2010

*"Patience is not the ability to wait but the ability*
*to keep a good attitude while waiting."*

— JOYCE MEYER

In early 2010, it was becoming apparent that it was time for some serious, professional help. My grandparents were getting worse, and I was so cash strapped that I was playing the lottery twice a week. A friend mentioned something about Medicare penalties over coffee, and it left me anxious and perplexed. He told me that when you applied for Medicare for yourself or a relative, any gifts or transfers of assets made within five years of the date of the application were subject to penalties.

I realized Kay and I knew nothing about Medicare penalties and very little about elder-care law, and I sensed that we might need a lawyer. Bob and Mary were also pressing me to set up a meeting so we could clarify all the expenses for the estate. I wasn't sure what type of lawyer would work best, but I soon met one at a networking event, so I set up an appointment.

The waiting area of lawyer Tabby McKinsey's office wasn't anything fancy. The furniture looked like it had been there since the Johnson Administration, but a few glass walls showed a nice view of the east side of Denver. Tabby was smart and confident, though she came across as the type of person who would speak nicely to your face but tell the staff what an idiot you were when you left because you didn't know the details of elder law. I still liked her.

I nervously looked up at the clock, stood up, paced, and found three or four brochures about elder care tucked in a plastic holder. I grabbed a few to peruse. Then out came Tabby. "Good to see you again," she said as she walked up and extended her hand. We'd already had a phone conversation that helped me bring her up to speed on my grandparents' situation. She guided me into the conference room and informed me that Bob was on the conference phone line. I took my seat, pulled out my notepad, and asked, "Where should we start?"

Tabby responded, "How about we review the Medicaid process? My understanding is that expenses have been incurred for your grandparents during the five-year look-back period."

"What's a look-back period?"

"These are incurred expenses that were not used directly for your grandparents' care. Or expenses not approved by your grandparents. It covers five years before the time they filed for Medicaid."

My stomach started to churn and my hands shook. "What do you mean by *approved* or *directly*?" I asked. "Do you mean they don't count toward this Medicaid penalty deal? Am I saying it right?"

"Kind of. The government penalizes based on the funds used for their direct care and funds for non-direct care."

I knew even less than I thought about this process. "Isn't Kay taking care of my grandparents for ten years considered 'direct' care? Or what about me helping them?"

"Not necessarily. Were there contracts signed?"

"Not for our caregiving. Why would we need a contract to do that? And what about the money Gram gave to my father as a gift?" Gram had mentioned before her dementia worsened that she had given my dad money. I continued, "That amount might have been given during the look-back period. I'm not sure how much it was or even how to find the total. It might be $50,000 once—or maybe a few times."

I had been assuming the money Kay and I used went under the heading of "caregiving," just as Gram had instructed, and would not be penalized, so I focused the conversation on the funds Gram gave to my father. I didn't worry about the money we used either way because Bob and Mary Smith had given us permission to use the funds. I said, "But I'm not sure when Gram gave Dad the money or if it was within five years. Would *those* funds all be penalized?"

Tabby went into a lengthy explanation about the process: "Medicaid penalties are different than other forms of spending. The money has to be spent directly for their care, otherwise it is a penalty."

As Tabby continued asking questions about accounts and use of the funds, my heart went into my throat. I was still confused but began to realize the money Kay and I had used could or would be penalized. The last fifteen minutes of the meeting were a blur because my attention was totally focused on what was "direct" and "indirect" care and on figuring out what we would do if much of everything we had spent on Gram's and Gramps's behalf was a penalty.

Tabby finished the meeting by saying, "You'll need to gather all receipts and financial paperwork and then get them to me. Oh, and one last thing: we'll need to set up a time for me to interview your grandparents. I need to understand their current state of mind."

• • •

After a short meeting with the grandparents at the facility about ten days later, Tabby pulled us aside. "As you told me, they are not capable of making their own decisions."

I responded, "What about all the agreements we made with them *before* they lost mental capacities?"

"What do you mean?" she asked.

Now I was even more concerned. "The funds we used were approved before they became mentally incapacitated. But their wills were never updated to reflect those wishes. The sale of the house, who could use what funds—all of that was never updated in the will."

I could see the concern in Tabby's face as if she were playing out the future in her mind. "So you're saying your grandparents cannot speak to the portion of money you used from the sale of their house?"

"But it was for their care!" I insisted. "Kay and I were taking care of them and putting our lives on hold to do whatever it took. We needed to use the money."

"None of that is in writing?"

"The sale of the house is, but the money to Kay for caregiving was not documented. We did track *some* of the expenses for Gram and Gramps, but not all. We should have tracked every dime, but we didn't realize."

"Well, I don't think it will be viewed as if they approved *anything*. We have a major problem and potential penalties."

The meeting with Tabby confirmed I was in trouble. As Gram would say, "deep doo-doo." Or as I would say, "deep shit." As a result, I needed to change course and create revenue, and it had to be fast. We sold some remaining XploreNet assets to a Canadian firm, but the legal fight with Tayson was dragging on with no end in sight.

I decided to put my expertise as a fundraiser to use. Every nonprofit in the country needs to raise money, and I had developed a successful fundraising process that I implemented for nonprofit leaders during my days with the Denver Active 20-30 Children's Foundation. I started by writing books in which I shared my experience with executive directors, development staff, and board members of nonprofit organizations.

It took me three months of following a hectic writing schedule to finish two books, *How Good Board Members Become Great Fundraisers* and *How Good Development Officers Become Great Fundraisers*. I didn't write the world's greatest book or discover a cure for cancer, but I was offering my expertise as an ace fundraiser.

Writing and giving seminars go hand in hand. Once I was a published author, I could get out on the training circuit. And once I was giving seminars, people wanted to buy a book.

• • •

In November, it was time to say goodbye. Funerals are always heart wrenching, and Gramps's passing and my opportunity and privilege to properly eulogize him was harder than anticipated. Only a few of the relatives knew about the impending legal battle over the estate, which was just beginning, but I felt intense pressure to show everyone who attended the funeral what a great man Gramps was, without seeming contrite or unoriginal. My intention was to authentically convey his true nature, even if some of the facts seemed impossible to believe—like never hearing him say a curse word in thirty-eight years. Not one time.

I started my eulogy by explaining more about Gramps. He was religious, but not preachy. He chose not to gossip, instead preferring to use his experience of living through the Depression to provide you with an anecdote or a quick comment that made you really think about your life and purpose. He truly lived Titus 3:2: "To speak evil of no one, to avoid quarreling, to be gentle, and to show perfect courtesy to all people." He took this verse to heart. I never heard him say a bad thing about another person—ever. My parents would have been low-hanging fruit for him to jump on the bandwagon of put-downs, but he never did.

His quiet disposition was so gentle that any sort of emotional out-burst from Gramps would make your eyes pop out. If the phrase, "Hell's afire," came out with a loud, muffled gargle, then you knew he was pissed. This phrase was as close to a cuss word or show of anger that he would ever demonstrate. He was my constant and consistent example, modeling how to live by your true values, your God spirit, and your appreciation for everything in your life.

Gramps had spent many years volunteering for several organizations, even participating in the voting system as a local polling judge for more than fifty years. Most people never knew he took care of a sick first wife until her early death or that he raised a daughter by himself from the time she was in middle school. He was proud of his life as a single father, as an electrician, and as a union man.

I ended the eulogy with a story about one of our many road trips during my youth. The typical setup was Gramps and me sitting in the front seat of his 1980 white Ford truck while my sister and Gram rode in the camper that sat on the flatbed. The classic truck had roll-down windows, a push-button FM/AM radio, and an intercom that connected to the back, allowing us to talk to Gram, or she could push the button on her end and talk to us. This was well before cell phones, so if the intercom didn't work, your only other form of communicating was banging on the camper wall as hard as you could or try tapping in Morse code. A last resort might be lighting something on fire so the smoke grabbed the driver's attention, but Gramps always said flames in a camper were never good.

Gramps and I sat in the front, having man-to-man talks. I don't remember too many details of his stories, but I did feel safe, loved, and understood. His stories usually covered the rules of life in rich and mean-ingful messages.

On one trip to Disneyland when I was fourteen, Gramps and I rode quietly as he drove through the hot Nevada desert. Gram's voice came over the intercom. "Dad, are you going to pull off?"

"Not yet." Gramps answered.

"But we're probably low on gas?"

"No, we're good."

"The kids are probably getting hungry."

"They can make it a while longer."

"*I'm* going to be getting hungry."

"We just had lunch. Are you sure?"

"Yes, I will be hungry again soon, and what about the hot temperature outside?"

"What about it?"

"Should you check to see if the engine is okay?"

"No, it's running fine."

Gram's voice continued to rise with each statement. "Dad I'm sure it's time to stop!"

"No. It's not. We are good."

"But you're probably getting tired, and that spot over there looks like a great place to stop."

We both knew there was no way Gram could possibly see out of the camper to identify anything other than a passing vehicle or two. And then it happened. Gramps simply leaned over and turned off the intercom. His eyes met mine and made the universal gesture for *Don't say a word about this!* He raised his hand with his forefinger meeting his lips.

I couldn't help but grin and then giggle. Gramps tried not to laugh, but soon he had joined me.

The next fifty miles were silent except for an occasional observation. It was nice. We stopped at a gas station, and as I started to open the door, Gram surprised me and came rushing around the camper toward me. When her eyes met mine, I could see her anger as she yelled at Gramps, "What happened to the intercom? Dad, why didn't you stop back there?"

And Gramps, with the calm confidence of a brain surgeon about to start a procedure, said, "Oh, sorry honey, the intercom went out. I'll need to check the wiring when we get home. I bet something got loose."

As the funeral crowd erupted in laughter, I knew Gramps was laughing somewhere. This story summed up Gramps's ability to keep Gram focused when her own anxiety started to take her off the rails. He always filled that role with her, even if a little white lie was required. He was rough, strong, and smart but at the same time soft, kind, humble. Gramps was easy to eulogize. I just presented the facts. The afternoon ended with a special moment as Gram tried to climb into the casket as it was being closed. There wasn't a dry eye in the place as we watched her beautiful last effort to show him love and stay with him. It was an authentic moment. It was true love. It was them. I'll never forget it.

• • •

With Gramps gone, Kay and I figured we'd be able to put all of our attention on Gram. Little did we know we were about to lose custody of her.

I had ignored the legal letters arriving during the weeks before and after the funeral. I didn't think they had anything to do with us, and I didn't want to deal with anything at that point. I was in denial about the gravity of the situation. As far as I was concerned, Kay and I were in control of the remaining estate because Gramps had passed and Gram was still alive. It was for her care and our inheritance, and the fight was starting to drown me emotionally anyway. I was lining up training and speaking engagements and didn't have time for more drama—but making assumptions about the estate was a big mistake.

I was dumbfounded when I received a short voice message while sitting in my car. It was about 8:30 in the morning of November 10, 2010, and I had finished an early business meeting downtown. The Smiths' opposing council had shifted the hearing about who would be the custodian of my grandfather—which I thought was canceled since Gramps had passed—to include a motion for custodianship of Gram. Kay and Mary had been in constant communication about Gramps and Gram over the past two years, so this new legal maneuver caught both of us off guard. I was surprised when the Smiths' attorney disagreed with how we chose to use the estate funds.

As I listened to the voice message, I thought, *How can this be legal?* Why should *they* have custody of Gram? I wondered what Bob and Mary had told the judge. The end of the message said the Smiths' attorney would be in touch about next steps. They would be requesting a sit-down meeting with me to go over the estate and the new custody procedures. Yet I *still* did not realize there was a problem.

In early December, as I headed downtown to oblige Bob and Mary's meeting request, I convinced myself this was a big misunderstanding and that they would agree they had helped us by giving us permission.

When I arrived, I was escorted into their conference room. Nate Lupton, my attorney, had already taken a seat. It was about ten in the morning. Nate was missing half of his thumb and the tips of two other fingers on his right hand, an accident from his pre-lawyer days when he worked on cabinets. Over the years, Nate had helped me complete business deals, contracts, and personal wills. Even though he had a problem with his hands shaking—which I later learned was caused by alcoholism—I trusted him.

The conference room's floor-to-ceiling windows behind Nate and me had no blinds, so the sun heated our backs. Before I could sit down, Ann Rossi, the opposing council, burst into the conference room and almost fell down as the door swung open. She caught her balance and then made a beeline toward me. I thought she was going to run me over. I didn't know whether to extend my hand or brace for impact. She met my open hand with a packet of paper. No handshake, just papers. "Take a look." was her greeting.

I turned my attention to these papers, stopping every now and then to look up and glance at the strangers in the room. "Who are all these people?" I asked.

"Oh sorry." Ann introduced a financial forensic specialist— a job I didn't know existed. Next to him was a Medicaid specialist, and next to her an elder-law representative of some sort. On the attorney's right side was a CPA. Bob and Mary were attending via speaker phone. I started to get the feeling this wasn't a meeting but an inquisition, and if all went well for them, it might end in my extermination.

Ann continued, "Do you know what you're holding?" She said it like she already knew the answer.

"I don't." I answered.

"It covers all the rules binding a power of attorney—what they can and cannot legally do. Bet you never saw these before."

"No I haven't. I didn't know there were specific rules around it. I was just doing the best I could."

"Yeah, I'm sure." Ann seemed smug.

"I probably should have known all the requirements," I admitted. "But I was worried about taking care of my grandparents and their needs. They were my concern."

"It never occurred to you to educate yourself about this type of document?"

"No, I was worried about a lot of other things. But thank you for sharing them." I made an attempt to look at Nate, but he was staring down at copies of the same documents. When I looked back at Ann, her eyes sparkled like she knew the final *Jeopardy* question. I didn't have a clue.

Sensing my confusion, Nate jumped in and said, "Ms. Rossi where is this going? You seem to have some kind of agenda for today. Please disclose where you're heading with these questions."

As Ann Rossi and Nate did a legalese dance of proper questioning processes, I looked out the conference window into the lobby. The strangest feeling hit me. I was sitting in the same office near where my desk had been some fifteen years earlier during my first corporate job out of college. I earlier remembered the building as it seemed to be the right tower and I could recall the floor, but now I realized we were meeting in the exact same suite. I was literally five feet from my former desk. Definitely one of life's ironies.

After the meeting ended, Nate and I stood in the elevator without saying a word. When we got to the lobby, we exited through the revolving door. "What do you think about this situation?" I asked.

Nate leaned against the glass wall, moved his hand to his shirt pocket, and took out a cigarette, nice and slow like he was in a movie. After carefully lighting the cigarette, he took a long, intense puff just like Olivia Newton-John did in *Grease*. As he blew out the smoke, he looked at me like I was a lost puppy and said, "Well, at least it's not terminal cancer, Will."

We stood silent, slowly smiled at one another, and all at once erupted into laughter. There was absolutely nothing funny about our meeting or the gravity of the situation, but we laughed. It took a minute for us to regain our composure. My laughter soon turned to tears. It was far worse than I had imagined.

Nate's eyes watered too. I think he truly felt fear for me—not as an attorney toward his client but as a friend who'd made careless choices himself. He knew I trusted too much. He was always telling me that I should do things *only* with a signed agreement. And now he knew I was a friend who was in a real shitty situation.

Nate lawyered up quickly and said, "You're going to need an estate lawyer. A good one. A cheap one, but a good one. I think I know just the right guy for you. His name is Leonard."

• • •

I don't think Len Dillard had any clue what he was about to get involved in. The first time I spoke to him on the phone, he made a crazy first impression and left me with more doubts than confidence. He was in the drive-through lane of some fast-food restaurant but didn't realize he'd answered his phone. I could hear him going into a full-on verbal assault of the drive-through attendant as he screamed into the speaker, "Goddamn fucking mayonnaise. No mayonnaise—and what the fuck?—you have fucking pickles on it too. Jesus Christ, I said no goddamn pickles. Can't you get my fucking order right? Holy shit, come on!"

In shock, I didn't interrupt the man. I wondered if I had dialed the right number.

I began to laugh nervously and listened for the sound of bullets, because surely Len's nine-millimeter was going to teach those burger-joint idiots a lesson. I wondered if I should dial 911 or hang up and pretend I never called.

Finally the guy realized someone was on the phone and quickly jumped on saying, "Oh sorry, this is Len." Surely he realized I'd overheard, but like a good lawyer he used a poker voice and glossed right over it. I identified myself, and he confirmed that Nate had told him I'd be calling.

After giving him a quick overview of the estate battle between me and the Smiths, we decided the next step was an initial meeting. As I approached his office, I was on edge because the craziness of our first call had put me in both a state of curiosity and concern about what I might find. Would he be dressed in camouflage as an antigovernment rebel with guns and dead animal-heads hanging all over the place? Or maybe I would find him with one of those signs that says, "Your soul may belong to Jesus but your ass belongs to the Marines"? Or would he be wearing a $3,000 handcrafted, three-piece suit and offering a fake smile and unauthentic smirk as matching accessories? I found Len to be somewhere in between, minus the nice suit.

It was as if I'd entered a time machine taking me back to the sixties or seventies. There was a vintage couch in the corner of his office next to some kind of old Hardy sling chair. The walls hadn't been painted in twenty years; a 1980s-era conference table caught my eye. It reminded me of the Studio 54 days with men in polyester suits and long sideburns. I could imagine Jon Hamm and the rest of the *Mad Men* cast sitting around the conference table making crude comments about a secretary's ass as they took slow, calm drags off their Lucky Strikes. As I sat down, I thought, *God, I hope this guy's seen a courtroom since this table was delivered.*

Len Dillard was a spot-on lookalike for *Seinfeld*'s George Costanza: bald head, similar facial features, but without the round, wire-rimmed glasses—except he was six foot two. His calm, slow-talking rhythm could easily put you to sleep.

Without even a handshake, Len asked if I'd brought the receipts he'd requested. I didn't say anything, just stood up, grabbed my large manila envelope, turned it over, and let all the papers come flying out. The receipts fell like confetti. They just kept falling and falling on the table. Len's jaw dropped, and his hand reached out and grabbed a few. He didn't say a word but grabbed up a few more, adding them to the ones in his hand as if he were a poker player picking up his cards after the dealer has dealt. Not a single word. He pushed his fingers over and through them. I think two minutes passed.

Finally Len looked up, and his face looked paralyzed. "Will, you'll need a spreadsheet for all of these. I mean—wow!—I mean every last one."

"Are you serious?"

"I wish I wasn't. You have a serious problem. Yeah, you have a *very* serious problem."

"We didn't try to hide anything. We just didn't track the expenses." I knew Kay and I were in trouble. But the question was: Will my problem be Len's challenge? Also, it was apparent he was in over his head. Len seemed used to dealing with typical estate paperwork or disagreements over who gets the dog or Momma's 1980s VCR collection of *My Favorite Martian* episodes. My problem was my failure to properly track expenses and categorize receipts. I had blown off getting everything categorized. I should have been tracking every single transaction, every cent of what I'd spent on our family and grandparents. The receipts included our personal expenses like groceries, cable, phones, utilities, and payments to my company for the sale of the house and work completed on it.

I grimaced in misery as Len explained that for the Court to understand where and why money was spent, I would need to have every penny accounted for.

"Every penny?" I calmly asked.

"Yes, and there will be penalties."

*Oh God*, I thought, there's that word again: *penalties.*

"Medicaid will go back and review the look-back period."

I interrupted, "Yes, I know. Five years, right?"

"Yes." He confirmed my fear with a nod of his head.

As I left Len's office, I was beyond emotional. I was a wreck.

# CHAPTER 16

# Do You Have a Warrant?

## February 9, 2011

*"The ultimate measure of a man is not where he stands
in moments of convenience and comfort, but where
he stands at times of challenge and controversy."*

— MARTIN LUTHER KING, JR.

The police banging on the door came two weeks after my unusual meeting with Len. Kay and I must have looked pathetic yet sympathetic (I hoped) as we stood in our living room with one officer holding my hands behind my back and another one holding Kay's arm. I had no idea why they were in our house. I kept thinking this was some weird home invasion by people wearing costumes. If they *were* the police, they must have gotten the wrong address.

The officer had a tight hold on me as he guided me into the corner. I stared straight ahead with my nose about six inches from the wall. I felt helpless and more confused than at any time in my life. I had this growing concern that my breakfast might exit my rear at any time. I'm sure I looked like I had seen a ghost.

I could hear the female officer addressing Kay. She said, "I'm sorry your kids have to see this. We thought they would already be off to school. We've had you both under surveillance to learn your schedules. I have kids, too, so I didn't want yours to see this. Do you have a neighbor who can take them?" I heard Kay give the officer our neighbor Celia's name.

Standing there, I tried to make sense of what was happening behind me and why these people, who were acting like police—I still didn't want to believe them—were in my front room. I wondered if it was a practical joke set up by my crazy high school friends Pauly and Murder (a high school nickname). But then I thought, *No way could they have pulled off this elaborate hoax. It must be that speeding ticket I forgot to pay last year.* Or was it possible Kay was doing illegal things behind my back? Could one of her sessions of Bunco—a fairly calm dice game that usually passes as a reason for older women to drink wine and share neighborhood gossip—have gotten completely out of hand?

The mental charades were escalating. I was going bananas with all kinds of weird scenarios flashing in my head like a scene from the movie *Inception.* One was of Kay cheating with a criminal in the neighborhood like the characters in some Saturday-night whodunnit from the eighties. Maybe they thought the guy was with Kay at our house.

Another wild thought placed her as a suspect like in some *Dateline* episodes we'd watched. Often a teacher, priest, or stay-at-home mom is leading a double life as a criminal. They get caught hiding a dangerous life filled with secrets, drug addictions, and/or bizarre behavior. Could my wife be one of them?

I could almost feel Kay staring at my back. Later she told me she thought the cops were here for *me.* "I thought you must have been looking at some weird, inappropriate websites," she said.

The female officer's phone rang, and as she answered it, I turned around and was face to face with four men and two women. Their expressions made me think I was supposed to give a speech. Maybe I could do something like Gene Hackman's halftime speech in the movie *Hoosiers*, and then the cops would run out the door, more motivated than ever to go to the correct house.

I am comfortably sure you've never had the authorities search your home, but like me, you've probably seen it on some movie or news show. The Hollywood situation is for them to come busting in, shouting, waving guns, and pushing people to the ground. It always looked scary, like something to avoid. Our situation lacked that kind of physicality, but it still scared the hell out me. I was trying to process the situation and figure out what to do next. My mind went into a crazy version of the fight-or-flee reaction, so I had to be careful.

I had crossed paths with the authorities when I'd broken the law a few times as a youth. A nice lady helped me put a candy bar back when I placed it in my pocket at the local grocery store at age five. I'm sure I busted some trees while illegally driving tractors and horsing around while partying during high school. These events, along with a few speeding tickets and an open-container fine when I was twenty-one, amounted to my life of crime.

As I tried to clear my head, Detective Starrett shouted orders to the others, using police codes, 10-23, 10-12, 10-26, and 10-106. I had no idea what the codes meant. When I asked why they had come to our house, she stopped me with the universal hand symbol for "not now" and turned back to her crew, continuing to say more codes. Each time I tried to speak, she ignored me like I was invisible. Then suddenly, Starrett stepped forward, ordering Kay to go into the kitchen. Turning to me she said, "You stay here."

I tried to talk to Kay—I even reached for her—but the detective blocked my hand and said, "Oh no. You *don't* touch each other or talk to each other." Then she started speaking like a lawyer: "You can leave at any time, but you can't come back. And if you leave, understand you no longer have a right to know what is taking place at your residence. You can go."

"We can go?"

"You can, but you cannot come back. Once you walk out the door, no reentry."

"This is my house," I stated.

"Doesn't matter."

"I still don't understand what's going on."

"That's not my problem." With an odd sneer, Detective Starrett turned and headed toward the kitchen. I remained where I was, thinking the police must be joking. I wanted to pop off in my best sarcastic voice, "Of course, the best thing for me to do right now is leave my wife alone in the house with you people when I don't even know why the hell you're all here." My confusion only grew when I noticed the logos on the police jackets were for the town of Western Ridge, but we lived in Commonwealth.

The detective's legal brief on our options to stay or go was not reassuring. My hands were trembling as I tried to come up with my next move. I'm a survivalist and a solution finder. My number-one priority became helping the cops understand that they had raided the wrong house. Rumors had flown around for the last year about a neighbor's teenage son, who might be dealing drugs. That family lived around the corner, so I reasoned that the police must have meant to enter *that* home.

When Detective Starrett came back into the room, I blurted, "Are you sure you're not supposed to be at Pierre's house around the corner?" I raised my hand to point out the window, looking like a reporter at the president's weekly White House briefing.

"*Sit down!*" Starrett yelled. "We have a search warrant for *this* house." She waved a piece of paper in front of my face.

"What? What is that?" I said.

"A warrant."

"A warrant?"

"Did I stutter? Yes, it's a warrant." She seemed to be enjoying this very much.

"A warrant for what?" I was dumbfounded.

"You know for what."

"What do you mean?" I said in a mumble-jumble tone, as she pressed the piece of paper into my hand.

"Take a look for yourself."

I stared at the page but became even more confused. "What? What happened with *what? Who*? " My hand was shaking so much it was hard to hold on to the paper. I raised it up to my face and read a few bullet points of legalese talking about "probable cause" and "power-of-attorney actions." I read it a few times and noticed the document had a judge's signature on the bottom of the page. Time stopped. This piece of paper said I had possibly committed crimes involving my grandparents' estate. Although I had never seen paperwork like this, it looked legitimate. I whispered to myself, "We just need to get to the bottom of this, and then the police will apologize."

Nothing was sinking in. I didn't believe what I had just read, and I wanted to jump up and down and say, "Do you know who I am? This is bullshit! Things like this don't happen to people like me."

With the warrant in hand, I collapsed onto the couch. The early-morning sun streamed in through the front windows, and rays bounced around the living room walls like tiny arrows. Even in winter, the sun's heat beat on the front of the house, raising the room's temperature. I was getting warmer, and the mounting mental and internal stress caused sweat to bead on my forehead. My hands continued to shake, and my heart pounded with anxiety and panic lasting a few seconds, coming and going every few minutes. Just to be sure, I re-read the warrant.

The officer was noncommittal—not suggesting I stay or go. I just sat there as she spoke, and then I said, "I'll stay." I wanted to lie down on the floor because normal breathing was becoming difficult. As I looked around the room, I felt lost, like being in a stranger's house. The last place I thought I'd find myself entangled was with law enforcement. In a split second, I wasn't just off the tracks, I had fallen off the mountain.

Detective Starrett went back to Kay in the kitchen while the officer managed me. He had a scar on his neck, and as I looked closer, it hit me who he looked like: my old business partner Trent. They could have been twins. He said his name was Detective Norton. Sam Norton had dark hair cut just above his eyebrows. With a stocky build and a permanent smirk, he could have been cast in *L.A. Confidential* or *The Usual Suspects*. Norton came into the room at the same time I sat back on the couch. The four officers who'd been standing around me dispersed, as if they were dogs released from being confined. They headed every which way: upstairs, downstairs, into the basement, and out into the garage. It looked and sounded like the mayhem at Walmart on Black Friday morning.

The police began boxing up anything that wasn't nailed down. They searched our computers and paper files. The house was filled with the sounds of file drawers opening, books dropping, doors banging open and shut, and officers barking orders at each other. Their communication with each other seemed like an amateur attempt at Pictionary. The scene was chaotic and loud. I felt my blood pressure rising, and the top of my head felt ready to explode. Like a small child who drops to his knees during a temper tantrum and cries at the top of his lungs, I too wanted to scream, "STOP!"

Officer Norton kneeled in front of me and gently presented me with the Miranda Rights paperwork. Then he handed me a beat-up pen. I heard someone questioning Kay in the kitchen, asking her to sign the same paperwork. I quickly asked, "Excuse me. Are we under arrest?"

The officer snapped back, "We're going to process you later, so let's talk." *Process* sounded like a bad word, even though I didn't know what it meant. We've all seen the thriller movie where some unlucky guy gets caught in some awkward position and is confronted by a detective who says, "Come down to the station so we can *talk things over*" or "Come down for an interview." It never goes well, so I followed the movie script. "Can I … talk to … call my lawyer first?" The words fell out of my mouth, accompanied by desperate gasps. A quick chat with our attorney, Nate, could not make this situation any worse. He had handled all my contracts and the sales of our companies, so maybe he could deal with this situation. Kay could barely hear me from the kitchen, but she followed my lead: "I think I'll need to … I better talk to our lawyer."

The officer looked like a kid who didn't get what he wanted at Christmas. I handed him back the unsigned piece of paper and pen, then sank farther into the cushions. As I looked out the window, a small cloud appeared, then it disappeared just as quickly. I remained seated, leaning forward to peer through the cherrywood blinds and noticed one side was closed while the blinds of the companion window were halfway down. The small opening allowed for a good view of the morning sun as it was rising in the sky. It looked chilly outside, but a beautiful winter morning nonetheless.

Norton was watching me—I nicknamed him "Scarecrow" because his odd facial expressions reminded me of the *Wizard of Oz* character— only without the sense of humor. He headed into my office, and when he returned, he had my wallet. He displayed my driver's license in front of my face. "Is this your license?" he asked with a stern voice. Then he pulled out my debit card. "This your debit card?" He moved it very close to my face, as if I had a vision problem. This became our game. Norton calmly asked an obvious question and then began spitting out odd accusations or making strange physical gestures. I confirmed that everything was mine while still in a surreal trance mixed with disbelief, sweat, and disgust. I lowered my head into my hands and tried to grasp what was happening. The process of moving from denial and isolation to anger was taking its toll.

"Who are the other victims?" Norton yelped, as he turned back around, still holding my wallet. He voiced the question in a tone of curiosity rather than accusation.

"Victims of what?" I was starting to lose it.

"We'll find the others," he said.

"What do you mean? *What* others?"

"Don't worry; we'll find them."

"There are no others!"

"We'll get to that."

The police were treating me like Tony Soprano, raping and pillaging the city for decades. I'm sure I heard three consecutive, descending notes: *da, da, daaaa*. What will the next question be? "Where were you on November 22, 1963?"

I went back to looking out the front window, and I thought how Kay and I should have gotten everything regarding the estate in writing. That included all decisions, contracts, everything. And I should have had witnesses sign each and every document.

I eavesdropped on Kay's conversation with the police by leaning my body as far off the couch and toward the kitchen as I could without falling on the floor. I was worried sick about her as the officers issued rapid-fire statements: "Nice house!" "What a lovely view of the golf course!" "What tee-box hole is this?" I was sure the onslaught was a shock for Kay. Although I couldn't see her, I imagined the emotional drain leaving her paralyzed. She was probably lost in her own thoughts sitting at the kitchen table. I bet she was almost crying now.

As the officers continued, she wasn't responding, and her silence was turning me inside out. Her strength was inspiring, although knowing her all these years I should have known. She's strong. She's courageous. She's incredible. She's special. But now she was in pain.

It wasn't right, because Kay had sacrificed so much to take care of her mom, Gram, Gramps, and then her dad. Everyone else always came first, and she put herself second. I felt terrible that I couldn't take away her fear or hold her in my arms to reassure her that everything would be okay. Worst of all, I knew it was *my* choices that had brought us to this point. My worst fear was that our marriage might not make it out of this unscathed.

I was so confused. I'd followed Gram's directions about selling the house and use of the inheritance. I had listened to my heart, yet I was in a mess. Every action we'd taken for them and for us felt right. It never felt wrong. I hoped Kay would be okay and that we would be okay, but my gut told me something different. I leaned back into the couch and prayed we'd still be husband and wife when this was over. We had a spiritual connection you only have with your soul mate, but how much can a marriage realistically take? *We'll see about "till death do us part,"* I thought.

About two hours had passed since the police started the search. A few cars passed by, and I wished I could jump into one of them and ride away. Or I'd like to be a fly on the windshield to hear the neighbors' reactions at seeing six cars parked in front of our house, some of them marked police cars and others unmarked.

I had calmed down now that there were no additional questions directed to me from the detectives. It was like they had given me a time-out. I was anxious to talk to my attorney, so I would look up every so often and, in a polite voice, ask again if I could call him. I figured at this point Nate might be my only connection to the outside world. Plus, he would know what to do with this mess. "Can I call my lawyer?" I asked. No answer. The officer just looked at me and smiled. So, as many years of sales training taught me, sometimes you just keep asking. This time my question was met with a surprising answer: "Yes." My anxiety took a break while I became giddy with the opportunity to finally speak to someone who could help.

I jumped up from the sofa and moved toward the officer who was holding my phone. I think I could have hugged him. I reached for the phone, thinking I could just start dialing, but the officer stuck his arm out and said, "Get back, and take a seat." He didn't push me, but his stiff arm helped me understand my place was back on the couch.

The officer turned around, and while holding my cell phone, he handed me my Bluetooth earpiece. "What's the name and number?" he asked. "I'll dial." He was showing me he was in charge and announced the names out loud, one after another, "Stop me when I hit on it: Brian, Colleen, Dave, Frank, Kenneth, Nate."

"That one! Nate! that's it!" It was like we were kids playing the Hot and Cold game—and he'd just found the object. The officer confirmed Nate's last name, and I thought, *Please, God, push the call button.* He didn't. Instead, he walked over to me, grabbed the earpiece from my hand, and turned around and walked out of the room. He didn't say a word. About five minutes later he came back to the room and said, "Nate. Is he your lawyer?" He handed me the Bluetooth.

I said yes.

He pushed the call button, and I could hear the ringing as I pushed the Bluetooth a little farther into my ear. I wanted to shove it through my skull as I lowered my head and listened. One ring and I begin to mumble softly to myself, "Pick up! Pick up! Come on, Nate, pick up!" After two rings, I began freaking out because Nate always answers pretty quickly. "It's okay," I told myself. "I'll hear his voice soon." On ring three I was about to lose my shit. Then I heard his normal, friendly tone, "Well hello, Will! How's it going?"

I quickly cut him off. "Nate, I need your help! Please don't hang up." I was stammering.

"What's going on? Are you okay?"

"Yeah."

Nate asked again, "Are you okay? What's going on?"

I tried to breathe. "The police are here, and they're searching. Searching everything. What can I …? What should I …? Do they have the right? Can I stop this? Please help." The words poured out in a rambling string of sound bites.

"First, slow down. I'm not sure I get what you're saying. *Who* is at your house?"

"The police."

I looked up to find the officers staring at me like I was the newest exhibit at the zoo.

Nate continued, "Are you sure it's the police?"

"Yes."

"Okay. Can they hear me?"

"No."

"Do they have a warrant, and have you seen it?"

"Yes, I've got some paperwork. It looks like a warrant."

"Is it real?"

"I believe so. I don't know."

"Are they looking at you?"

"Yes."

"How many are there?"

"Not sure. Maybe four to six. Could be more."

"And are they all wearing underwear?" Nate and I could joke around together. My nervous chuckle confirmed the drastic situation.

He continued, "Do you know why they are there?"

"Not totally sure, but the warrant talks about my grandparents."

"Are they taking you in? Have they arrested you? Read you your rights?"

"They said they would 'process' us later. I don't know. I don't know what they're doing. Nate, I have nothing to hide. Should I just answer their questions?"

"Oh no. Stop talking. Just answer *my* questions. Don't say anything else. And be short with me. Remember, your words can get twisted fast in this type of situation. You're under stress. Let me help you. We need to figure out the next step. I'll call Sharon. She's a criminal defense attorney I've known forever. I'll get back to you right away. Don't say anything else."

"I won't." And with that I looked at the officer, nodding to let him know Nate had hung up. Then I told him Nate would be calling me back. I handed him the Bluetooth and put my head in my hands, holding it like a beat-up soccer ball.

The officers were creating loud noises as they moved from room to room, packing boxes. A tall officer came in and traded places with Scare-crow. The new guy moved a chair up rather close to me, but then he moved it closer to the couch and almost touched my knees. It was like we were starting some theater improv scene, but then he reminded me again that I was still subject to two key rules: I could leave the house but not come back, and I couldn't leave my front room unless I needed to use the bath-room. The main caveat was to not talk to anyone.

This officer looked about my age. He was young and fit, seemed to be kind, and reminded me of one of my best friends, Stu. I did what I knew best, trying some small talk to bond and build rapport. It was breaking the rules, but I couldn't help myself. He looked straight ahead as I asked for his name. He didn't blink—just continued staring straight ahead.

It was like I was speaking Chinese. I asked for his name again. Still no answer. Then he burst into a weird speech that finished with, "What the fuck, man? No talking! I'm not your fucking friend, and while we're at it, where is your cash, your jewelry? Do you have guns in the house?"

I instantly questioned, "Cash? Jewelry? What guns?"

"You heard me. Where are they?"

"The only jewelry we have is on my wife's finger."

"Don't screw with me. Where is your safe?"

"What safe?"

"Where is the cash?"

"What are you after? The only jewelry we have is my wife's wedding ring. Do you want it?"

"And the safe?"

"We don't have a safe."

"We'll rip down every wall, tear out every picture to find it," he said. "Should we start with the ones in here?"

"You can do that, but you won't find a safe. Actually, now that I think about it, that would have been a good idea for an upgrade when we built the house." I couldn't help but throw in a snarky comment.

"What about the basement?"

"Nothing there, but that would have been a good spot. "

"This isn't fucking funny. How much cash do you have here?"

"Whatever we have is in my wallet."

I leaned back in the couch when the officer leaned back in his chair. I wasn't sure if we were done since he had gone silent so abruptly. So, I asked if he was from the area.

"What did I say? I'm not allowed to chit-chat, man."

The interplay reminded me of the times with my Dad when I tried to start conversations with him—only instead of looking at me he would grab another cigarette. He and I would talk if the subject was up his alley—like about gravity and the universe or tectonic-plate movement—but if it interested me, then he was out.

By late morning on most days, I'd be doing my sales calls, preparing content, and practicing my presentations. I was surprised when Scarecrow suddenly popped back into the room. He walked toward me fast, like a fire drill was taking place, but stopped, turned, and looked out the window as if he were pondering his life. Next, he turned around, looked directly at me, and leaned toward me, acting like he empathized with me. Then he gave me a partial grin and bluntly said, "Your Dad killed himself."

"What!?"

"You heard what I said."

I didn't know if that was a statement or a question.

"Let me rephrase that: Did your dad kill himself?" As he said it again, he made odd movements, pointing his head toward the window, then swinging it back toward me like he was on drugs. He continued, "Well, he did have terminal cancer, right?"

"He did."

"He was really sick, stage IV?"

"Of course he was."

This guy was being an asshole and was completely out of line. But what could I do?

By early afternoon, the direct sunlight from the east that kept the living room warm was now making its way toward the backyard, leaving the front of the house in partial shade. The accompanying temperature drop wasn't the only thing making the room feel cold. It was like I was sitting in a morgue, feeling dreary, stoic, and silent. I couldn't muster the courage to ask the officers to turn up the heat, and lack of movement made my feet go to sleep. I was reaching the last stage of grief: acceptance, the point when reality hits. For me it felt like I had hit bottom. Not a junkie's level where someone wakes up in their own vomit in some unknown neighborhood or under a bridge after downing twenty-four beers or shooting up another full needle of meth. My bottom was different from the druggie's because my fall wasn't because of addiction or bad luck. It was totally on me.

I started to think about the mistakes I'd made managing the estate. Yes, I had reached out to Bob and Mary and attempted on several occasions to work out an agreement with them regarding the use of the grandparents' funds. But it was a mistake to assume Bob and Mary knew we'd pay back anything that was considered compensation to Kay for caregiving or the contract on the house. I had never denied using the money, and they had full access to all accounts. In addition, Mary and Kay had monthly updates over the phone to review the situation with Gramps and Gran.

Then Norton came back to the room. He started on me again, "Do you want the media here? We can have more show up," he added with a sharp snicker.

I stood up and tried to look around him but couldn't see any television trucks or people out the window. "What are you talking about?"

"They'll be here soon."

"Why would the media be here?"

"They like to cover stories like this."

"Stories like what?"

"They like to see the good guy gone bad. You know, one who fucks up. Loses his reputation. Or maybe his life. They should be here shortly."

"You mean the press likes to take the good guy down."

"Don't worry, they're on their way. They'll be here soon."

"Who will be here shortly?"

"The media."

"Like reporters?"

I fell back into the couch and started to consider that maybe Scarecrow wasn't full of shit and that the media *would* be here soon. I thought everything I had worked for was slipping away. All the early mornings and late nights meant nothing now. God only knows in what light the media would paint our story. I was sure they would address the real issues of elder care in our country and Kay's uncompromising promise, dedication, and sacrifice to everyone around her. She did it all for so many years without asking for a dime. The media would tell the true story because they tell *all* sides of *all* stories.

At about one-thirty, the police moved Kay into the front room with me. We were together, but we weren't allowed to talk. It was so strange. I was five feet from my wife—I was staring at her—but I couldn't say a word. Even though she tried to remain still and show no emotion, I could see the concern and stress in her eyes and the tears slowly welling up in them. It was horrible. I couldn't hug her. After being together for almost twenty-seven years, occupying the same room and not talking or touching felt alien. I used my eyes to convey how incredibly sorry I was for this fiasco.

Detective Starrett kept returning to the front closet, which was about ten feet from the front door and ten feet to the left of the couch. As soon as she opened the front-closet door, she would turn and head back to the kitchen or walk upstairs or downstairs. She returned after a few minutes to repeat the whole thing: opening the closet door again and looking in. Either she was doing some weird workout or was lost. Watching her was exhausting, like witnessing someone with OCD caught in their cycle. The frustration on her face grew more intense each time she returned. Then she slammed the door, turned, and looked at me like she was possessed. She yelled at us like a small child whose toy has been taken away. "*Where are the rest of the files?*" she screamed.

I kept quiet, not sure what to say. Her behavior reminded me of my mother's mild schizophrenia. My mom would often ask the same thing over and over while rooting around the house looking for something she had lost. As she searched, she would become even more angry—similar to what the detective was doing now.

Starrett continued, "Did you hear me? Where. Are. The. Rest. Of. The. Files? You need to tell me where they are."

"What files?

"Where are the *files*?"

"I don't know what you're talking about. If you'll just tell me what you're looking for, Detective, I can help. We have nothing to hide. What files are you looking for?"

"Where are they? Where are the rest of them?" She kept repeating herself like someone with dementia.

I started to stand up. "Tell me exactly what you need, and I'll get it."

"Just sit down," Starrett snapped. She looked as if she were going to say more, but then just before opening her mouth, she stopped, spun around, and left the room. Within a minute, she was back, ranting again, "I need to know if this is all the files."

"I don't know, what files do you need?" I repeated.

Detective Starrett's eyes dropped, and her shoulders slumped. "Feel free to go, by the way. You can leave anytime you'd like." She never said exactly what she wanted.

I thought, *Fat chance of us leaving now. We're in for the entire show.* Kay and I were in survival mode, and staying in our living room seemed to make the most sense, although going outside to get fresh air sounded tempting. I wondered if the police would ever leave.

Kay and I were sitting down and staring forward, but we still weren't allowed to talk. My mind shifted as I considered *how* the police would be leaving—by themselves or with us in tow? "Officer, how much longer?" I asked.

Detective Starrett answered with a question this time. "Would you like to come down to the station?"

"Are we under arrest?"

"No. But it would be good to talk."

"Talk about what?"

"We can sit down and hear your side."

"Our side?"

"Let us hear your thoughts on the situation with your grandparents. I'm sure you can tell us your side of the story."

"We'd be happy to do that."

"We can schedule a time for later this week if you'd like." Her tone had changed to friendly and warm.

I smelled a rat. "Yeah, sure, we'll talk to our attorney and set up a time."

"Doesn't have to be formal," she added. "Just give us all the details."

"Are we in trouble?"

"I can't answer that. This is an investigation."

I didn't respond.

"Why don't you call me and make an appointment when it's convenient for you?" Detective Starrett reached out her hand and gave me her business card. An appointment was usually what I tried to set up when doing a business deal, attempting to close sales, or bring in dollars. Maybe she would show us a PowerPoint presentation or a flowchart depicting the case on the whiteboard. She might even add in a motivational speech or a training workshop to add value, covering the finer details of preparing the best party dip one could ever imagine. Really? An appointment?

I didn't say anything else, wondering if the detective was fucking serious. This thing went from an intense search that gave Kay and me the impression we were in real trouble to Starrett suggesting we set up a convenient time to meet and get to know one another. All of a sudden it seemed like we were part of some networking group.

Like an old-fashioned Wild West shootout, I stared at her, and she stared at me. She didn't respond but turned around and headed toward the door. She was the last to leave, following her posse out. About five feet away she stopped, turned back, and stated, "You have my number."

After the detective had closed the door, Kay and I sat there speechless. We were frozen, trapped in our own thoughts, each trying to formulate a next step. It felt like someone had died. I felt dirty from total strangers rummaging through our home, touching our belongings, invading our life. I jumped up, hugged Kay like never before, and we both cried for a moment. Then we laughed a weird laugh—like aliens had just visited. I started to inventory what the police took and what was still intact. I moved from one room to the other, noting the missing laptops, phones, and most of our files. They left us with our driver's licenses and one debit card.

"Let's go down to the station and clear this thing up," Kay said as she took a seat in the kitchen.

"Clear it up, babe?"

"We didn't do anything wrong. Let's go down and tell our story."

I was skeptical. "Won't they just twist our words?"

"Gram and the Smiths told us we could use the money from the house sale as we saw fit!" Now Kay was getting angry. "Even during our trip to Vegas, Bob told me we shouldn't feel bad because businesses *always* have problems, and he said we should use whatever money we needed. He added that Gram said we could use the money to support her and Gramps and to help our family. I know the truth. Mary and Bob know the truth. They know us and our intentions. We did *not* use the money without permission."

I stood up and started to walk toward the bathroom. I was still sweating and shaking when the phone in my office rang. I ran to it as quickly as I could, nearly tripping over the edge of my desk and knocking over the chair. My arm hit the phone, and it slid across the desk. I looked at the caller ID while picking up the receiver. "Nate! Hello. Hello. Nate, it's you! They're gone."

"Are you guys okay?"

"Yes, a little shook up. But we're okay."

"What did the police say when they left?"

"The detective said to make an appointment to come in and talk."

"Really. No arrest is good. What'd they take?"

I gave Nate the play by play. As he started to ask more questions, I interrupted. "Nate, we talked it over and we'd like to go down and meet with Detective Starrett. We know we can clear up this misunderstanding."

"You mean go in and talk to the cops?"

"Yes, we have nothing to hide. She said to come in. We did nothing illegal."

"It seems the police disagree."

"Nate, we want to get this over with. We'll tell them the entire story—the truth—and exactly what happened. We didn't steal anything. Kay's name was listed on all the bank accounts, debit cards, everything. Gram gave us permission to handle all the finances and use the money for ourselves if we needed to."

Nate sighed. "Well, you can go to the police station, but first let me give you the legal side. You must have done *something* wrong for a judge to sign a search warrant. He found enough evidence of something illegal to agree to the search of your house. The law is not about ethics or helping your family, it's about rules and strict wording. We're talking actions and consequences. Courts are guided by strict wording on many cases—not emotional realities." He took a deep breath and continued. "The courts look at everything from three sides: the cops' version, your version, and the truth. They are most interested in the police version, not yours. Have you ever watched TV shows like *Criminal Minds* or *Dateline*? The police always twist your words during the questioning process."

Nate proceeded to scare the hell out of us with his tales of crazy interrogations, based on personal experience and past clients. As he spoke, Kay and I just looked at each other, listening intently. I could see the fear in Kay's eyes as Nate helped us understand our situation. It hit both of us that our family, including our children, were now in for a long haul. Her emotions were coming purely from motherly instinct, while mine were pure guilt.

"I'll get dressed and meet you at the station if you still want to go," Nate said. "You guys are not just my clients but my friends. Let me tell you one more story before you decide. I had a situation with my wife several years ago. We were arguing, and it got heated. It was loud. We both had a few too many drinks, and a neighbor heard us and called the police. No real reason for them to call because nothing got physical—just a heated argument between husband and wife. Generally when the cops show up, they're looking to arrest someone. They have quotas and budgets to maintain. In our case, when they arrived, they decided to take me to jail and charge me with domestic abuse. I stayed in for a night, and it was a nightmare trying to get the charges dropped. I had to spend money for legal fees to a defense attorney, and there was the mental trauma of dealing with the entire situation. If you're charged with something, it could take many, many years to reconcile it. In my case, the cops made me feel like I was a wife beater. I can go with you if you want, but I'd advise you not to go meet with them at all. Let's just us sit down and figure this thing out before we talk to anyone."

"But the truth is the truth."

"Will, this is going to be a long haul. The entire legal process and the resulting impact on your life could take ten to fifteen years in the end."

I felt my blood pressure skyrocketing. Nate assured us that talking to the police would only complicate the situation, not radically change it or make it go away. "Remember the cop interviews/interrogations during *Dateline*? Those sessions are not fun."

At the end of our conversation, Nate gave me the contact information of Sharon Maddox, his defense attorney when he and his wife had their situation. Then he recapped: "Whether you did something wrong or right, it gets twisted quickly. The cops have a job to do, and the district attorneys live on data, stats, winning percentages, and conviction rates. Perception becomes reality, and along the way the truth comes out from time to time. Hell, you don't even know what evidence will be allowed and what will be suppressed. Sharon Maddox will do a good job for you." Nate had twenty-five years of trust in her.

After talking it over, Kay and I decided that meeting with Sharon was a good next step and, at this point, maybe our only step.

# CHAPTER 17

# You Could Get Ten to Twelve Years

**2011**

*"Down these mean streets a man must go who is not himself mean,
and who is neither tarnished nor afraid."*

— RAYMOND CHANDLER

K ay and I arrived at the address that defense attorney Sharon Maddox had given us. Our meeting was two days after the search. The women who greeted us in the reception area had us take a seat in Sharon's office. The décor felt calm, more like the inside of a mountain cabin or meditation retreat than a legal office. Sharon had all the typical degrees and certificates of legal achievement and business accomplishments hanging on the wall in nice frames. The feeling was almost too personal and too relaxed. I hoped to God she was a pro.

When she walked in, my first impression of Sharon was part actor Susan Sarandon combined with legal commentator Nancy Grace. She had brown hair with short bangs; black, circular glasses rested on her pale-white cheeks. Her smile went ear to ear as she shook our hands with a firm grip. I wasn't sure if the smile was natural or contrived.

She got right down to business, grabbed her pen and notepad, and started firing away. "So, Nate says you guys gots a little problem." She had a deep Southern drawl, which, like her smile, seemed genuine, though it could have been a clever disguise to make her seem like a clueless Southern girl who was really as sharp as a Leatherman tool. "Nate said you had an unexpected visit at your house two days ago from the police poo." She grinned as she finished *poo*, waiting for us to laugh. I was feeling uncomfortable.

Without preamble, Sharon blurted out, "You could get ten to twelve years in prison if found guilty." She was not going to ease us into the process. She grabbed a state law book from the shelf next to her desk. The book covered classes of crime, explanations of punishment, and legal guidance. As she thumbed through it, she looked part thrill seeker, part lunatic. I wondered if she started all her conversations like this. Was it to scare us, or was she just horrible at people skills?

Her eyes darted at the pages while she took a quick break every few seconds to look up at us. She was flipping through the book and pointing to different paragraphs. She seemed lost.

"I know it's here somewhere," she muttered. "I reviewed it after our call. Oh, yeah, baby, there it is: class 5, 4, and 3 felony levels. Don't worry: class 1 covers murder and the electric chair. Wait, I was wrong. Colorado does euthanasia."

She thought that one was really funny. I didn't. I stood up from my chair, bent over the front of her desk, and looked down at the book. When she lifted her finger from the page, I replaced it with mine. I read the lines for myself, and as I did, my stomach sank into the bottom of my feet. This was the first of many anxiety attacks. I didn't throw up, but my face must have looked like I was about to let it fly.

"Are you okay, Will?" Sharon asked.

I fell back into my chair and threw my arms up into the air. "So how do we plead?"

"What? What do you mean?"

"How do we plead? Don't people usually plead something in these situations?"

"You already want to plead? But if you did nothing wrong, why would we do that?"

"We didn't do anything wrong," Kay said.

Sharon continued, "Well, maybe not, wrong or right. The real question, kids, is did you do something legally or was it illegal. We won't be looking at the ethics or morality of it, just the legality."

I said, "I know we made mistakes and maybe we broke some laws, but it wasn't on purpose. There was absolutely no intent whatsoever."

"A jury may need to decide that."

"A *jury*?"

"Yeah, we'll let a jury take a look-see."

"What about the media?" I asked. "What will we do? What will they be saying about us?"

Her face said it all: I was completely full of shit or had just been diagnosed with multiple personalities. "Come on! Really?" she replied. "The media? Why would the media get involved? They don't care about stuff like this. Really, you guys? The media getting involved? Me don't think so, honey."

Over the next thirty minutes, Sharon helped Kay and me see what the process going forward would be like and that our lives would be turned upside down should there be charges. Just when we thought the meeting was coming to a close, she had another surprise for us.

"I can't represent both of you. The state of Colorado says that's a no-no. I'll represent Kay, if she'll have me. And I'll have Jack, my partner, represent you, Will. We've discussed your case, and he said he'd like to defend you." She stood up and walked around her desk, waving us to follow her to the next office like she was a restaurant hostess.

Jack Tillman was a dead ringer for John Wayne. Heck, Jack could have been his stand-in. I noticed the Green Beret information on his wall alongside pictures of his kids. He seemed like an old-fashioned tough guy who now served the innocent and defended the guilty. At least that's what I hoped—that he would be a good guy to have on my side. I figured he'd understand me. He'd get it.

I summarized for Jack what we had told Sharon, and he said the next step was to have his investigator, Nick Hopco, do some investigating. I didn't realize defense attorneys had their own investigators.

When our session with Jack ended, I was so numb I couldn't move.

Kay snapped me back into the world. "Will, let's go," she said. As I started to get up, my knees were shaking, ready to buckle at any moment. I'd just put our lives in the hands of people we'd known for only sixty minutes. They didn't know us or our history, and the cost in money and time was still unknown, but I knew it would be significant. As we left, I felt doomed.

In the coming weeks, my thoughts of suicide started. I had battled mental health issues for most of my life, figuring it was probably genetic from my mother. With each passing day I drank more, and my depression worsened. I daydreamed about killing myself so Kay would get the life insurance. There was plenty of money to end this nightmare. I started to plan how I would do it, looking at what methods would be quickest and cleanest.

Reading the life insurance documents caused me more confusion than clarity, though. I was worried Kay wouldn't get the money if my cause of death was suicide or that she'd have to battle for years in court. I'd recently upgraded my insurance to over a million dollars, and I wasn't sure if that counted in the contestability period. I didn't understand the fine print. What type of lawyer do you approach for guidance? Do you just call and say, "Good morning, I'm thinking about killing myself and need to feel good about the insurance company paying on the claim to my family? If you don't pay out, they'll hate me even more. Can you help me?" I even made an appointment with a lawyer who handled life insurance claims. I never went.

Kay and I were starting to argue about little stuff—unimportant things that didn't matter much. Still, the volatility of the situation was expanding. Fear of the unknown and what might be coming at us from the authorities was increasing anger and frustration in both of us. My own feeling was more like guilt, while I'm sure Kay blamed me and felt disappointed in me. I had urged her to use the money. We were hanging in, but the pressure was mounting.

Getting out of bed was getting harder. A week had passed since our meetings with Sharon and Jack, and I wasn't sleeping more than a few hours each night. I was exhausted. My mind would not turn off, running through all the crazy scenarios about potentially going to prison, losing my wife and kids, falling into the abyss. I turned to the only thing I had left, God.

I began to pray again, and my prayers were more intense. They were real now. Before this debacle, I'd prayed like I was checking off a task on my to-do list. And, as the character Andy said in *The Shawshank Redemption*, "Get busy living or get busy dying." Caught in between, I was feeling more desperate than inspired, so I added journaling to my process. One night while journaling at my desk after a quick prayer, I looked up at my bookcase. A quiet whisper in my heart said, "It's a mile." I had no idea what that meant. Should I go to Mile High Stadium, grab an airline ticket, or go for a Rocky Mountain hike? The book that caught my eye right then was *The Science of Mind*, the book I had taken from Gram's house when we started working on it. Maybe the whisper was about Mile Hi Church.

On a beautiful spring day, the third Sunday in February of 2011, Kay and I attended a ten o'clock morning church service at Mile Hi Church. Ironically, my Gram had taken me to this very same place when I was about ten years old. The white, mushroom-shaped building had given way to a new and larger facility. I'll never forget walking through the front doors and feeling an overwhelming sense of love that I still can't put into words. It was so peaceful, like three or four people were hugging and squeezing me all at once. It felt good.

Soon we were attending regularly. It was a Sunday escape for Kay and me. I would sit near the back with tears running down my face. The entire service was like therapy. A very unique place, Mile Hi is more therapy, inspiration, and self-development than religious dogma. People there spoke about all religions and all different views, and combining those discussions with science made the teachings just our speed. The group was diverse, open to all genders, races, and sexual orientations and preferences. I appreciated their open hearts. It was truly a spiritual place. I felt welcome there. Even the minister, Dr. Roger Teel, at times seemed like he was talking just to me. He was incredible, and he delivered amazing words.

Afterward, lunch as a family gave us a chance to discuss topics the kids had covered in their classes, and Kay and I could impress upon them our undying love for our family. It was both fun and a break from the anxiety. I was starting to feel the joy I had desperately searched for in all the wrong places. During the week we had discussions about the court case and the fearful nightmares, but on Sunday it was gone. The services were saving us, saving me, keeping me from taking my own life, and keeping us together as the fear and anxiety mounted. That first visit to Mile Hi helped prepare us for our first meeting the next week with Nick, Jack's private investigator.

# CHAPTER 18

# What About the Neighbors?

### February 2011

*"Nobody can do for little children what grandparents do.*
*Grandparents sort of sprinkle stardust over the lives of little children."*

— ALEX HALEY

"**A**ll you would have had to do was write an IOU and this would never have happened." The words of Nick Hopco, our legal investigator, pierced me like a well-sharpened arrow; he might as well have stuck a real one through my chest. I stared straight ahead out the window. Jack had set up this first session to help Nick understand our situation. I was learning that the role of an investigator for a defense team is to get to the truth. Nick would help the defense make a judgment on moving to trial, plea bargaining, or a little of both. Both Kay and I met him, six days after our meeting with Jack and Sharon, at a Village Inn north of town. We sat in the booth, and I stared across the street at the building where we had started our initial internet service provider, XploreNet. I was thinking about those startup days as Nick rattled off his preliminary findings and opinion.

Kay bumped my hip under the table, and it snapped me back into the moment. I said, "Sorry, Nick. Yes, I can see how if we'd written IOUs for every time we used Gram's funds to purchase something that would have helped us. But what now? Plus, the reality is that not everything was an IOU situation. I don't suppose you have a time machine, do you?"

Nick continued. "That simple step would have saved a lot of headaches. You had the legal right to do what you did with your inheritance."

"I didn't tell our relatives the total amount of money used because I felt most of it was compensation for the house contract," I explained. "Why would I have to pay those back? And now we could get charged with a crime. Do you think that will happen?"

Nick had spent thirty-one years with the FBI as an investigator, and he looked like an agent or an accountant. His focus had been on white-collar crime and financial fraud, and he'd seen a lot. He had completed investigations and testified in court as an expert witness in some large trials that got media attention.

His job now was to investigate the case, investigate us, interview witnesses, and examine potential evidence as if he were a detective in order to find whatever the DA might also dig up. In the end, he would try to figure out what really happened. His most important job was to help us explain the evidence to a jury, should a trial take place. Nick glossed over my question about the charges as if I had never asked. He said, "Let's start from the beginning. Can you help me understand what happened?"

I had already explained our case so many different times to so many different people in the last month, that when someone said "start from the beginning," I died inside. I just hated those words. But the good thing about repetition is you end up knowing the story *very* well. By now I could go through the details without thinking, but I was still always on the verge of emotional breakdown. I was so embarrassed by the entire situation. My face always felt like it was on fire, and then my eyes would water.

I told Nick about using the estate money for our living expenses after the house was sold, and only when we had very few other choices. I reflected on how the relatives gave us permission to use the funds. We were to be paid by the estate for cleaning up the house, taking care of the grandparents, managing the estate sale, and selling Gram and Gramps's house. I also told Nick how we agreed on almost everything using oral agreements and handshakes, with very little in writing. The only exceptions were a few emails between us and the relatives and a signed real-estate contract.

I finished my summary by saying, "The irony is that we've given money and resources to almost every member of the family—to the tune of thousands of dollars. We've donated to the local community and probably spent 5,000 hours volunteering. Yet now we're facing the fight of our life."

Nick asked, "What about PeakView Senior Living? Did the employees know you? See you? I think it's important to establish how much time and effort you invested in taking care of your grandparents."

"Oh yes," I said. "The staff saw both of us every weekend, and Kay three to five times during the week."

Kay chimed in. "They made jokes like, 'Don't *you* live here by now?' or 'Do you pay rent yet?' And I would talk to my friend Toni about how I was doing all the tasks for Gram and Gramps that she had also done with her folks."

"Would the staff be good witnesses?"

"Yes, they should be *great* witnesses," Kay answered.

"Did you fill out a log book or visitor register when you went there?" Nick asked.

"I did early on," Kay said, "but then I was at PeakView so often I just walked in. They all know me."

"That's great. We can get copies of the book. What about your grandparents' neighbors at their old house in Heartwood?"

"Yes, they all knew us well, and many helped us by calling or communicating if something happened," added Kay. "Sometimes they called us late at night or early in the morning to say Gram or Gramps needed help. They knew we'd be there right away."

"People from church?"

"Sure," I said. "They knew how often we took care of them."

"What church was it?"

"We attended Gram and Gramps's local Methodist church, often because the short ride from their house was safer with us driving."

"Did the other relatives know how much time you were spending with them?"

"They did," Kay said.

Nick checked his notes. "Jack told me your relatives said you should have been paid. He thought they said four to eight dollars an hour sounded fair. Isn't that way below minimum wage and far less than most in-home nurses receive?"

"We disagreed with the four dollars per hour," I explained. "We received estimates of thirty to sixty-five dollars per hour for a live-in nurse or someone with similar caregiving skills."

"And your relatives also agreed you could use as much money as you needed in your situation. Is that right?"

"Yes, during two trips in particular," Kay said. The first one was to Glenwood Springs and the second was during a family trip in Las Vegas. They were very clear on us using the money. But it was confusing. I would review the monthly bank statements with Mary, Gramps's daughter, and I assumed she was also reviewing all the bank and financial statements. If Mary or Bob had a problem with how we were managing things, they would have said something." Kay paused and sighed. "But I guess they must have just been talking on the phone without even looking at the statements. I assumed the Smiths were okay with everything. Of course, we still should have been more transparent on everything—I realize that now." Kay looked so worried. "We should have tracked every dime."

Nick nodded. "Another one of Jack's notes says hiring a nurse would have cost between five and eight thousand dollars per month. But instead you tried to serve this role, correct?"

"We tried several outsourced nurses when Gram and Gramps were still living at their house, but Gram wouldn't have it," Kay said. "It had to be me. Even when they went to PeakView Senior Living they still wanted me there. *Someone* had to help them." Kay's voice wavered with emotion. "I spent as much time helping them while they were at PeakView as I did before."

Our meeting ended on a not-so-positive note when Nick said, "This is a tough and complicated situation. I'll need to interview the list of witnesses you provided, but I'm worried the relatives might not tell the truth. This seems like a "she said / he said" situation. And with very little in writing, you risk them not remembering what they agreed to. Let's reconvene next month."

That spring I had to change my role with Talus, stepping down as CEO but remaining a board member. This move enabled me to focus on contracting as many nonprofit-fundraiser training sessions per month as I could to cover the cost of lawyers, investigators, accountants, and consultants. I believed deep inside those charges would never come.

Nate had helped us put together a good legal team, and I wanted to thank him. I hadn't heard from him for a month. Each time I'd reached out, his voicemail was full, and an email reply never came. I did not know what to do, and I thought maybe he had left the country. He always replied to me. The weeks went by and still no answer. This was bizarre and not like Nate at all. I wanted him to know how grateful I was for referring us to Sharon and Jack. Nate had helped us more than he knew.

I rarely looked at Facebook, but I figured I'd see if it showed where Nate was or if something odd had happened. There it was—his obituary—posted on his page. *I didn't know he was born in Schenectady, New York,* I thought. My relationship with Nate was like many of my relationships:

more shallow then deep. I was more worried about my own bullshit than in staying in touch with friends.

When I read the news, my mind raced with frustration and disappointment. I had missed his funeral by two weeks, and I was angry that I had missed the opportunity to speak at it. I would have talked about how fantastic he'd been to Kay and me. A real angel from heaven. In our darkest hour, he kept us calm. Nate was never just our lawyer. He had cared about us, and we knew he would do anything to help.

Now what would I do? A potential trial would be around the corner, and Nate was gone. He could have been a third party to the proceedings, giving me an honest opinion regarding evidence.

I saw a link on the web page to reach out to his family, so I did. I received a message from his wife, Anna, the next day. *Will, it's great to hear from you. I had you on my list. Do you mind setting up a time to come get your files?*

I met Anna at her office, where she was a paralegal for a large Denver law firm. As she walked toward me, I could see her eyes were red. She was holding a Kleenex to her face.

"Anna, so good to see you," I said. "My God. I'm so sorry you've lost Nate. I didn't know about the funeral or I would have been there. I miss him. What happened? I didn't know he was ill. I hadn't heard from him for several weeks."

She paused, looked away, and then looked at me. "You didn't know?"

"Know what?"

"Will, Nate killed himself."

The news ripped through me, and every muscle in my body clamped down. "I don't know what to say," I stammered. "Wow. I'm so sorry, Anna."

"His drinking had become worse in the last six months to a year, and he decided it was time to move on."

"Oh." I felt sick. "He had a drinking problem?" Nate had been in silent agony too, trying to anesthetize his way out of it. Why didn't he say anything? Why didn't *I* say anything?

"You didn't know that either?"

"Maybe I was in denial, but he never showed up drunk to anything. He never smelled like booze. Nothing. I never saw him drunk or even take a drink—not even buzzed. Never. I guess he hid it well."

"Yes, he loved to crawl into a bottle of Scotch and forget the world."

As I listened to Anna talk about Nate's final days and the way she found him, I remembered our last few phone calls. Nate kept mixing his words and didn't sound very coherent. He told me he had a back problem and the pills made him feel funny and woozy.

"Anna, I'm so sorry. Is there anything I can do for you?"

"No. I'm a little lost right now, but I'll come around. Nate always said you were one of his favorite clients even back in the days when he helped you sell the internet and tech companies. You and Kay were kind to him."

"We felt the same about him."

I knew I would miss Nate greatly. He would have been a support person for me—someone to bounce ideas and fears off of, but now he was gone. Meanwhile, my own mental health was worsening, and I had to get ready for a trial—if that's what was coming.

# CHAPTER 19

# Are You Ready to Say Goodbye?

**November 2011**

*"All our dreams can come true if we have*
*the courage to pursue them."*

— WALT DISNEY

**N**ate's passing hit me hard. I was dealing with many similar thoughts of suicide, drinking more than I should, and fearful of the future. I, too, wanted to crawl into a bottle. My choice was vodka. I thought it was normal to think about taking your own life, especially under the circumstances I was dealing with.

Ralph Waldo Emerson wrote: "Our greatest glory is not in never falling, but in rising up every time we fall." The problem was I could barely survive each day—much less "rise up." I woke every morning to the horrible reality of the situation, knowing I had to be preparing for a game I'd never played before. I didn't know the rules, especially the unwritten ones.

I took some comfort in reminding myself that all games have unwritten rules. The only thing I understood about the legal system is you do *not* want to get caught in it. Once the police and the district attorneys have you in their crosshairs, there's little chance of escape.

I kept my depression and desperation hidden as well as I could, but my sense of doom and my regret for what I was putting my loved ones through was unbearable. Kay and I were going along pretending life was normal—that everything was great. Each day that passed with no news about legal charges was a victory.

And then everything got more complicated. One day Kay said the unthinkable: "I'm pregnant."

I froze. I hoped I'd heard wrong. "Say that again?"

"I'm pregnant."

"You must be joking."

Kay was putting on a half-smile while doing her best to hold back tears. This was no joke.

"I really am pregnant," she said. "We were irresponsible at age fifteen and now again at forty. I've taken two tests already this morning. I can't believe it."

I went stone-cold silent, thinking about the unimaginably awful timing. How could I confront the irritability, discomfort, illness, and insanity of pregnancy—and that's just me!—while potentially preparing for a trial? I looked at Kay like someone had shot my dog, "But I thought we were in the safe zone."

Her tears turned to a slight chuckle, then she burst into ironic laughter. "We'll have to name the baby Safe Zone."

Kay always tracked her ovulation schedule on a spreadsheet, which was not the greatest idea. Part of the spreadsheet was called "Safe Zone," meaning she would not be ovulating. But her tracking was off, and now we were expecting a third child.

"I know when it happened," Kay grabbed my arm.

"Me too." Then we simultaneously said, "Our anniversary weekend. Shit!" It would be the gift that keeps on giving.

• • •

A few months later, our family life became even more complicated. The phone rang, and I recognized the number. "Hi Cali," I answered. The baby girl Kay and I had given up for adoption twenty-four years ago in high school was calling.

Kay and I were reunited with Cali in 2006 after waiting for eighteen years. When our daughter Helen was born, we mailed the birth announcement to Cali's adoptive parents. We wanted her to know she had a biological sister in the world. We decided Kay would email Diane, Cali's adoptive mom. She finished the message and hit send. The reply came a couple of days later, and it blew our minds. Diane replied that their family was overjoyed at the news. And, they were excited to meet Helen and for Cali to meet us. They had prayed for this day. Diane said she had kept all the special moments in Kay's and my life—graduation announcements, our wedding announcement—and all the birthday cards we'd sent every year to Cali. Diane had stored them in a box and gave them to Cali on her eighteenth birthday. That day, Kay and I held each other as tears of joy flowed. Later that year we met Cali in person, and now we talked to Cali a few times a month on the phone.

When I answered the phone, Cali said, "Hi Will, can I ask you something?"

Cali being so matter-of-fact scared me. I asked, "How is LA?"

"Not good."

"Why? What's going on?"

"The girl I came here to live with is not making money doing acting."

"Oh, yikes. She's not doing acting?" There was no need for Cali to say more. I got it. Many girls in LA end up making money in desperate ways other than acting. Cali was almost twenty-four, but her dreams were big and her timeline for "making it" as an actor was massively unreasonable.

"I've been here three weeks, and you were right: it's going to be a long, hard road."

As she described a few auditions and her nights waiting tables, I wondered how she thought she could succeed in LA so quickly. People spend eight, ten, fifteen years trying to "make it big."

Cali cleared her throat. I could hear the nervousness in her voice. "You always said I could live with you guys if I need to. I don't want to go home to Florida, so can I move in with you for a little while?"

It was going to be awkward, having our twenty-one-year-old biological daughter live with us, especially now with all the legal headaches. And there would surely be more than a few bumps ahead in the road because Kay and I hadn't raised her. But without hesitating, I said, "We'd love to have you here."

Kay was upset because I didn't discuss this decision as a family, but my heart screamed that Cali needed to be around her siblings. Even if her time with them was short, it could be valuable to them and an amazing experience for everyone.

Cali must have hit the road right after hanging up because the next morning, I opened the door to see her standing in front of me. Peering over her shoulder, I could see her car, filled to the roof with all her stuff. It looked like her "visit" would be more long term than short. We smiled as we embraced.

"So great to see you. How was the drive from LA?"

"I got here faster than I thought, about fifteen hours," she said. "I got some sleep in St. George, Utah."

I was excited for Cali to get to know her sister, now six, and brother, who had just turned three. I was willing to overlook all the concerns of her fitting into the family and the worries about whether the kids would warm up to her. They were much younger and in different stages of life, so my hope was that they would appreciate having an older sister. Most importantly, my intent was for them to start a relationship.

Cali is a beautiful young woman. You can see her dark roots under her dyed-blonde hair, which accentuates her cheek bones and hazel eyes. She's not tall, but she often wears high heels that boost her up three or four inches. She's full of confidence and looks a lot like her beautiful biological mom—combination gorgeous and supermodel. She's competitive and driven, yet nervously uncertain at times. Not as in lacking confidence, but more like a person with lots of talent and an underlining fear that she might be great.

Cali and Kay locked horns soon after she moved in. We hoped Cali would help around the house and babysit from time to time, which would take some burden off Kay, who was still going to PeakView almost daily. Cali got a part-time job at a local restaurant and wasn't available as much as Kay had hoped. I'm not sure Cali ever did feel welcome with us—in fact, she probably felt like an outsider, which made me sad. It must have been hard trying to melt into our family dynamic in her mid-twenties.

A month passed, and Cali and Kay were getting along better when another life event occurred. It was yet another death. They say life experiences come in threes. When people you've known your entire life start dying, it screws you up. This time is was Kay's dad. He made his transition right before Christmas. Ed's passing didn't exactly cause me to panic thinking about my own mortality, but I felt a loss of my personal history. It was a kind of longing to go back in time to when the parents were young and I was innocent. You miss them and you miss who you were when your parents were healthy and young. I yearned to be thirteen years old again with my entire life ahead of me.

I remember sitting at dinner with Kay's parents when I was thirteen. They had often taken in Sadie and me while my mother was off barhopping or dealing with some new mental-health issue. Kay's parents were very good to us, so when Kay and I started dating, they were a new, interesting family for me. The whole family actually ate at the table, together. They spoke to one another during dinner, rather than the way my family stared at the TV while eating off banged-up TV trays. They enjoyed being together and talked about things that mattered, like the events of the day, sports activities at school, and even a national news story or two. I was used to spending most of my evenings sitting in my room watching TV by myself and dreaming of a better life.

At five foot two and 100 pounds soaking wet, Ed had been more racehorse jockey than NBA forward, and he always had a look of uncertainty on his face. It might have been boredom rather than uncertainty because he spent so much time sitting at the kitchen table with a cigarette in one hand and a cup of coffee in the other. He never said much, which I guessed was either because he was terribly shy, a great listener, or didn't give a shit about the conversation around him. Other family members would babble on for hours about a family drama or the local news, but Ed just sat there. I always joked we needed to check his pulse once in a while to make sure he was still physically with us.

Ed taught me something special that I didn't fully understand until after he was gone. Life is not about being the loudest, proudest, or most victorious. He didn't have a drive for career achievement or financial gain. His days were not about how many tasks he could accomplish or the number of people added to his Rolodex. Ed demonstrated the power of silence. His life was about noticing, observing, and listening. Because of him I finally understood Gram's saying, "God gave you two ears and only one mouth for a reason."

Ed's silence was so refreshing. It was like a sweet meditation, a quiet moment on a mountaintop, or a yoga retreat in some mystical location. When he did talk, his words had substance, and I paid attention. We'd talk about NASCAR, him growing up in the Midwest, his cabinetry work, or the Rockies' baseball season. Also, he was one of the few people I knew who didn't have to add his two cents regarding personal views or opinions. I liked Ed from the start.

"He's gone!" Tears once again rolled down Kay's face as she took the call from her sister about the news of their father's passing. He had been under the care of home hospice for a few months at the house of Kay's sister, Lynn, whom the kids had nicknamed Auntie Sis. Each day had been touch and go.

When we arrived at Lynn's house, Ed's body was still on the floor. The hospice nurse was working to get him onto the bed so his daughters could properly say goodbye.

As I took a seat at the dining room table, the nurse came to let us know Ed was ready for Kay and Lynn to see him. Then the nurse added something I'll always remember. She said, "Funny how when we see people go through the last phase of life it makes us—well, me—feel good. If they can do it, I will eventually make it through too."

I agreed, smiled, and then turned to head back to Ed's room. Kay had taken care of him most of her life. In the beginning, her caregiving was mostly emotional support, but later it became physical and financial support as well. She paid his bills, gave him our Chevy Blazer to drive, and showered him with love and attention.

God love Auntie Sis. She is a natural redhead with shoulder-length hair, though now it's dyed blonde most of the time. At about five feet tall with ivory skin and blue eyes, she's spunky. She can be impatient one moment and then willing to sacrifice her day or time to help her kids or grandchildren.

Auntie Sis is the elder sister by twelve years. Although Kay was adopted, they could be mistaken for blood relatives. Her heart is similar to Kay's—filled with lots of empathy. She had looked after Ed during the last few years and had him live in their house. Because Lynn helped their father, Kay was able to focus on taking care of my grandparents.

As I said goodbye at Ed's funeral, I knew the best way to know a man is to look at his children. If your kids are great, it shows you did something right.

# CHAPTER 20

# Who Is the Father of These Children?

## 2012

*"If nothing is going well, call your grandmother."*

— ITALIAN PROVERB

As 2012 began, each day was filled with fear of what other changes would follow. Kay's mom and dad were gone. My dad was gone. Cali was living with us. What was next?

I traveled to do speaking engagements and trainings about fundraising and nonprofit management, and each time I got in front of an audience, I wondered if the people in the audience could read my mind. Did everyone know what Kay and I were dealing with? I sat anxiously during my meetings and phone calls with clients, scared to death they were going to find out I was being investigated. Even walking past people in the airport terminal, I wondered if they somehow knew my situation. It was exciting to help all the nonprofits, but at the same time, it was strange to function like a fugitive.

Kay and I continued holding on to our optimistic view of the investigation and had faith it would resolve itself with no charges brought against us. The longer the investigation went, we reasoned, the better. It was more blind hope and denial than reality and common sense. Those stages, similar to dealing with grief, ultimately gave way to anger.

By late January, I had reached the bargaining and depression phases of our life upheavals, and was almost ready to deal with the last stage of acceptance. One day Jack, my attorney, called while I was waiting for a flight to Tulsa. Assuming the worst, I answered the phone with an angry tone, but Jack had good news.

Turns out, he had a brief encounter with the DA at the annual county Christmas party. He told me he quipped to the prosecutor that they should get together in a month to discuss our case. He was hoping the DA would see there was no reason for charges. The idea of a meeting with the DA as the drinks were flowing must have seemed like a good strategy. Jack was confident we could win a trial because he'd beaten this DA in a several cases over the last fifteen years, and he felt their mutual respect could lead to a productive session. The DA agreed to schedule a meeting.

February came and went, marking the passing of one year since the police search of our house. My panic attacks were increasing, and tension was destroying my health, but on the positive side, Kay and I were growing and changing together. We appreciated each other more; we loved our kids and friends more. The weekends were fun, filled with family time. We were becoming a closer family. Kay and I were dialed in to each other, and I was starting to learn how to be a better father and husband. I was finally prioritizing family first and letting everything else come second. We argued less, and we started to accept the fact that charges might be coming. Our attitude could be either positive or negative. We had a choice.

My weekday training sessions, speaking engagements, and book sales were great distractions. I felt alive again teaching a room full of trainees or giving a keynote speech to a large group. The problems and demons disappeared for a few hours. I consulted with clients in different parts of the country, and my fundraising seminars were about ways to increase donations, to carve out a planned-giving program, to increase the amount of money raised, and to advance the best skills for a development officer of a nonprofit. My speaking engagements covered topics that ranged from fundraising for nonprofit board members to the economic state of fundraising in the US. I spoke in places like Boise, Albuquerque, Salt Lake, Phoenix, Dallas, Spokane, Chicago, Atlanta, Boston, New York, and Miami.

Though I wasn't selling millions of my books (*How Good Board Members Become Great Fundraisers* and *How Good Nonprofit Officers Become Great Fundraisers*), I was enjoying meeting nonprofit leaders from all over the country. I was starting to be known nationally as a great nonprofit trainer and outstanding public speaker. In one year, I completed fifty-two talks. Educating others so they could raise more money and complete their mission was fulfilling for me, and the money I made from the trainings helped pay the legal fees Kay and I were incurring to defend against what I felt was an inevitable trial.

Airports and hotel rooms, however, were no fun. I didn't sleep well in the beds, and my drinking was getting heavier with each trip. The nightly alcohol binge dulled my senses. I'd do whatever it took to get up and finish the sessions. Often hung over, I would drink water up in the front of the room like I was lost in the desert. Whether I felt good or not, the show went on. I was making a name, creating a brand, selling myself, and generating important revenue. Sometimes the room contained fifty people; sometimes I spoke in front of a thousand. At times I received nice fees—$4,500 on one occasion—at others I did presentations for free so I could sell more books, sign new clients, or book more workshops.

My unorthodox tools were targeted at the average development or fundraising person to help them break out of their comfort zone and overcome personal barriers. Instead of traditional training methods, I opted for skits. My most popular one was playing a doctor. I wore a white medical coat and a costume stethoscope while walking up and down the aisles helping the audience understand the main components of a good thirty-second commercial, using a script and a closing. The idea was that a good fund-raiser, like a good doctor, connects with a donor's personal concerns by asking the right questions to give a proper "diagnosis." The crowds loved it, laughed, and had fun.

The downside of speaking gigs was being away from home. My absence during the week made it tough on Kay, who was managing the kids plus Gram by herself. And Gram's condition was getting worse. We felt like we were the only ones in the world dealing with this issue of being in the "sandwich generation," but we were far from alone. I learned that every sixty-seven seconds someone is diagnosed with dementia or Alzheimer's disease in the US. In 2021, the Alzheimer's Association estimated that 6.2 million Americans age sixty-five and older were living with Alzheimer's dementia.

The even scarier statistic involved caregivers. Fifteen million people were providing 17 billion hours of care. Some estimates showed 470 billion hours per year of help. Kay and I didn't fit the typical profile, which is usually a child supporting a parent and a median age of 49.

In the spring of 2012, Gram's physical regression was starting to match her mental decline. Though I wanted to spend time with her, watching her continued decline each time I saw her made me sick and angry. I hated to see her like this. Plus, I was losing my patience. "Please stop asking me the same goddamn question," I whispered under my breath each time I walked into PeakView. Upon my arrival, the awful smell was always the first thing I noticed. In spring, it seemed like a mixture of overcooked lunch food combined with bodily fluids; in winter the odor was more like dirty laundry mixed with a wet dog.

Each time I visited Gram, my frustration and guilt expanded. It was an overwhelming test of patience. I'd make it over on a Saturday or Sunday with my main goal of completing two hours without wanting to jump off the highest building or to grab a sharp knife and shove it through my throat. I usually found her in the main group-living area, sitting in a large red chair and smiling into space. I would stop and look at her, thinking to myself, *Here is this incredible lady who at one time was a magnificent, glowing, beautiful creature with a razor-sharp mind like a college professor or a brain surgeon, but who now asks the same questions over and over like a broken record.*

It was hard to believe that only a few years before, Gram and I would talk for hours about politics, major social issues, or religion. No topic was off the table. Now she would spend an afternoon with me, her grandson, and her great grandchildren, repeating herself while I struggled with all my might not to show my frustration. She looked through me more than at me.

I searched to find new things in the room that I hadn't noticed before as I tried to keep my conversation with her interesting. I loved her, but these sessions were a detriment to my own mental survival. I would try to improve my interactions with her by pretending to be different characters with each of my answers. I might be Exciting Will or Bored Will. My favorites were Southern Will, Boston-Accent Will, Slow Will, or Smiling and Happy Will. Even Chicago Will or half-drunk Will kept me focused. During a bathroom break or a quick lap down the hallway, I got a few seconds to gather myself, and then I was able to return to the room and try on a new character.

The worst thing to bear was when Gram would stare at our seven-year old daughter, our four-year old son, and, later, our baby. She would look at Kay and back to me, and then look at each one of us again and ask, "Who is the father of these children?" We tried to laugh at it—and initially it *was* funny—but as time went on, the visits became grueling. They cut through me. Sometimes Gram asked a question fifteen or twenty times in a few minutes. She would wait for me to answer, or if I paused she would smile and say, "Of course *you* are the father, dear." It probably helped that all three look like me.

During some of our visits, she would have these moments of clarity like the real Gram was there and we made contact. A slight feeling of hope would jump into my chest, but then, like changing a channel, it would jump back out.

One time Gram blurted out, "Will, just tell the facts, tell your story. Tell it like it happened. Tell the truth. It will be alright. Everything will be alright."

Kay and I looked at each other with dropped jaws, "Did she really say that?" I asked.

"I think she did," Kay said.

"Do you think she knows about the investigation?"

"No, probably not."

"But maybe she *does* know."

It was like Gram knew all the bullshit we were going through, but as soon as I tried to answer her or dig for more, she was lost again with that look of uncertainty. We all knew that look. Somewhere, deep inside, the real Gram wanted to help, but the disease was too much, too strong. Her mind was too far gone.

She could still talk about her youthful days in Utah, living on the farm. She would mention her parents, at times asking where they were, but then she'd act as though she had not said a word. Gram's parents had been gone for fifty years, but it was a great moment of lucidity for her, so we'd urge her to continue the stories. There wasn't anything she couldn't remember prior to being thirty years old. She talked about her dad working with the cows, her younger sister getting in trouble, or her mom making some interesting dinner out of milk, water, bread, sugar, and some odd prayers. The prayers made the meal better. Gram talked about her high school days and the early part of her marriage to her first husband, Bill.

When Gram became tired, and my patience was spent, my pretend, one-man show would come to an end. As I left I would tell myself, *Don't remember her like this; remember the lady who helped raise you. Remember the dynamic community leader, the intelligent and thriving woman, the God-loving and caring human being.*

This was easier said than done, and when we would leave, the kids would ask, "Why does Gram keep asking that same question over and over, Daddy?" I didn't know how to answer them.

• • •

May 23, 2012, was complicated and amazing for two reasons. First, our fourth child, another daughter, was born. We named her Francine, after Gramps's first name, and we called her Frankie. Second, after an eighteen-month investigation, the county issued the paperwork for our arrest warrants. Both Kay and I would be charged with a crime: one count of theft. But we wouldn't learn this for thirteen more days, and we were enjoying our new baby girl while the summer was in full gear.

At work I was sharing an office and training room with a good friend and signing up new clients. On June 5, my sister called over and over. I let her calls roll into voicemail, thinking I'd get back to her after I finished a client call. I was excited to be signing a contract with a large, nationally known nonprofit, and the rings interrupted my thinking.

After the fourth call, I was so frustrated that I ended my client call and answered Sadie's. "You okay?" I asked. "Why do you keep calling?" She didn't respond right away, began stuttering, and then with a crackling voice asked if I was alright.

I wondered why she asked. As we both remained silent, I thought, *Not again*, figuring someone else must have passed away. Then Sadie took a deep breath and said something that filled me with confusion, pain, and fear. More fear than I had since telling her about Kay's pregnancy in high school.

"The local news just called me," she said. "They say there's an arrest warrant out for you."

"What? Are you serious?"

"You didn't know?"

"No! No idea."

"Does your attorney know?"

"He must! Well, I'm not sure. Are *you* sure it's true?"

"She seemed legitimate. She said she was a producer for the evening news."

"Are you *serious*?" I was having difficulty breathing.

"They wanted me to comment, but I said I had no comment because I didn't know about it."

I grabbed the sides of my head; I wanted to disconnect it from my body. "You've got to be shitting me!" I shut my office door so the other people in the office wouldn't hear. I was shaking. "I haven't heard from Jack or Sharon—from anyone. I'll call right now and get back with you."

I hit "end," leapt from my chair, grabbed my stuff off the desk, and bolted toward the exit. I was in such a panic, my only thought was to leave. The receptionist said goodbye, but I just muttered something random and sprinted out the door to my car. I remember my hands shaking as if I had Parkinson's disease. I could barely put the key in the ignition.

I took out my phone and started frantically dialing my attorney. Jack answered and I yelled, "What the hell is going on? My sister just called me and said a news station called her. They said there's an arrest warrant for Kay and me! I thought they weren't going to charge us?"

Jack sounded unfazed. "Oh, yeah. Sharon was supposed to call you."

"She didn't. What's happening?"

"Where are you?"

"Why does that matter?"

"I'm about to tell you. Where are you?"

"I'm driving from my office in Lakewood. Jack, you said there might not be charges, so what is going on?"

"I guess the DA decided it was necessary."

"Necessary?"

Jack raised his voice, "Will, we told you from the start they don't do a search unless they're serious. Now listen. Drive slowly."

"What can we do? And how did the media find out?"

"I'm sorry Will, we're stuck. The warrant is in the public domain. The news has access. Someone from the DA's office could have just emailed or faxed it over to them." He paused. "Here's the deal: don't get pulled over. If you do, they'll take you in to whatever county you're pulled over in because of the warrant. So drive slowly, safely, and follow all laws of the road. Once you get home, we'll figure out what is next."

"But what about the media? I think they'll want to do an interview."

"No! I wouldn't do that. The media will *not* tell the true story or offer a fair or balanced approach. You and Kay are the villains now, and they'll make it look as bad for you both as they possibly can."

The more Jack talked, the more screwed I realized we were. I didn't know whether to cry or scream. He was so calm, but I thought I was going to throw up. My reputation was gone.

"I know this is a new role for you both. But this is the reality of where you're at now."

I drove home like an old lady, scared to death of breaking even the most insignificant driving law. As I puttered along the main highway, I turned on the radio and "Renegade" by Styx was playing. The lyrics rang out, and I sang along, "Oh Mama, I'm in fear for my life from the long arm of the law." My tears were mixed with cynical laughter. I hit the off switch.

A few hours later, Uncle Don and Auntie Sis arrived at our house. The minute they walked in they started to cry, which made Kay and me cry. Their eyes were filled with fear and love. For the first time since the day Kay told me her parents knew about our teenage pregnancy, I felt completely out of control. There was nothing I could do. I could run, but I wouldn't be able to hide. I thought about packing up the family and making a run for Mexico. I seriously thought about it for about fifteen minutes, thinking through a few steps. That always goes so well in the movies.

Then I headed to my basement with a belt in one hand and a bottle of wine in the other. I stood on the last step and looked up at the large, steel, ceiling beam and thought about how I would hang myself on it. I intended for the wine to help the process. I could swing the belt around the beam, tie it tightly around my neck, and be done. I realized how devastated my kids would be to walk down the steps and see their dad hanging there. So I just sat there and drank the wine.

That night at seven-thirty, Kay and I did the only thing we could and headed down to the Richland police station to turn ourselves in. Jack informed me that under Colorado law you can turn yourself in at any police station in the state if there is a warrant out for you. He said our best bet was to go to a station with low traffic, as this would also allow us to speed up the booking process and potentially avoid the media.

We were sure the media was ready to ambush us if we went to the Western Ridge station, which was home base for the police officers who had conducted the search. Western Ridge would probably delay the processing until the cameras arrived or would have a cross custom-made for my height and would arrange for my hanging to be set up in the front lobby.

Kay's lawyer, Sharon, met us at the Richland station. We heard our names called after about an hour's wait. The officers took us back to a small room. There were three officers standing like they were in a manufacturing plant, working the assembly line. They filled out our profile information, cleared a search for other warrants, and proved who we were via our driver's licenses.

One officer began to process Kay. He took a swab and inserted it into her mouth to obtain her DNA. She joked as he swished it around saying, "Can you at least buy me dinner first?" I actually cracked a smile. He grinned, even though you could tell he was trying not to.

Next, they had Kay stand against the wall for the mug shot. I stood against the opposite wall and tears ran down my face as they took her picture. The officers had no reaction. I wanted to point fingers and try to justify our actions for a brief moment of vindication, but I'd never lived my life as a victim and I wasn't about to start now. They continued taking Kay's fingerprints and then moved on to me, repeating the process.

It was all over in about thirty minutes, and we headed home. The drive home with my sister was quiet. Sadie and Kay sat quietly in the front while I was in back wishing the seat would open and suck me down to the farthest depths of hell, never to be seen again.

Each of us was trying to comprehend in our own way what had just happened. I was thinking at least this step was over and we could start to get ready for whatever was next. I had no idea the circus was just getting started.

• • •

The next morning my phone rang from an unknown caller. I let it go to voicemail. When I listened to it, the female voice said, "I'm a producer with *9News* and we'd like to talk to you. Find out what *really* happened, and why you were arrested last night. Will, you can explain everything to us about your grandparents' estate. Please call me back. We're going with your story on the five o'clock newscast. It's the lead story."

I was frozen, holding my phone up to my ear and staring at nothing. I thought, *This is funny and ironic, because after helping thousands of children and hundreds of charities around the country, my path to the lead story on the evening news is this ridiculous family drama.*

Now our friends, the community, and anyone with a TV who lived within a hundred miles would see our story. And anyone with internet access could watch. It would be the media-circus version. Not the truth. Not *our* version.

That night at 4:50, I prepared for the spectacle. Seconds seemed like minutes as the time crawled along. At five o'clock, *9News* didn't disappoint. We were the lead story, and their "Denver entrepreneur accused of bilking grandmother" headline was nuts. They made it sound like Kay and I were flying private jets around the world and buying cars and mansions.

Our mug shots appeared on the screen, followed by flashing logos of businesses whose services we used: Comcast Cable, United Power, King Soopers, Netflix. Another part of me died in that instant. Just imagine one of your worst nightmares unfolding in front of your eyes on your TV set. A family disagreement, meant to be argued behind closed doors, on display at center stage for your local community.

In my terrified state of mind, I hoped there would be a major disaster so that cable lines and satellites stopped working. No one would get hurt, but they couldn't continue to watch this. As the broadcaster finished our segment, I melted into my office chair.

Texts started to roll in within minutes of the story. If I worried the messages would be hurtful, I could relax. I looked at my phone, and the first text said, "We got your back." Then I checked my voicemail. "I saw the news. Netflix? Really? Isn't that $7 per month?" There were a few not-so-kind texts, but 98 percent of the messages were from supportive friends and family reaching out. It was amazing and touched my heart.

The next day opened my eyes to several new challenges. I had out-of-town trainings to do and needed to be in Idaho in two days and in Dallas on Friday, but the arrest paperwork said I could not leave the state. Sharon and Jack suggested we make a motion for an emergency hearing to get a travel permit approved.

Sharon met me outside the courtroom at one o'clock to represent me because Jack was out of town. She had some notes and started asking me about where I needed to travel.

"I have to be in Boise on Thursday. Dallas is Friday, but then I have Oklahoma in a week. I *have* to be able to travel."

She nodded but then broke into a smirk. "Holy shit balls, you were right about the media. The lead story on the five o'clock news? Wow, I didn't realize it would be that big of a deal! I've seen Ponzi schemers, rapists, and murderers get less coverage. Hell, Jack represented a witness to a serial killer escapade, and even that didn't get this type of coverage."

I sat down on the bench next to her and said, "I don't get it either. So what now? Any ideas on how I can save my career?"

Then Sharon said something that initially pissed me off, but in the long term it meant something. She stood up, put her hand on my shoulder, looked me in the eyes and said, "Honey, you just gotsta put one foot in front of the other. Who said that famous saying—a journey starts with something? The first step, I think it is."

*There is no way she just said that*, I thought.

Sharon continued, "Anyway, that's all you can do for now, darling."

"That's all you've got for me?"

"Don't know what else to say."

But she was right. What else *could* she say? Sharon's words would come back to me over and over during the next few years.

As the two of us walked down the hallway to enter the courtroom, I had this incredible experience. It was like a blanket of energy was thrown over my shoulders or someone was hugging me. It felt so good and positive. It was a spiritual moment. It was God connecting—or maybe it was Gram.

For that moment, the fear was gone, and anxiety fell away. I was free. I could float in the room. Even though I felt like fainting, I just kept moving. Whatever I was going to do, I wasn't going to stop. I kept telling myself, *Just keep walking, and don't stop. One step at a time.*

Sharon and I took our spots behind the podium, and the judge began. The DA, late to the hearing, rushed in, tossed his briefcase on the table in front of him, and began. He started off by grumbling about his day: "I had to move all kinds of things around to be here, Your Honor."

The judge didn't react. Instead, he read off the charges of one count of theft and finished with, "And now you'd like to travel." More of a statement to me than a question.

"Yes," Sharon said. "Mr. Young must travel."

The judge looked at the DA asking, "And you are objecting to this permit? Why?"

"Yes, we are, Your Honor." The DA then began an odd explanation about some parts of the case and then ended with a bizarre, one-minute monologue that was crafted like it was from the screenplay of the 1947 Hitchcock film *The Paradine Case*. He acted like he had channeled Gregory Peck, offering the same fierce, awkward look on his face while mustering his attack. "We think Young might have done something illegal with *9News*."

Sharon and I looked at each other, simultaneously blurting out "What!?" It wasn't proper courtroom procedure, but we were thrown off guard with this wild accusation.

The judge looked at us but didn't say a word. Then he looked back at the DA, paused and said, "Okay, please continue."

The DA was silent, looking down, so Sharon piped up, "Your Honor, this is very strange, and it's the first we've heard of it. I'm failing to see what *9News* has to do with anything?"

The judge replied, "*9News* is involved? I don't see that anywhere in the charging documents."

The DA answered, "They are not."

The judge asked, "What does *9News* have to do with this?"

Sharon added, "They are covering Mr. Young's story, along with many other media outlets."

The judge spoke to the DA, "Do you mean *9News* has filed a claim against Mr. Young?"

"Oh no, of course not. They are covering the story, and Mr. Young did consulting work for their nonprofit foundation arm a few years back."

The judge was confused, "I don't think I'm following. Did *9News* file something?"

"No," the DA said.

The judge decided to let it go. "Okay. Is there anything else?"

The DA added a couple of points stating that I was a flight risk.

The judge closed the hearing by ordering me to go through a flight-risk analysis, and then we'd return to the courtroom in two hours with the results.

My next stop was to meet with a person in charge of analyzing me to see how much of a flight risk I was. Would I take off for Mexico? I kept thinking about it. They gave me a questionnaire that included questions on how long I'd lived in my current location, where I was from, did I own a home, where my family was located, and how long I'd had my business.

As we arrived back in the courtroom, I noticed the DA was not at the podium. A young lady who looked about sixteen years old handed the result of my flight-risk analysis. The judge read off the results and said, "This is the highest score I've ever seen in my courtroom. I'm not sure why we're here, Mr. Young."

Then, in almost an apologetic way, like he was cutting a player from their high school basketball team, the judge looked at the young lady and said, "I rarely do this, but this situation is different. I'm going against the State and allowing Mr. Young to travel. I've never had such a positive score before. Then the Judge turned and looked at me saying, "A word of advice, Mr. Young: if the charges are true, then you'd better do as many speaking engagements as you can in the near future. Good luck, Mr. Young."

There were no further objections.

# CHAPTER 21

# Are You Shitting Me?

## Summer 2012

*It is said that the world is in a state of bankruptcy,*
*that the world owes the world more than the world can pay.*

— RALPH WALDO EMERSON

Preparing for a trial is a combination of mental strain and a gut-wrench-ing, emotional roller-coaster ride. "It ain't like the movies," I remember telling one of my friends. Ever since that first meeting with Sharon and Jack back in February 2011, their office had given me the creeps. Unfortunately, I now had to use it for preparing our defense.

Law offices come in two types. The first type is extravagant—made to resemble an episode of *MTV Cribs* with gold-plated paneling, imported Italian-leather furniture, and an original Picasso. The lobby of this kind of office would make a great venue for a wedding or a blow-out party. On the opposite end, an office can be drab, old, and outdated—the sort of place one might go to die. Unfortunately, our attorneys' offices were more like the latter.

Jack laid out the rules. "You'll be able to work down in the basement. Maria has set everything up for you. You'll find the discovery boxes, additional files, pads of paper, sticky notes, and highlighters."

I'm sure my weak, affirmative reply sounded as if I were headed to my death in a dungeon. I would soon learn that in a case like ours, the "discovery," or evidence, becomes critical. It doesn't tell the entire story, but for the prosecution it's a safety net. Prosecutors can speed up the process, using certain parts to emphasize a particular pattern in the story that strengthens their argument, or they can slow down the defense by taking some bit of evidence out of context to try to make a key point. In the end, a file or a certain piece of evidence could substantiate the prosecution's arguments. Also, prosecutors can have certain evidence thrown out, which could mean the end of the defendant's chances.

For the defendant, discovery can help clarify their version of events, provide an example that will connect with a juror, or be the lifeline to the truth. The materials in our case were vast. Half of the documents were obtained by the police during the search of our home, while the other half were obtained through warrants. There were financial records and personal histories for both my grandparents and Kay and me. Those records went back many years. The documentation included bank statements and interviews with potential witnesses like my business partners, assisted-living personnel, my grandparents' neighbors, and many others. There were nine discs containing the digital versions of every page. More than 88,000 sheets of paper took up nine two-by-three-foot white boxes.

My discovery routine went like this: I would arrive at Jack's office and head downstairs after my normal business hours were finished, usually around two or three o'clock in the afternoon twice a week. There were eight steps to reach the basement, where I would turn left, then make a quick right to find the boxes stacked on four long shelves. My stomach churned every time.

Other than boxes, the fifteen-by-fifteen-foot room contained an old black desk, a phone, a desktop computer, a printer, and a bookshelf. The smell was a combination of mothballs mixed with dust and dirt. Depending on the time of year, a small window provided some sunlight or gave the appearance of a black hole. It was located on the wall behind the chair. The room quickly became my personal insane asylum.

I preferred to look at hard copies rather than the digital versions because I could touch them. Most days I would pick up where I'd left off, reviewing the next piece of paper in chronological order. Each document was labeled with a five-digit number. Apparently, Edwin G. Bates patented this number process back in 1891, and now some modern version helped me keep the pages in order. The number near the bottom of the first page started at 00001 and the last page ended at 88441. It was overwhelming.

Depending on the topic and how I felt, I would review as many pages in a box as time allowed. If a file seemed irrelevant, I'd quickly thumb through it. Jack told me my goal was to look at each and every page. I wanted to tell him my goal was to keep reviewing and not end up hanging myself in the corner. My outlook on the case would change constantly, depending on what documents I viewed. Some days I felt ecstatic, while others plunged me into a deep depression.

• • •

Kay and I found ourselves with another pressing issue in late 2012: our financial situation was getting worse. We were using our savings and cashing out investment accounts to pay our legal bills, financial consultants, and investigators. Now it was time to seek relief.

God bless Ted Cole, who explained to me the ins and outs of bankruptcy. I started to snicker, thinking how he didn't know about the degree and extent of our legal issues. Ted was a young bankruptcy/real estate attorney who looked more like a sales rep or Silicon Valley techy than legal guru. His short, blondish-brown hair and casual jeans with tennis shoes gave the impression he was relaxed, cool. He didn't know it yet, but he was about to help me complete the trifecta, adding bankruptcy to estate probate problems and criminal charges. I wondered how his tone would change once he heard the depth of our case.

Ted started explaining, "There is Chapter 7, Chapter 11, Chapter 13. You have several options, and everyone uses them for different reasons."

I didn't interrupt—just let him wear himself out.

He finally finished his excellent presentation with a cheesy smile and said, "Where should we start? And maybe you should begin by telling me your situation."

"Yes, that's a good idea, Ted," I said with a sarcastic smile. "We probably should have started there. I'll just jump in." I told him the details of the last eight years and, just as I predicted, the color went out of his face. As I finished, his eyes opened real wide and then, like someone who realizes he's about to get hit in the face by a baseball, his lips puffed out, his eyes scrunched, and his cheek bones met his lower eye socket.

"Are you shitting me?" he shouted. "Sorry, I didn't mean to say that. That was unprofessional. But come on. Really? You're joking?"

"It's okay," I said. "When I think of this situation, I say a lot worse."

He added, "But are you serious?"

"Unfortunately, I wish I wasn't."

About two months later, Ted and I had one more meeting to conclude the bankruptcy process. This last meeting was with either a court judge or a judicial officer who decides if your bankruptcy case can be adjudicated. (We were scheduled to meet with a judicial officer.) As we sat in the lobby waiting, Ted outlined the meeting agenda, explaining the typical flow and the standard questions we'd probably get. Both Ted and I were in for a big surprise. The court official is part of the Department of Justice, so many of the inquiries included questions about our criminal case. I was flabbergasted.

The judicial officer started, "Did you use any of the estate money to buy assets?"

"What?"

"I have an email from an attorney asking me to ask you if you did. Mr. Young, let me remind you that you are under oath."

"What do you mean by assets?" I asked.

"Did you use the estate money for cars, homes, furniture, jewelry, something of value?"

"Absolutely not. No, we didn't buy any assets."

As we left the meeting, Ted just looked at me and said, "Sorry. I had no idea they would ask those questions. I've never had that happen before, and I didn't even know they could do that."

"It's okay," I reassured him. "This whole thing is a lot of firsts for us."

• • •

In late December, as we completed our individual Annual Goal Boards, Kay and I took a minute to reflect on 2012. We talked about lessons learned and what could be coming down the pike. The last year had a lot of ups and downs. One day the two of us would be having a knock-down, drag-out fight, then the next day we'd be holding each other as tight as possible. We were scared to death, but we still held on to our faith. In the annual review, we dug down deep to find the positive side to the entire situation.

Less than a month later, in January 2013, Gram passed. As sad as it was, her death gave Kay and me a chance to breathe. I'm ashamed to say it, but the legal drama had screwed me up so much that I found myself acting more like a forensic accountant than a loving grandson. Kay and I kept telling each other everything was going to work out.

# CHAPTER 22

# Is It Goodbye for Now?

## 2013

*"I don't want money, and I don't want medals.*
*What I do want is for you to stand there in that faggoty*
*white uniform with your Harvard mouth and extend me*
*some fucking courtesy. You gotta ask me nicely."*

— JACK NICHOLSON AS COLONEL JESSUP IN *A FEW GOOD MEN*

I wish I could say Gram's last days were spectacular and filled with deep, two-way conversations between generations, leaving a lasting impression of joy and remembrance. But I can't.

My wish was for this amazing lady to have a fairytale ending—something of substance and deep meaning. She deserved a dignified conclusion. I leaned down and quietly whispered, "Gram, its okay to go."

I had been sitting with her in her assisted-living room every night for several nights in a row. I always sat on the edge of her bed and held her hand with one of mine under hers and the other on top. Kay would join me for a while, but often left early so I could spend one-on-one time with the woman who raised me. Gram's hair looked greyer than ever, and her lips were dry. She was dehydrated, and she showed no facial expression. She still looked great for ninety-five, but her skin was starting to look like plastic.

The room smelled horrible, like dirty laundry and a port-a-potty. The nurses kept a humidifier going and played pleasant classical music to give the room a loving presence and to distract visitors from the side effects of impending death.

Gram's mental capacities had been completely gone for several days, and now her physical body was hitting the last stage. The nurse came in, stopped, looked at me, and said, "Honey, she's going to hold for you if she knows you're here."

It was 10:45 p.m. on a Thursday night, and Gram's eyes were glassy and empty. It was like she had already left, but no one had told her body. Some of her vitals were still functioning, but her breathing was becoming fainter, with the inhales coming every five or ten seconds, followed by a delay and then an odd, smooth exhale. I prayed she wasn't in pain or scared.

"I love you Gram; thank you for everything." I kept saying it over and over. I didn't know what else to say, "I love you Gram. Thank you for being a wonderful grandmother. You're as good as there is." She would take another breath, and I would continue, "I love you Gram, we'll be fine. You can go now. I'm sure the others are waiting."

As her breathing became more difficult, a gasp would be followed by a period of silence, and then the exhale turned into a gargling noise. Her repeated gasps were just like Gramps in his final moments. Another gasp would follow, but the delay between them was extending.

I was so tired, but I couldn't leave her. I was so heartbroken, realizing she would be passing. Even though the incredible lady I knew had mentally left a long time ago, the thought of not seeing her made me sad.

The nurse gently urged me again, "She's going to hold on. She has no consciousness, but she still knows you're here. They always know—some kind of God thing."

I swore I felt Gram's fingers tug on my hand as I told the nurse she was right. I realized that as long as I stayed, Gram would continue to fight. That was just her being her.

My sister had left with Kay about thirty minutes earlier so that Gram's last minutes on Earth would be spent with me. I thought that was fitting. I stood up and headed for the door, but something told me to stop and turn around. I went back to the side of her bed and started to apologize for the last four years. I had no idea how much of it she actually knew about. I apologized for the lawyers, all the drama, and, most importantly, the unfair treatment of Kay by the authorities. After everything Kay did for the grandparents, she was charged with a crime. She was Gram's angel and Gramps's "jewel of the family," but Kay was being tortured.

I knew it was my last chance, so I bared my soul. As I spoke, one memory after another popped into my mind, from my childhood to the present moment. The experience turned spiritual. I was filled with so much love as I stood by Gram's bed with tears rolling down my face. I continued to stand there, looking at her empty eyes and recapping all the great times and how grateful I was for being her grandson. It was now 11:15, and I knew I had to go.

"Gram, I'm going to leave now." I was choking up and could barely finish the sentence. "I love you. Goodbye for now." Those were always her words when we said goodbye.

I lifted Gram's hand, kissed it, lowered it again, and neatly tucked both hands together on her stomach. I stopped a few times near the doorway, thinking I should go back—or maybe go back to that nine-year-old kid I used to be and tell him to not screw up the management of the estate when he got older. But would he have listened to me? I kept putting one foot in front of the other, finally exited the room, and made my way to the car.

During my drive home, the nurse called to let me know Gram had passed. It was literally within minutes of my exit from the building. She made sure she made the final decision, got the last word in. The timing was her choice. She left on her terms. Just as I would have expected.

We had her funeral a few weeks later at the same place we had laid Gramps to rest. On a beautiful Friday morning, about thirty people showed up. The attendees were mostly her friends from church plus our immediate family. Mary Smith was there as well, but it was hard to act like everything was normal. It wasn't. Gram's niece attended from Salt Lake City, and the same minister who presided over Gramps's funeral presided over Gram's.

Eulogizing my grandmother was as tough as it had been when I spoke about Gramps, but I walked up to the podium and began. I started off reading the long list of nicknames that grandmothers are called. Gram never cared much for any of them—Nana, Grammy, Granny, Nanny, Mamaw, Mawmaw, Mimi, Baba, Bebe, Gigi, Geema. The audience laughed and it set the tone for my message. That was the relationship between Gram and me, one minute serious, the next making fun of grandmother nicknames. We were both kind of cynical and smartasses in a lot of ways.

I talked about all the great memories, the trips, the holidays, birthdays, and especially Christmas. Gram made Christmas special by purchasing wonderful gifts for Sadie and me. She cooked lavish meals with all the fixings, and the table was always decorated just right. My parents never had the money to buy many presents, so Gram filled in. As I explained the depth of our relationship to the mourners, I said the gifts were great, but that what I remembered most was her advice.

I told everyone that Gram mailed me a letter during my first year of college. When I opened the envelope, a poem that touched my heart fell out—along with a $100 check. Then I read the poem aloud at the funeral. It's called "The Guy in the Glass," by Dale Winbrow. In short it says, "You can fool the whole world down the pathway of years, but you can't fool the guy staring back from the glass."

The poem and note arrived toward the end of my second semester in college. It had been a tough transition from high school to college, so Gram's letter and her heartfelt phone calls made a big difference in my life. During one call she told me: "God. You. Kay. And someday your kids. That is the order you live by, Will." She enunciated the words as if she were giving a Sunday sermon in front of a thousand people.

Gram was always there for me. She continually told me I had to satisfy the man in the mirror, number one, above all else. She added, "You'll know what is right; listen to God; you'll hear it." She just didn't talk about things, she walked the walk. I believed her. I listened. I learned. She was a person of both commitment and action. I didn't know until later in my life that she had raised her first husband's nephews, who were ten and twelve at the time, after their parents died in a car accident. She never complained about having to help or when life hadn't been quite fair to her.

I finished the eulogy by reminding the audience that she was a spitfire, and wherever she was now, her spirit would not be sitting down or staying calm. No, she would be controlling everything and everyone she possibly could control. And she'd be doing it with a smile or smirk, depending on your preference. That was Gram.

• • •

A month after Gram's passing, Jack insisted that we meet with him and Sharon at their office to go over next steps. We had been waiting for fifty-five minutes.

"What the hell are they discussing?" I asked Kay as my patience waned. It was Saturday, February 23, 2013, and our trial was six weeks away. We had put Gram to rest, but now we were about to take on the fight of our lives.

Jack's office door was cracked so I could hear them talking, but it sounded more like whispers than audible sentences. Finally Sharon popped around the corner and said, "You all can come on in now. We're ready for you."

I was surprised to see Nick, Jack's investigator, and his paralegal, Maria, sitting there. This seemed more like an intervention than trial preparation. I was under the impression we were going to strategize for the battle and discuss next steps. Their faces told a different story, and their expressions made me think we were sheep headed for slaughter.

As we sat down, Jack began with a long monologue about the decision we would make today. He acted like a newsman reading a teleprompter, sitting behind his desk with his hands folded on the top, all proper and professional.

Within a few minutes, it became clear his soliloquy was 50 percent heartfelt and 50 percent cover-your-ass legal notice. He recapped his meeting with the DA from the previous week, touching on the major points.

"I didn't know you had a meeting with the DA," I said.

"Yes, it was informal. This is often done in this type of case."

Jack and the DA, Kathy Cline, had reviewed the case and the evidence in detail, covering key occurrences in the timeline as well as potential testimonies of key witnesses. They pissed at each other from different angles. It sounded more like seven-card stud than a legal meeting to find resolution. Mostly the DA wanted Jack to know how her team would win, stating the details of their path to victory. This was the county's approach at bluffing and the process of attaining a 95 percent plea-bargain rate, which was one of the highest rates in the entire country. Jack tried to impress her with a counter-argument, but in the end she must have won.

"She's admitted we can win," said Jack. "Good chance of it. But she influenced me with her confidence."

"Isn't this just poker?" I said. "Aren't they all good players? The best ones never blink." Then I added, "We didn't get a chance to tell you, but Kathy Cline married a friend of ours from high school. He was four years older then us. This is crazy, but my sister was best friends in high school with her husband's little brother, who died in a car accident back in the late '80s."

Jack looked at me like I'd kicked his dog. "What? What are you talking about? Are you serious?"

"I know, you can't make this stuff up! This is crazy shit."

"You mean to tell me the DA on your case—Kathy Cline—married your high school friend?"

Kay nodded. "Yes! Can we get her tossed from the case for conflict of interest?"

Sharon started to laugh.

"Probably not," said Jack. "Well anyways, she knows her stuff, she knows this case, and she's really good. If they hadn't changed DAs I'd feel differently—that we could win—but here we are."

"So you're saying we'll lose?" I went numb.

"No, I'm not saying that. I believe in you guys." Jack's voice started to rise. "I'm going to talk to you like you were my own son. You're not much older. What I'm saying is trials are not about what really happened. The truth often takes a back seat. Trials are about the stories, images, and the feeling that you, the prosecutors, and we attorneys can leave in the mind of the jury on that day. That is a subjective, risky thing."

"You've seen the emails from Bob and Mary?"

"Yes, I know they say you could use the money. Those are incredibly important to this case, but you didn't have formal, signed agreements. There were emails, maybe handshakes, and, best case, verbal assumptions and borderline verbal agreements."

"We did have a written agreement on the house."

"I know," Jack repeated. "The question becomes what happens when the Smiths are on the stand?' We don't know what they'll say."

"But the emails and the house agreement are our proof." My voice was shaking with anger. "We didn't break any laws or steal anything. I used my inheritance!"

"I know, but we've got to look at the entire case. And at the law—how it reads. I can't kill someone and then say, 'My neighbor said to do it, so it's okay.' We can only ask the Smiths certain questions. Do you think they'll tell the entire story? Will they tell the truth about what happened?"

"I don't know."

Jack continued. "Come on. Look, if we tried this case ten times, we'd probably win four out of ten or five out of ten. I think worst case would be three times out of ten. You only get *one* shot at trial. We would be at the mercy of the jury pool or whomever we get that day. The jury I had two weeks ago would have been perfect for you guys. But we don't know until that day. How much are you willing to risk? Are you willing to go forward on a coin flip? Does 30 to 50 percent sound good? It does in stocks and baseball batting averages, but not in a courtroom. This is your life—potentially decided by odds like a coin toss."

By the time he finished, I was on the edge of my chair, ready to vomit. Yet at the same time, I was searching my heart for more argument points, more justification for moving forward. I was damn set on overcoming my own gut. "I think you're telling us our choice. It's obvious."

Jack finished in his most serious tone. "*Listen!*" He pounded his hand on the desk. "Listen to me. It comes down to this: the DA is promising that if you lose she will push—no, that's being too nice—she will *fight* for prison time. Maybe not for both of you, but for you, Will, for sure."

"We have to say we broke the law? We have to accept a plea deal?"

Up until this point, the meeting had seemed choreographed so that each person could add their own opinion of the facts. Now the real emotion kicked in. The competitor in me said to fight on, never give up. I didn't say a word as the anger built in me. I wondered when Jack and Sharon had lost their faith in me and Kay. After some time of silent tension, I yelled, "You guys just don't *get* it! You don't get us, or this case! *You don't!*"

Jack tried to stop me, raising his hand in protest. "Now, Will …"

I cut him off. "Have you two been listening to us at *all*?" I abruptly stopped talking and stared at each of them. What I saw written on their faces was fear—fear for both me and Kay. Time stopped. It was another spiritual moment for me. I looked at Jack, and he smiled at me as the tension in the room melted. "Will, the DA's office will try to put you in prison. Listen to me." He lowered his voice to almost a whisper. "If the judge thinks you should not have gone to trial for any reason, then *he* might put you there. What if he thinks you're lying or justifying an illegal act? The media will be in the courtroom, and that tends to push judges to do things they might not otherwise do."

I sat back, closer to surrendering. "I thought you said you believed we were right—that we were innocent?"

"I do, but the law doesn't work like that and neither do prosecutors, judges, or trials. You are not innocent until proven guilty. The public likes to use that term, but it's not real. It's not about what's fair or right or even what was ethical for your grandparents. There are many other things that get tangled in the process. If your grandparents could speak on your behalf, this would be totally different. The law doesn't care how many hours you spent caregiving or how much you sacrificed. It may not matter that you legally inherited everything. It could come down to the letter of the law—as small as the wording in the law. If you were in Adams County or some county other than Thomas, we'd push to go to trial. For God's sake, Thomas County has one of the highest conviction rates and plea-bargain rates in the country. I think it's damn near a 97 percent plea rate and a 98 percent trial win rate."

I asked, "What about Kay? I can't risk having our kids being taken from her. Not for anything. Not even to make a point or for redemption."

The tears slowly came down my face as I looked at Jack and recapped the story, covering all the financial issues, what we understood, and why we took the action we did. As if saying it one last time in a poetic, emotional rage would make me more right or increase their faith in us. My meltdown was a last grasp for straws. I started to shake and said, "We gave everything we had; we offered everything."

Sharon turned toward Kay and asked what she thought about pleading. Kay's eyes were watering. She just sat there, staring out the window, not making eye contact. She was so overcome with emotion that no words came out.

Jack looked at me, "Will, I know the Smiths stayed at your house and borrowed your cars when they came to Colorado. They were in Michigan taking vacations while you guys kept all the plates spinning, even though Mary was Gramps's daughter. You all were friends, but they didn't know how much you sacrificed. That's part of the problem. They didn't know the truth of how bad the situation was for you guys. And they probably didn't know how much money you were using."

I turned and looked at Maria, Jack's paralegal, and said, "How about you Maria? You know this case better than anyone. What do *you* think? No bullshit."

Maria looked at Jack, then back at me. Her eyes looked afraid, but she took a deep breath and looked at Jack again. He motioned for her to go ahead. She began rattling off a list, like bullet points, of our catastrophic mistakes and other reasons that would cause us to lose: "You used the money after your grandparents' mental state changed. Their wills were never updated. You should have paid Kay like a nurse with payroll stubs. Very few items had "IOU" written on them. The out-of-state relatives will claim they knew nothing. And your father is now dead, and dead people are not good witnesses."

We were done with wishy-washy words like "I think" or "maybe," "might," and "probably."

Maria summed it all up in two words: "You'll lose." Her words were powerful. Everyone in the room felt the gravity, and we trusted her. As a good paralegal with more than twenty-two years of experience, she knew the game. And she knew every detail of our case. She was acting like judge and jury.

Jack broke the silence, "Will, the Department of Justice is like the casinos in Vegas. It looks like you can win, but the house always wins.

What if those emails are not allowed into evidence? What if several of your witnesses are not allowed to testify? What if what we think is certain discovery is instead discounted or disallowed? What if the witnesses don't tell the whole truth?"

When the meeting was over, Kay and I stood in the parking lot and hugged each other. We held on tight. After an emotional, two-hour lunch, we knew what we had to do. The trial, set for April 8, 2012, was just around the corner. Sometimes you must make your last stand while you're still standing.

# CHAPTER 23

# How Do You Plead?

## March 2013

*"Change the way you look at things,*
*and the things you look at change."*

— WAYNE W. DYER

As I opened the door to the courtroom, it was unusually quiet. At other hearings the courtroom was packed, but not today. There were only the DA, our attorneys, and the court reporter, no one else. (Jack told us later that the DA had been kind enough to set our hearing for Friday, March 29, using fake names instead of ours so the media wouldn't know to attend.)

At 3:10 p.m., the judge entered, and the attorneys began the process. Kay and I looked at each other through tears. I grabbed her hand and knew in my heart she was hurt. She was mad at the situation, mad at the authorities, and mad at me.

Two nights before, Kay and I had a knock-down, drag-out fight. I had been drinking heavily, and I threatened to kill her. Several years later, when she was fourteen, my daughter Helen reminded me of this. She remembered me throwing a large candle (about six inches in diameter) on the floor like I was spiking a football, and saying, "I'll kill you or myself!" All the stress and pressure had taken such a huge toll that I was striking out against my angel, my best friend. It was one of the few times during this entire ordeal when I emotionally attacked Kay.

Then, in the courtroom, a slight smile came across her face as she squeezed my hand. In a calm whisper she said, "I love you." Once again, my wife saved me. I looked forward as the DA began to talk to the judge.

God bless Jack and Maria, who had created a document detailing the entire case: who, what, when, and how. Almost ninety-two pages described the "why" in a professional, well-thought-out format. The judge was hearing the real story behind the case, and Jack's thirty years of defense-attorney experience showed. His past trials in front of this judge made everyone feel comfortable.

"Jack," the Honorable Judge Monarch said, "it's good to see you again." Judge Monarch looked about sixty and seemed like someone I'd like to join for coffee or to play a round of golf with. In another life, he could have been one of my investors, clients, or neighbors. We might have had a networking lunch together.

Jack proceeded, "Yes, Your Honor. Thank you for this opportunity to introduce you to Will and Kay. I wish it were under different circumstances, but I need to set the record straight and clear some things up."

Earlier that morning, Kay and I had continued our conversation about whether taking a plea deal was the best option for us. I laughed inside, wondering as most people probably do, *Why would you plead guilty if you're innocent?* An innocent person would fight until the end. Several of our friends told us that innocent people never give up. But reality is not always true, and perception is not always wrong. Plus, the legal system would topple if *everyone* went to trial.

Jack finished his presentation by stating, "Your Honor, the Youngs are good people who've made an incredible impact on the local community. But they made several mistakes, and now they're accounting for them."

The judge took off his black-rimmed glasses, wiped his face, and asked an odd question: "Now Jack, can you tell me where they were culpable?"

I thought *What in the hell is "culpable"?*

Jack answered by covering all of our defense positions, which were privileged attorney-client information, and he emphasized the mistakes we had made. Every detail, the good, the bad, and the critical part of how the law was or might have been broken. He covered our good intentions but also showed where we fell down.

The judge made a few notes and then asked us to stand. After he read over the charge, he finished with the question, "How do you plead, Mr. Young?"

I stood silent. My knees started to shake, so I reached out to grab the table in front of me, thankful it was solid enough to hold me in place. Jack could see I was struggling and asked if I was okay. I looked at Kay, back at Jack, then back to the judge.

"Mr. Young," the judge said with quiet empathy in his voice.

"Your honor, I'm sorry I'm ..." I just couldn't say it. As the sweat dribbled down my forehead, those simple words wouldn't fall out of my mouth.

"Mr. Young what is your plea? You need to make it official for the Court."

I started to stutter. My throat was closing off, and I held in the tears, though my eyes felt like they could explode at any moment. Then I corrected my posture, flexed my shoulders back, straightened my tie, looked forward, and blurted, "Guilty. Guilty, your Honor." Kay followed me with the same plea. There was a deathly silence in the room. The only sound was the court reporter typing on her laptop.

That night I slept maybe an hour, and in the morning Kay and I decided to take the kids to the park. We could focus on them; it had been awhile since we'd been able to do so. Getting some fresh air and a clear head would feel great. On the way to the park, we stopped for lunch, and as we sat down to eat, Kay's phone went off. As she looked at the text, her face turned white.

"What?" I said noticing how pale she looked.

"My sister."

"Your sister what?"

"Her text."

"What's going on?"

"My sister is texting me that our plea is ..."

"Is *what*?"

"It's all over the news."

"Oh shit." I was stunned. I wanted to crawl in a hole and cover it over me.

All the major news stations in Colorado had broadcast our plea as breaking news. Within minutes, a fire-fighter buddy of mine texted that he heard about it on the radio while *en route* to a fire call. A good friend said he saw it on the TV in a bar while having lunch downtown. Again, Kay and I were the major news story.

We raced home. My gut told me the media would be on its way to our house. Auntie Sis and Uncle Don met us in the driveway, and within fifteen minutes of arriving at home, a news van parked in front of our house. I had just finished closing all the window blinds and doublechecking the locks. Then a second news-station team arrived. The reporters began pounding on the front door.

As I peered through the peephole, I could see a female reporter holding a microphone and a male cameraman. When I didn't open the door, they decided to walk around to the side of the house. They came back, knocked one more time, and then headed across the street to our neighbors' house. The other news team looked like trick-or-treaters carrying a camera instead of a candy bag as they walked the neighborhood. All the reporters were going house to house, hoping to interview one of our neighbors. They were desperate for a comment.

As the *Denver7 News* crew trekked the neighborhood, the Channel 4 CBS Denver team got out of their van. After making their assault on our front door, they set up shop on the sidewalk and started filming our house. As the reporter began speaking into the camera, I turned away from the front window and headed toward the kitchen. The rest of the family was huddled in there. For now we were safe, but I realized the media wouldn't stop their pursuit anytime soon. They got another chance eight weeks later when our sentencing hearing took place.

# CHAPTER 24

# The Sentence

## May 2013

*For to be free is not merely to cast off one's chains,*
*but to live in a way that respects and*
*enhances the freedom of others.*

— NELSON MANDELA

J udge Monarch was ready to pronounce a sentence. He directed Kay and me to stand. My arms shook like someone with a fever as I pushed away from the table. I slid back my chair and stood as straight as I could. The courtroom was so quiet I could hear the blood pumping through my arms, starting at the bottom of my head, flowing down my neck, into my arms, and then pumping back out again.

"William Young, I sentence you to six months in the county jail to begin a week from today and you are ordered to pay restitution," said Judge Monarch. "Kay Young, I sentence you to seven days in the county jail." Part of me was relieved he didn't say I was going to prison, but the other part of me thought six months seemed like a long time. Kay looked at me with dazed relief and whispered, "seven days?"

Though my sentence was just around the corner, Kay's sentence didn't start until January of 2014 to make sure one of us could be home with the kids and that the family would be together for Christmas.

Judge Monarch was very gracious to give us sentences that didn't overlap and to have Kay spend only a week in jail. I believe it was his way of making an already difficult situation easier. It was like he knew the truth of the situation and thought we had already been punished enough.

Also, my six months in jail would be cut in half if I behaved. With the "good time,"—the county's phrase for how quickly I could finish my sentence—I could be done in ninety days.

• • •

On May 20, 2013, I arrived at the Thomas County Jail at 8:40 in the morning. I sat in the parking lot staring at the homely jail building. It looked like a gigantic silo, fairly new and about five stories tall. It was designed to look as dreary as possible.

When I walked in the front doors, I found a seat near the middle of a room. I had been given one week to get my affairs in order. Judge Monarch called it "a stay of execution." Death seemed like an extreme sentence, but at the time I would gladly have accepted it. I was still thinking about taking my own life. My career of helping nonprofits, raising money for startups, and serving on nonprofit boards was over.

The jail's chairs were made of a hard plastic connected by a metal pole, and sitting on them was similar to sitting on concrete. I looked around the room and noticed a few people, but two of them caught my attention: a Hispanic man and his son sitting about three rows in front of me. The older man appeared to be in his mid-sixties and the young man in his twenties. I thought how nice of the older man to sit with his boy or grandson before the young man turned himself in. I wondered why the young man was there. What had he done? Was it a DUI? Domestic violence? Theft?

As I looked at the faces of the others who were waiting, I wondered about their situations too. How did they get here? What conundrum were they dealing with? Where did their meltdown begin? I also thought *This silly legal system needs to be blown up and redesigned.*

Half an hour passed, and I was feeling very anxious not knowing what was ahead. I tapped my foot; I fidgeted. You hear stories about jail, but you don't know the reality. Like everything in life, you can watch a movie set in a prison or read about it in a book, but until you live it you have no idea.

Finally an officer appeared, a Hispanic man in his early fifties, I guessed. His salt-and-pepper hair was cut short, and his green-and-grey uniform was perfectly ironed with all his badges appearing in their correct places. He took a few steps forward, paused, lifted his clipboard, and adjusted his glasses. In a very loud, clear voice, he announced "González!" To my surprise it wasn't the young man who headed over to the officer but his older companion.

Then the officer called, "Young!" I heard, but I didn't want to move. I sat there as he yelled again, "*W. Young!*" I stood up fast, like something bit my ass and headed toward him, falling in line beside González. In the past, my name had been called to accept awards, to present grants, to win elections, to begin an interview, to start for a sports team. Now I was being called to go to county jail.

The Hispanic man and I stood there awkwardly looking at each other. I had this anxious sense of fear coming over me when the officer told González to turn around and place his hands on the desk. He then turned toward me and instructed me to do the same. For the first time in my life, handcuffs were placed on my wrists. The officer checked our pockets and then led us toward a large, brown, thick door. I'll never forget the loud noise the door made. It startled me when the lock popped and the door slid open, sounding like a car backfiring. We proceeded through, and then it closed.

It's hard to put into words that moment when the heavy door slams behind you for the first time. The crash is explosive and ghastly, making you jump. The body jerk is a reflex motion. Now I knew why Andy Dufresne's face, in the movie *The Shawshank Redemption*, looked like he was constipated as he made his way inside the prison gates.

When I had watched prison movies in the past, the buzzing sounds, banging cell doors, grinding noises, and flashing lights would send chills down my spine. I had watched *Shawshank* more times than I could remember, and now I was living a scene from it.

In some odd way, thinking of Red, who ended up being Andy's friend in prison, kept me calm. Red described the first time he saw Andy: "He strolled like a man in a park, without a care or a worry in the world, like he had on an invisible coat that would shield him from this place. Yeah, I think it would be fair to say … I liked Andy from the start."

I hoped I could figure out how to stroll and that the other inmates would like me too. But now I wanted to curl into a ball and cry., *How many doors are there, and how deep into hell are we going?* I wondered. We passed through another large door, and then another. Each time the booming sound took my breath away. González cringed every time we heard the crashing sound.

With each step, I felt a deep loss of control, and a primal fear grew inside. We walked single file because the hallway was narrow—maybe five feet wide. I looked up to notice several people sitting behind the windows that lined the walls. They were perched about ten feet up, like a raised bank teller at the drive-through, only they weren't smiling. As we went deeper into the facility, I wasn't sure if we were going down or just straight ahead. My sense of direction disappeared. I wondered if I'd ever see the light of day again.

After another door opened and shut, I entered an octagonal-shaped room. It contained a few chairs in the middle. There were three sets of windows, each about five-feet-square, that formed three-fifths of the octagon. People sat behind each of the windows.

The officer told me to sit down, and as I sat, my eyes watered from the pain of the handcuffs. Unless you have a *Fifty Shades of Grey* fetish, sitting with cuffs on is almost impossible.

The officer ordered González to sit next to me while he took our paperwork to one of the windows. When he came back, he instructed us to line up by an open door and said we would change clothes in there. This is the point where you trade in your street garb for the famous orange gear you see on TV. It makes a true fashion statement as it is accessorized with a set of white underwear, white socks, and brown sandals. I actually smiled for a quick second when I thought this would make a great, new, fall-fashion look for the world. My attorney Jack had told me a little about this step, so I was prepared by having nothing in my pockets and wearing only a simple button-up shirt, dress pants, and loafers.

After changing, González and I looked like cattle moving through the National Western Stock Show. Next, we formed a straight line at the retina-scan machine, which looked like an optometrist's tool. The device is used to take an image of your eye, which was later used to check us in and out of the facility to prove our identity.

Printing was next, including fingerprints, knuckles, palms, hands, and wrists. It seemed like overkill. My knuckles did not print correctly, so the officer had to keep rolling them over and over. I told him I was forty-two and it was my first time in jail, and I must have sounded like I had won a local golf tournament.

He just smiled and said in a smartass tone, "Congratulations!"

*Fuck you!* I thought, but I didn't say it.

Their jail's process was high tech, reminding me of the onboarding process of entering a spaceship in sci-fi movies. We went from one station to the next in a very controlled, orderly process. Like a space-movie plot, the jail needed to analyze inmates' mental state, so my next stop was with the psychologist, a Black woman who wore grey glasses. She pointed her nose down to avoid the bifocal effect and looked at me over the top of the frames. "Are you William?" she asked.

"Yes."

As she questioned me, I could tell her intent was twofold. First was to make sure I wasn't nuttier than a fruitcake, and second to calm me. I was neither. Her questions were followed by warnings like "There are some rotten apples in here, so be careful." She put me on notice for what *could* happen, but usually doesn't. She mentioned that jail was not as awful as in the movies, though some bad things did take place. Then she said those magic words, "Would you like to make a call? You get one."

"Really?" *It is like the movies*, I thought. "Oh, God yes. Yes, definitely," I said.

"Must be your first time, honey?" she said with a slight grin.

"How can you tell? Is it my shaking hands or scared voice that gave me away?" I matched her grin.

The psychologist moved the corded, 1980s-style push-button phone over to me. Then she asked, "What number do I dial?"

I gave her Kay's cell. Kay answered, sounding as anxious as I did. You'd think I was Tom Hanks calling after his years as a castaway cradling Wilson the volleyball in my arms. "Hi Baby! It's me, don't hang up!" I didn't know the prerecorded message warned callers a person from county jail was calling.

She interrupted. "Hi Baby, you okay?"

"I'm okay. I'm going through ... well, they call it 'processing.' I'm wearing this killer orange wardrobe." I chuckled. "I was thinking I'd miss out on the orange gear since Jack said I would get to wear my own clothes. But apparently everyone goes through this initial step called "classification." Seems more like atonement than classifying."

"When do you start work release?"

"I don't know. I'm with the therapist, and she said maybe within a day or so. Maybe two days." The psychologist smiled at me. "Or more than three days, maybe."

The psychologist kept smiling and said, "Sometimes longer."

Kay said, "Why do you have to do that? Why so long?"

"I know, I didn't understand any of this stuff. I thought I went to work release right away."

I looked at the therapist, and she nodded to let me know it was time to hang up.

"Baby girl, I've got to go. My time is up. Love you! Hug the kids. I'll call you the next time I can. No idea when that will be. Call Sadie—let everybody know I'm still breathing, at least for now."

My next stop was the holding room. This lovely room was made up of white concrete walls, a toilet (no doors, just bricks about three feet high around the commode), and a TV hanging from the ceiling in the corner. The room was built for ten guys, but about fifteen of us were smashed together.

González and I sat by each other like we were each other's life preserver. His face showed he was as freaked out as I was. Some of the guys looked like they had been up all night, while others still seemed drunk from the night before. Most of them didn't say much. Just sat there.

I looked in the white bag the officer handed me to find something they called a sandwich. I could not tell what type of meat was on it or if it was meat at all. "Spam," I said out loud. González laughed as he took a bite of his.

There was a pay phone on one wall, and one or two guys used it during the four hours I was there. Then an officer stepped into the entrance and yelled, "González, Young, Mendoza," followed by several more names. He instructed us to go to the door and follow the officer to an elevator. We stepped in, and it stopped on the fifth floor, opening into a large room that looked like a hamster cage built for humans. It was appropriately nicknamed the "gerbil tank." It had white ceilings and twenty-foot-high concrete walls, painted brown, on three sides. The front walls were glass. There were two levels with a few tables and chairs at the bottom, a TV hanging in one corner, and then several doors on the second floor with numbers on them.

An officer sat at a desk lifted about ten feet above us, and he was barking orders down at us. The other officers lined us up against the glass and handed each of us a brown blanket, white sheet, an orange toothbrush, toothpaste, soap, a comb, and a cup. The blanket prevented the other items from falling to the floor. They placed the whole package into our arms as if it were a newborn.

The officer continued directing, calling out each person from my right to left. I don't remember the names, but I still remember the scared looks on most men's faces. Finally, he got to us. "González. Young. You're both in Unit C, cell number 7D38."

We took our place in line as an officer pulled out his keys, walked over to a door, put the key in, unlocked it, and motioned for us to enter. I followed González up the maroon, metal stairs, relieved he would be my cellmate.

The size of the cell made a lasting first impression. It was small—like *real* small—maybe ten by ten feet. My closet at home was larger. There was a metal toilet in the corner, and it was connected to a metal sink, making it one unit. The phrases "sink and shit," or "crap and wash" popped into my mind. I told González to take the concrete block, like a simulated bed. I would sleep on the floor next to the opposite wall in a device resembling a small, rubber boat.

The cell walls were made up of six-by-ten-inch white blocks. The color of everything in the room was a drab grey and white. The cell made Gram's plain, out-of-date basement bedroom look like a winning design-show entry.

I sat down on the mat inside the rubber boat while González took his place on his concrete block. We both looked around the room, and then I broke the silence. "My name is Will. What is yours?"

In broken English he answered, "Familia and amigos calls me Gonz."

"Good to meet you," I said. "Well, not a great place to meet you, but you know what I mean. This is crazy. I can't believe I'm here. It's like an out-of-body experience."

He stood up on the concrete block and, without saying a word, started looking out the small rectangular window just above the block. He pointed out the window saying, "That my place there." I stood up, thinking maybe my initial happiness about having Gonz as my cellmate was off base. He might be loony tunes.

I said, "What do you mean? Which building are you talking about?" He was pointing at a restaurant on the hillside about two or three hundred yards from us.

"That is one of my restaurants."

"Are you serious?" I thought, *Oh God he's delusional!*

"*Sí*. Isn't that funny?"

"How many do you have?"

"I have ten." Gonz went on to tell me his entrepreneurial tale, explaining where each of his restaurants was located and how long he'd been in business.

After he finished, I asked, "How did you get in here?"

He made a gesture with his hands like he was driving a car. "DUI."

"Oh no."

"I come to a place where they stop cars and I no stop, I just turn away. My last DUI was twenty years ago, so I receive sixty days. Why are you here?"

I laughed, "Now that's a story. I guess we have a little time in here for me to tell it." As I recapped, he listened intensely, either from being really interested or because he did not fully understand due to the language barrier. I hoped for the prior.

We had to stay in our cell eighteen hours per day, giving us two three-hour periods to be out. At specific times, the guards ordered us out of our cells. The first time I came down the stairs I could see the metal carts full of light-brown trays. We were told to grab one filled with disgusting-looking food and head back to our cell.

I mostly slept while in the cell and sat at one of the tables while out of it. After the first few nights, the sleep was some of the best I'd had in a long time. The stress of the investigation and charges and ending with a plea had taken a toll. When not sleeping, I just laid there staring at the wall, thinking about Kay, my incredible kids, Gram, Gramps, and our whole saga. I wondered if we'd lose our house. I thought it ironic that my mom never went to jail, even though she did some weird, shady stuff and hung out with some criminals.

Being in a cell had its ups and downs. One minute it was like meditating, and then the next I fantasized about clawing out my own eyeballs or making a perfectly formed swan dive from the roof.

I spent my limited time outside the cell either watching TV or making small talk with Gonz or a couple other guys. Most of the stories that inmates told were not of harrowing tragedy but mild offenses. They were all harmless. I figured out quickly I was in the pod with the docile offenders.

The pod directly across from ours had lots of drama, though, with guys yelling at each other, making obscene gestures, and fighting. They looked like gang members. It seemed like a crazy place. I split my time watching the crazy show next door and listening to guys in our pod yell into the pay phone. I think some of them thought the computer voice would talk back to them.

The first night seemed to last forever. Mine wasn't as bad as Andy's in *Shawshank*, which gave me solace. I remembered how Red conferred, "The first night's the toughest, no doubt about it. They march you in naked as the day you were born, skin burning and half-blind from that delousing shit they throw on you, and when they put you in that cell—when those bars slam home—that's when you know it's for real."

I wasn't naked, and didn't get deloused, but I could connect with the fear of the bars slamming. In the movie, Red added, "A whole life blown away in the blink of an eye. Nothing left but time to think about it."

The lack of a watch, phone, clock and the lights on constantly made me lose track of time. I actually slept all night and guessed it was close to morning as the sun rose. During afternoons I was able to call Kay, but only when the pay phone was not in use. I let her know I was okay and that I had a good cellmate.

By Day Three, after two nights in jail, I was ready to go to work release. During the second night they woke me up at two o'clock to swab my cheek for a DNA sample. The Richland police had already taken mine, but early-morning wakeups allowed the officers in the jail to instill more punishment.

My third morning brought more frustration. I longed for my own clothes and to get released for work as soon as possible. My patience was wearing thin. Odd noises at night, along with the bright lights inside the cell, were driving me crazy. I could hear people screaming from above, and the smell of cleaner mixed with body odor was hard to handle. It usually sounded like three or four parties were going on in different places within the facility, typically starting at midnight and ending around three o'clock, I think. I couldn't tell what time it was or where I was. I could feel my anxiety and fear grow with each passing minute. Jail was like a haunted house combined with a three-ring circus. I was ready to go to work release and take on whatever was in store for me.

# CHAPTER 25

# Do You Know English?

## May 2013

*"It is time for parents to teach young people early on that
in diversity there is beauty and there is strength."*

— MAYA ANGELOU

On the afternoon of my third day in jail, the officers finally moved me down from the holding area (aka "classification") to the work-release pod, and let me change out of the orange gear and into my original clothing. All those of us on work release left the holding area in single file, following a narrow hallway that took us into a large open space with several pods connected to each other. Each pod contained inmates based on their classification. The system was classified by low, medium, and high risk.

Accompanied by five other men, I entered the low-risk pod, which was now where I would be sleeping in one of the enclaves called "caves." My first impression was the pod looked more like a two-story college dorm than a traditional jail cell. The officer behind the desk said, "Have a seat right there, fellas!" He pointed to an aluminum table with six seats all bolted together about a foot from each other.

I sat down and clasped my hands in front of me like I was going to pray. It felt odd to have nothing in my hands or pockets, but I had to leave all my belongings back in the holding area.

The deputy walked over to our table and gently threw hard-bound rule books at us, saying, "Go ahead and read every word—and no talking! Is that clear?" We each mumbled something close to the word "yes."

"I said, 'Did you fucking hear me?'" The deputy's cussing sounded so premeditated that it made me smirk. He didn't see the humor in my gesture, so he stared at me like Superman does when attempting to pierce iron or steel.

I looked down and started to read the book. One of the first rules was not drinking alcohol at any time during your sentence. With my recent alcohol issues, I wondered if I would be able to follow that rule. And I could only imagine this group of men all lit up on alcohol. They'd kill each other or try to burn the place down.

The book covered what you'd expect, from the items you could bring into the pod to the contraband and the required behavior while in the facility. We were allowed to be out of the facility for a maximum of sixteen hours in a twenty-four-hour period. And, we had to stay inside the facility for at least seven hours before we could sign out again. We were also required to remain inside the jail for a twenty-four-hour period each week, or seven-day cycle. As I continued to read the booklet, I started to grin when I read that work-release inmates can earn "good time" (days deducted from your sentence) at a rate of one day earned for every day served. It said the calculation of your good time didn't start until you were transferred to the work-release facility. *I'll be done in ninety days, thank God*, I thought. Or at least I hoped so.

I was hesitant to stop reading and look up, but around page fifteen, I couldn't help myself. I used the booklet to hide my eyes, raising it just below my brows so I could scan the room. I found several more aluminum tables built as one large furniture piece, each with several connected chairs. The base was cemented to the floor. Each table had either six or ten seats. In front of me was the deputy's desk, set up like a high school teacher's desk, with a small storage closet and a large bulletin board. To my left was what appeared to be three toilet stalls without doors. Each was enclosed by a three-foot-high brick wall on either side. To my right was a 1980s laundromat washer/dryer set and an enclosed area with a basketball hoop. Three nice-sized, flat-screen televisions were mounted on the walls in the upper corners of the room, about thirty feet high. The only color visible in the entire pod—other than the dark-chocolate brown of the entrance door— was white. Later on, I figured out why everything was painted white: it got dirty. Dirty areas need to be cleaned, and not just occasionally but all the time. We inmates would constantly be cleaning.

The room was empty because most of the inmates were still on the outside at their day jobs. Even though we were told not to talk, several guys bitched and moaned in a whisper to each other about why they were here. One guy complained it was his fourth time in jail; another said it was his third. The others were newbies like me. I counted three DUI convicts and two unpaid child supporters at our table.

As I continued to read the rule book, "He" made his first appearance. Appearing as a combination drill sergeant and college history professor, a man wearing a dark-green uniform shirt and brown pants began barking orders. His uniform was perfectly pressed, and his hat tilted to the right like it was held on by glue. It was like he popped out of the wall and began yelling. I guess he needed no introduction.

"All of you stand up now and follow me!" he bellowed. "I need you to pay attention. No fucking around, no talking. Just follow me. Are we clear?"

We all jumped up without a sound. The man's nametag said Officer Neyers, and his thick-lensed glasses outlined by black frames made his face look unfriendly—or maybe it was his growling voice and screaming tone that scared me. His raised eyebrows with his sagging cheek lines made him look like he had a permanent frown from years of yelling at people and making them feel like shit. When he took off his hat, the light in the room bounced off his bald head like a mirror in the noonday sun. His horrible handlebar mustache, which looked like Will Ferrell's in the movie *Anchorman*, made his face look fat. His salt-and-pepper hair rimmed around the outside of his head reminded me of a meaner Archie Bunker. It was obvious we wouldn't be best friends.

Neyers led us through two large doors that slid open like a barn door and into a room called the orientation room. "Take a seat!" he yelled.

I tried not to make any kind of eye contact. I walked quickly past him and grabbed a back-row seat. Gonz followed, taking the seat next to me. The room was narrow with about four rows of tables and chairs. It was a tight fit with little legroom. A large whiteboard hung on the front wall.

Officer Neyers stood in front like a college professor reviewing essays and explained the work-release rules, fees, and overall hell expected to come our way. "You'll pay a daily fee based on your income—a minimum of fourteen dollars a day. You'll stay out of trouble, or you'll go back up."

This work-release fee was new to me. Apparently, most counties have come up with a way to obtain money from inmates. They charge a daily fee that must be paid weekly in order to participate in a work-release program. The county fee structure started at fourteen dollars a day and went up to seventy dollars per day.

Neyers ended his motivational speech with, "Do you hear me? Let me say it again: you'll go back upstairs and back to the regular jail with no work release and no fresh air or sunshine. No alcohol or drugs of *any* kind. We do random tests on all you numb-nuts, so don't screw it up. We'll catch you, and you'll go back up."

He then had us fill out each field of a two-page form, which included our contact information and three references. "You'll need to write in three people who can vouch for you," Neyers said. "These are people who would be a reference. Do you know what a 'reference' is? We will be calling them, you fucks, so no bullshit numbers or fake names. Do not waste my time! They better know you and say something nice about you. That might be hard for most of you to find three people who give a shit, but they better say something good. You got it?"

We all answered, "Yes."

"I didn't hear you."

"Yes!"

Then Neyers stopped talking and moved quickly around the first-row table as he headed toward our back table, slipped, and almost fell down. He caught his balance just in time to stop to the right of Gonz's chair. I didn't dare laugh, but it looked like a Steve Martin comedy routine. The officer straightened like a pole was shoved up his ass and looked at Gonz. Suddenly he bent down, adjusted his glasses, and began his assault. "Do you know English?

"Yes, I ..."

"I said, 'Do you know fucking English?'"

Before Gonz could answer, Neyers interrupted him and gestured at me. "Why are you looking over at him while I'm talking?" he demanded. "Are you talking to him?"

"I confused on the ..." Gonz stammered.

Interrupting Gonz again, Neyers gave the "stop" hand signal. "I'm not going to explain this to you in fucking Spanish. This is goddamn bull-shit. I only speak English." He grabbed Gonz's pen and started using it like a pointer. He pointed at the whiteboard, then back at Gonz. Then again at the board, and back at Gonz. I thought he was going to stab my cellmate with the damned pen.

Neyers yelled, "Do you get me, amigo?"

Gonz looked dejected and disoriented, so I did the only thing I know to do: I opened my mouth. I never learn. "I'll help him," I said. I've always been one to take on the bully in the playground.

Neyers definitely didn't like that, and now his sights were on me. He took one step over, positioning himself directly in front of me. "Well look at this! Are you his fucking mom?"

"No."

"Did I ask you to help him?"

"No, but ..."

"Fine! Okay, Mr. Helpful, you help him then."

Neyers turned back to Gonz and threw the red pen at him, missing him by inches as the pen bounced off the desk and into the back wall.

It felt like a contrived act, but I didn't care. I was shaking. My courageous act to help Gonz drew him closer to me as a friend and confidant, but it put me in Neyers's crosshairs. I would pay later for my act of kindness, but in this moment I started to realize my journey to this place was as much about helping other people as it was about helping myself.

Neyers finished his Knute Rockne speech with more administration details. Once my references were verified, I would have two hours to drive home and gather all my belongings that I would need over the next three months. This included all my clothes and hygiene products like toothpaste and shampoo. I would be allowed to go shopping during my sentence, but that involved calling from the store phone—which was required to display the store's caller ID—and leaving a message on the jail's special answering machine. This would be an embarrassing process if one of the store employees was standing there listening. Also, if I was late, they'd issue an escape warrant. I would have preferred Neyers's closing lines to be, "Let's win one for the Gipper!" No such luck. Instead what he said was, "Get the fuck out of here and don't fuck up!"

I ran to my car as fast as I could. I couldn't wait to see Kay and the kids. I pulled my cell phone out of the car's center console and dialed Kay. She answered on the first ring. We talked like we were on our second or third date. I started rambling, explaining the last three days and the fear of what might be next. When I got home, I loaded my bag as fast as I could. She followed me around the house so I could pack and talk. I conveyed to her the ironic peace and rest I received while lying in the classification cell. It was crazy that so much worry and anxiety were combined with restful sleep and contemplation. After the stress of the last four years, it was almost like a meditation retreat. Now I understood what Kay meant when she joked about being in a car accident and having to lie in the hospital for a week.

I spent as much time as I could with Kay, waiting until the last possible moment to leave so I wouldn't be late. I raced back to the facility, arriving with a few minutes to spare. As I parked the car, I looked across the parking lot and saw the line. This would be my intro to the next step in the work release process: getting in and out of the facility.

I've encountered numerous awkward situations in life, but making my way *back* into jail took the cake. It starts outside, where you take your place at the end of the line, which that starts inside the building. If you're lucky enough to get the first eight spots in line, you'll get to sit in a chair, but if you arrive later, you'll stand outside in a winding line with about a hundred guys. It's not a big deal since no one shows any signs of eagerness to get back inside.

At exactly six o'clock, the re-entry process starts when an officer opens the first door. As you make your way into the building, you pass the chairs and then enter a room with glass from ceiling to floor. The deputy asks you to empty your pockets and take off your shoes, then your pants. Then the fun starts. He asks you to turn around and squat, spreading your butt so the deputy can see if you're hiding any contraband up your ass. Some of your pride is left intact because the deputy does not physically touch you, but the moment is beyond weird.

The guard on duty started giving me a hard time right from the start. "Nice shoes," he said, eyeballing my flip-flops. "What do you do?"

I muttered, "I thought I'd wear these so I can get through this line quicker."

"I like that," he chirped with a smirk. Most of the guards started to like me once they knew more about my story and saw that I was a professional guy—the exception rather than the rule in this hellhole.

If you pass the butt exam, then you enter the room where you started in the morning: the cage. You sit on a concrete bench, then one by one, the deputy reviews everything you've brought in. He grabs keys, shakes your jacket, picks up your shoes, and checks inside your bag or backpack if you have one. No phones, drugs, food, or technology of any kind are allowed. Since it was my first time out, the staff took a detailed look at every one of my items.

Next, it's on to the retina scan. You now wait in line in the hallway by the first gated door, where you're required to sit on the floor as close to one another and as tightly against the wall as you can get.

At exactly seven o'clock, the first door to the pods slides open—and not one second earlier. The big door-crash signals everyone to stand up and make their way into the hallway that is in between the next door and the cage door. When everybody is accounted for, the door behind you closes while the one in front opens. The entire group heads down the narrow hallway, again in single file, which widens as you get closer to the pods. It reminded me of a stockyard.

You're not done yet. Now you must stand outside the door of the pod with the attendant in the glass booth, which is located about ten feet above the floor like the booth in *The Wizard of Oz*. You wait until everyone is lined up next to the wall in a straight line before the door opens. A buzzer sounds, and the first person in line grabs the door while everyone follows. You've made it! You're back to where you started twelve hours earlier.

As time went on, I started to get to know other inmates, smiling when I saw them in line. We weren't best friends, but a nice "Hello" or "How was your day?" broke some of the tension and boredom. But tonight was my first re-entry, and dinner was next.

I couldn't help but people-watch during my first dinner in the work-release pod. My God, it was an interesting crowd. I estimated there were about sixty guys in the pod—about 60 percent of them Hispanic, 30 percent white, and maybe 10 percent Black. One Asian completed the diversity of the group. The Equal Employment Opportunity Commission would be proud.

Sleep was hard to find on the first night of work release, and I wondered again how in the world I got here and how slowly my time in jail would pass. The next morning, I was up early, showered, got dressed, and expected to leave. Taking a shit while everyone can see you from the chest up was initially humiliating. After a week, I barely noticed.

On my second day in the low-risk, work-release pod, I got in line for the release process, but they said I couldn't leave because they were checking my references and making sure my paperwork was correct. As the hours passed, I asked several times about my status, pleading with them to let me go. The answer was "soon," but it wasn't happening. All I could think about was how worried Kay would be if I didn't come home for work release as planned.

# CHAPTER 26

# What Do You Mean "Your Book"?

## May 2013

*"Everything can be taken from a man but one thing:*
*the last of the human freedoms—to choose one's attitude in*
*any given set of circumstances, to choose one's own way."*

— VIKTOR FRANKL

Another hour passed as I waited to get out and go home for my first day of work release. Then suddenly, the guard called my name and started my introduction to the normal, daily morning-release process. It was a menial procedure, involving the usage of half of a Number 2 pencil without an eraser to fill out a small, white piece of paper about eight inches wide by four inches long. On this sheet, you wrote down where you were going, for what reason, and when you would return. Then you signed it. Once completed, you took your place in the line at the entrance door to the pod. Every fifteen minutes, the officer inside the glass booth unlocked the pod door.

After going through, I made my way toward the next door. Just as when you come back into the jail, you wait with other inmates, and the big crash tells you it's time to move toward the outside gate room. Once again, a line formed at "the cage," where a quick face-to-face meeting with the on-duty guard was next.

After I stepped up to the retina scan to validate my identity, I gently glided my paper form through the small opening, which reminded me of a bank-teller window with metal wiring instead of glass. If the officer liked my answers—and verified with court paperwork that they were correct—he would hit the buzzer, which opened the door. I could leave.

I started to lean toward the door, expecting the buzzer sound, when the guard said, "Oh yeah, you're the guy." His odd smirk gave me the impression something was amiss.

"Yes, sir," I said. But I thought, *They get me now. They realize this whole case is a mistake and it's time for me to go home.*

The deputy said, "Hold on there Young, let me grab Neyers."

Oh God, what would *he* want with me? My offer to help Gonz was about to bite my ass. I hoped this wasn't about retaliation.

Neyers traded places with the deputy like they were teammates in a game of charades. He sat down, looked at the form, and then—with his eyeglasses sliding down to the tip of his nose—he looked up at me. As he pushed his glasses back in place he asked, "You work from home, Young?"

"I do."

"Well, not sure if that's going to work out for us. You might need to get a different job."

"I *have* to work from home," I said. "It's my own business. It's all I have."

"I don't care. Well maybe you'll have to get an office or rent one from someone you know."

"What?"

"You'll do what I tell you."

"Sir, I don't understand. I have to work at my business. I can't take on the additional cost of rent for an office."

"Why don't you have a seat, and I'll be back in a minute."

As he went to the other side of the cage, I started to sweat. Like a used car salesman pretending like he is meeting with his manager, Neyers made me wait for several minutes and then reappeared. He came back, slowly sat down, cleared his throat, and stated, "Well, Young, here's the deal. I'll let you go tomorrow. I'll give you two hours to get all your financial paperwork. I want to know who your clients are, how you make money, how much money you make. I want bank-account paperwork and any other financial statements. The whole shebang. Bring as much evidence as you can. Got it?"

"Are you serious?"

"I'm as fucking serious as a heart attack."

"Yes, sir."

"If your release form is filled out correctly and you have all the paperwork, then I'll let you leave again tomorrow morning."

"Okay."

"Wait, do you understand me?"

"I do."

Frustrated, I headed back to the pod.

The next day, I raced home. I had just two hours to retrieve all my financial statements, client files, and any other paperwork that would prove my employment. Finally, on Day Three of my work release, I filled out my release form and completed the release steps to exit the pod and the hallways. As I approached the gate, Neyers saw me and asked, "Do you have all the paperwork I asked you to bring? You're not going anywhere again until I see and confirm it. All of it."

"I do." I passed along all the information I had collected at home the day before, including my financial documents, client paperwork, speaking engagements, contracts, and a copy of my book.

He grabbed the paperwork and then picked up the book. "What is *this* for?"

"It's my book."

"What do you mean 'your book'? Are you reading it? Why are you giving it to me?"

"I wrote it."

"You wrote a book?"

"Yes."

"Well big fucking deal—you're a writer. I don't care about that crap. Keep it." He passed it back to me with a shit-eating grin on his face. I wondered if I should offer him an autographed copy. He didn't say a word as he reviewed the documents, taking a look at each piece. He stopped and gathered his thoughts. "Well Richie Rich, you'll be paying the max daily work-release fee each week."

"Are you kidding?"

"Did I stutter? You'll pay seventy dollars per day."

"But that seems excessive."

"I'm not kidding. You'll pay the maximum amount. It's based on your income. Now head to dinner."

After dinner that night, I began what would become a nightly ritual. When I arrived back at my bunk, I started journaling. The small, county bunks were not created for comfort. I tried to write with my rear on the six-by-three-foot mat, which was about two inches thick, and my legs dangling over the side. The frame and bottom under the mat was made of a thin metal. It was hard to sit on and not much easier to lie on. Tonight, my first thoughts were on the monthly release fee. I would have to pay $2,100 per month to stay in the program. I was going to pay that much to stay in jail, be released each day, and then come back at night. I wrote in my journal, "Day 3: *WTF!?!*"

Most of the inmates sat at the tables and either watched TV or talked while I sat on my bunk. I soon added reading to my evening ritual. I would read whatever they allowed me to bring into the facility. I perused the library cart, but most of the books were fiction or fifty years old.

The repetitive writing on how much I loved and appreciated my family stirred deep feelings I'd never connected with—or maybe I thought I had, but the link was rusty. I knew I was connecting because it hurt.

I kept thinking of Gram's advice and her constant positive approach with me. Thank God she never saw me in here. I remembered Gramps telling me to stay busy and do what an authority figure tells you. It was like he was telling me to "Keep your head down."

I was a fish out of water, while most of the inmates were recurring guests. Many seemed like they were old friends. Most of them had done something stupid and were broke financially and emotionally.

As I listened to their conversations and observed their behavior, I understood the extent of the fracture in our ridiculous legal system. Rehabilitation is more of a pundit's talking point than a real thing that happens.

As the first weekend approached, I realized the days were not just slow, they literally crawled by with a minute seeming like an hour, an hour like a day, and so on. I started to get upset each evening, so I'd lie down, take deep breaths, and remind myself that my time here was not long. Only eighty-five days left.

The next day, I had this incredible moment of déjà vu while sitting near the front of the pod room on one of the aluminum chairs. I sat there glancing occasionally at the TV show that was playing—there was no sound because I didn't have earphones yet, and you could only hear the TV with earphones. Suddenly an overwhelming feeling came over me. The white brick walls reminded me of my high school math classes. We had a similar brick pattern, size, and color. I was stunned. Had I been through this already? I could see my old math teacher yelling, "Willy, you're pathetic at math and sports."

I was filled with amazement and uncertainty. I kind of freaked out. Was I destined to be here in jail, or had I already gone through this experience? Even the guard looked familiar, like I knew him—or maybe we knew each other in a parallel universe.

With the passing of each day, I felt more of the dreary feeling. This place carried a perceived perception that one should be negative, act disrespectful, or be mean. The gloom and doom influenced me to emotionally shut down, and the false premise didn't speak to reality. The guys in here were not evil, mean, or hateful. A few were lifetime criminals and bad dudes who kept doing dumb things like selling drugs, driving drunk, or not paying their child support. But most acted like they were tough, using ideas or concepts learned from TV shows or personal relationships about stereotypical male masculinity. Their *real* need was to receive kindness, friendship, and support. Hearing a kind word now and again would go a long way toward building up their psyche. None of them would admit it, but they were all desperate for love.

• • •

As the second week started, I was excited to get home on Monday and celebrate the first birthday of my youngest daughter, Frankie. During the first week, every time I arrived at home in the morning was a celebration. I was so excited to see Kay and hoped I'd get to see the kids before they left for school.

This day was no exception. The morning began with me filling out the usual release form and heading to the cage. I followed normal procedure and passed my paper to the female guard. She looked at it, turned around, and grabbed my file from a cabinet beside her. "Nope, it's a holiday," she said. "You work for yourself, Young, so you have the day off. Congratulations—we're giving you the day off!" She had a smart-ass tone.

"But I own my own business."

"So?"

"I need to go."

"No, not today. Go back to your pod."

"I *have* to get out today."

"I don't want to say it again," she said. "Go back *now!*"

I turned around, my head sagging to my shoulders, and plodded back. (Later, I came up with the idea to send in faxes that showed a Saturday work schedule so I could leave the facility. It worked for about six weeks until Neyers stopped it.)

I wouldn't be released on Memorial Day, so Frankie's first birthday celebration had to wait a day. When I made it out on Tuesday, I enjoyed a piece of cake with her—her first piece of cake. This happy moment turned out to be brief. I almost forgot I'd have to return to jail that afternoon.

During Week Two, I was introduced to my babysitter, aka my probation officer. As I sat down in Andrew Simpson's office for our first meeting, I noticed the banners for the St. Louis Cardinals and Miami Dolphins on the wall next to his computer screen. Andrew was in his late thirties or early forties, but his goatee made him look older. He started the conversation by saying, "You made it through the hour-long intake process."

"Yeah, it was interesting. They herded us into a conference room, presented some simple material, and fielded questions. There must have been a lot of people with drug violations because there were lots of questions about drugs—people asking what they could and couldn't use, or when it was okay to use. Apparently, these people will not be 'former' drug users or 'recovering' alcoholics for long."

Andrew laughed, "How is work release going?"

"Okay, it's only been a week and a half, but I'm starting to get the process. Some nights are a little crazy. Like last night there was lots of noise and I didn't sleep well. It sounded like a party was going on in my cave and around the room. I have no idea where some of the noises were coming from. Upstairs? Beside us? Outdoors? Is there a basement in this place? It was both male and female voices, and I thought I was dreaming at first, but then I became lucid enough to know it was not in my head."

"You were hearing the other inmates. There are quite a few on each floor."

"The loudest part was around 2 a.m. I'm looking forward to sleeping again."

Then Andrew proceeded to throw a wrench into the conversation. "I've reviewed your paperwork, and you're not going to be able to do your own business any longer."

"Pardon me?" *Here we go again,* I thought, wondering if Officer Neyers was waiting in the next room.

Andrew continued, "You need to do a W-2 job."

"I can't change from my business. I make good revenue doing what I do."

"We need to be able to track your income. See what you're making."

"Do you mean see a payroll stub?"

"Yes, that's what we need."

"We use a payroll company, so there is nothing to worry about," I said, trying my best to convince him.

"It might still be best to find a regular job."

"I'll never make the same money doing a minimum-wage job," I said, taking care to hide my anger. "Not sure how much money I'd be able to pay the court—twenty-five dollars a month at best. And I won't be able to take care of my family in any way, shape, or form."

Andrew sighed. "I didn't want to have to do this, but I will bring in my boss."

"Great, you can bring in whoever you want."

"Okay. Sit tight."

Andrew returned with a man wearing a terrible forest-themed tie, brown khakis, and a white shirt. "William, this is my boss, Mr. Eric Dixon. He's filled in on your situation."

Dixon said, "We need to see your income, so a W-2 position is what we'll need you to take."

"I understand," I replied, "but as I told Andrew, we use a payroll company, so I can show you payroll stubs. And minimum wage isn't going to work unless you want me to pay twenty-five dollars a month instead of over $2,000 per month right now." I paused to let that sink in. "I figured the county would want the higher amount. Let's do a hearing in front of the judge," I suggested.

Dixon said, "We don't have to do a hearing, but make sure you bring in the pay stubs each time you meet with Andrew."

Andrew and I would continue to meet every four to six weeks for three years while I was on probation. When he left his position, a new guy named Ronald took over. Although subsequent probation meetings never matched the level of drama of my first one, each time involved some surprise question or demand. Ronald like to keep Kay and me on our toes. (He was Kay's probation officer too.) As long as the court was paid, nothing else mattered. It was always paid. In fact, Kay and I paid every dime of the restitution back.

The summer moved by slowly. Later, Kay called it "our lost summer." During my second week in jail, I began writing a sitcom with a work-release story line, using my fellow inmates as characters. It occurred to me that most people have no knowledge of work-release programs in the US, and the exercise helped me remember the guys who came and went during my time.

I tried to meet as many inmates as possible, learn about their unique situations, and help them if I could. Invariably when we first started to talk, their lack of self-esteem showed right away. I could feel their childhood misgivings, struggles with authority, unfortunate decisions, and/or irrecoverable accidents. I'm sure many of their early years established a baseline for emotional distress and a disconnection. A few even sought me out and asked for advice on how to start a business. One particular young man, who was maybe in his twenties, saw me reading *Success* magazine and asked what I liked about it and if he could read it after I was finished.

Over two weeks, I wrote an episode for my sitcom called "7D-38 Work: Capture and Release." The main characters were good, bad, and some ugly, based on members of both the pod and cave around me. Most were in their early to mid-twenties; several were in their late fifties and early sixties. I seemed to be somewhere in the middle age-wise. When I talked with them, I was pleasantly surprised by how nice and engaging they were, with only a few exceptions.

I'm lucky the guys in my work-release pod were fairly stable emotionally, even though we were crammed into a small area, called a cave. The cave is where you slept. The pod was made up of eight caves, four on the bottom floor and four on the top floor. My cave was on the bottom floor next to the emergency exit. Each pod had an opening that faced the main area, which contained the aluminum tables. There were four bunk beds that lined two of the walls. At the end of the bunks were eight lockers, like the type we had in high school. The third wall had only a small, barred window. Most of my time was spent talking to the other seven guys in my cave.

A bright light in the middle of the cave's ceiling stayed on 24/7. I had the top bunk closest to the cave opening. The occupant of the bunk directly below me rotated every few weeks and ranged from an alcoholic in his late twenties who suffered two grand mal seizures that required paramedic attention, to an eighteen year old who looked about twelve and who returned each night covered in oil from working in a car shop. His beady, blown-out pupils let the world know he was still using. I never knew what he was taking. I guessed meth. A failed drug test sent him away.

The bed behind me and toward the outside wall had Paul, a Hispanic man in his early forties with a wife and several kids. He was getting his life together when a third DUI and a night of uncontrolled anger landed him in jail again.

Below Paul was Dave, a guy in his late thirties who was missing his front two teeth. He was a former drug addict with multiple theft convictions. He didn't seem to have a home because he talked about leaving the state as soon as he was released. He looked like a young version of Gramps during his Navy days. Although the similarities disappeared when you saw his missing teeth and his lack of any morality during conversations with him.

Across from Paul and Dave on the top bunk was a kid named Cliff, who was very odd and often made fun of by other inmates. He looked like the actor, Josh Gad, who voiced the character of Olaf in *Frozen*. Cliff wouldn't talk about his offense, but apparently he had injured a younger child, a family member. I never asked and really didn't want to know.

Below Cliff was an older gentleman, who became a friend. "Caveman," as we called him, was about fifty, although years of drug abuse made him look in his late sixties. He was a self-confessed drug addict in recovery, with a self-deprecating sense of humor. He had found himself homeless, so he stole money to survive. Although he was never caught on the thefts, a third DUI put him in here for a year. He had about six months left when I arrived.

Next to Cliff and Caveman, toward the opening of the cave, were Nick and Mendoza. Nick was a nice construction-business owner who was paying for his second DUI. Mendoza, who had the top bunk above Nick, now worked at one of Gonz's restaurants. He had been convicted of using a girlfriend's credit card to go on a high-fashion spending spree. I'm sure marriage wasn't in their future plans.

Gonz, my initial "classification" bunkmate, was placed in an upstairs cell. We would talk during meals, but he kept quiet and stayed on his bunk most of the time.

Writing about each one of my cave-mates helped me pass the time. One of the other inmates, who did not sleep in our cave, looked like Donnie Wahlberg, one of the singers from New Kids on the Block. I would think about their song "Hangin' Tough" each time he would walk near me, and it made me chuckle. I'd think up sitcom story lines using each of my cave-mates as a main character.

Your mind starts to go a little crazy in jail, but with each passing day, I found myself relaxing and becoming more comfortable with the system. However, it's a natural human reaction to feel penned in like a caged animal.

My other routine for passing the time in the evenings and on week-ends was walking around the gym area, a room with glass halfway up the wall that looked like a cross between a zoo cage and a hamster bubble. The top half of the walls were made of grey bricks. The gym had a basketball hoop and a pull-up bar. The wall behind the basketball hoop was topped at the seven-foot mark by an open-air, chain-link fence that went straight up to the thirty-foot ceiling. There, we could see the clouds and feel fresh air coming in.

My nightly walk followed a circular path around the gym room, passing the fenced area and brick and glass walls. I would think about Gram and Gramps and all the wonderful experiences we had together. I prayed that Gram would not be disappointed in me. I thought about how my mom had not reached out to see how I was doing in jail. The hundred-foot circumference of the gym gave me a chance to get deep into my thoughts. Although the track was small enough to make me dizzy, it was just wide enough that I did not lose my balance. I would switch directions each night. I bet I walked more than 100 miles during my time.

As the second week ended, I was writing more about the treatment I saw in the county jail. It boggled my mind how the inmates were treated by the guards. Degrading and belittling prisoners was the norm, though I thought it inhumane. There was a total disregard for the inmates' feelings or circumstances of their lives. Gram had taught me to treat everyone with respect and make gratitude and kindness your first reactions. But I saw the guards causing as much emotional damage as they could.

Though there are documentaries and occasional news features that give the public a taste of jail and prison life, I was receiving a first-person snapshot, unfiltered by the media, of our broken "justice" system, a weak link in our government agencies.

Between the ages of eighteen and thirty-five, most of these men arrive in jail with little money and even less support. Most spend six months to two years in jail and can barely pay their fourteen-dollar-a-day minimum jail fee. Lack of skills, inability to improve their status, and growing mental instability only exacerbate their problems. It's a win if they hold down any low-paying or minimum-wage job during or after work release. Ninety percent have permanent or temporary positions doing manual-labor jobs, such as construction work, for seven to fifteen dollars per hour. Most of their pay covers jail rent. There's nothing left, making it hard to move their lives forward. They are more than stuck between a hard place and hell, and they have zero chance of improving their circumstances. It is a vicious cycle. If inmates fail to pay their fees, they end up in "general population" (no work release), where they just take up space. The work-release program helps many of them feel like men and gives them some freedom because they get to leave jail for several hours a day. They make money. They contribute. They have value. I knew only one guy who wanted to get kicked out of the work-release program. He broke a rule on purpose and spent his one and only day outside of jail binge-drinking alcohol. Like some inmates, he decided he did not want to go to a job. When you are with the general population in jail, there is no release, no fresh air, no daily freedom.

Prior to my incarceration, I had no idea work release existed. Administrators and wardens use words like "education" and "rehabilitation," yet from my viewpoint, there was little of either. There was, however, a minister or a priest—I wasn't sure of his religious affiliation—who stopped in once a week for a thirty-minute group session. I saw one or two guys head over to the meeting room.

On my second Friday night in jail, I was thinking that I made the right choice by bringing an incredible book called *Man's Search for Meaning*, written by Viktor Frankl, a Holocaust survivor. The officer on duty had taken a quick glance at it, reprimanded me for not having a receipt (inmates can only bring in new items purchased from a store), and handed it back to me.

I got in some reading before we had to clean the entire facility, which was our Friday-night ritual. Viktor's words moved me as I read, "Man's ultimate challenge is to push forward even when he lacks all or any ability to control his current situation." Although my situation was nothing like a Nazi concentration camp, I still felt helpless in many ways.

However, Viktor's words kept me calm as I read, learning about the horrific stories of the Jews who were killed, raped, and destroyed in those concentration camp hellholes. Reading Viktor's journey made me sad, angry, and grateful. His words gave me peace and confidence. I realized I could make it through my time, and I understood that many people have had it a hell of a lot worse than me.

And, as I continued to write each night, I used the word "experience" to represent my situation. It was probably a bullshit word to keep me sane—but maybe it was true. This was not what I thought jail would be like, but I was starting to change.

In many ways, the experience was worse than my expectations, but in other ways, it was so much better. I ended up struggling with the loss of control, the disrespect from the guards, and the bizarre negative environment. However, as I look back through my journal now, I see that my evolution started in Week Two.

During Week Three, I read Daniel Pink's book *Drive: The Surprising Truth About What Motivates Us.* Pink argues that human motivation is largely intrinsic, and the traits of motivation fall into three buckets: independence, resolution, and proficiency. He saw emotional issues similar to what I observed among inmates inside the facility. The men had self-esteem issues connected to negative self-image. Their negative views connected to false behavior, and they made changes in behavior that ended up with less-than-desirable results. It became a form of self-fulfilling (and chilling) prophecies for these guys. The worst inmate attitude usually spiraled downward and did not get better while inside jail walls. It only got worse and worse.

As Daniel Pink pointed out, many times a person's downward spiral starts inside. The slippery slope is always present as they lose any sense of who they are or what they could become. Outside of jail, the guys I knew were joyriding, strong, unyielding. Inside jail, they were starving for something more: real connection, brotherhood, stability, love, and kindness.

During Week Three, I continued my nightly journaling while sitting on my bunk. The writing helped me feel at ease. Each day I became a little calmer, but when I left the facility or came back inside, the anxiety was as strong as ever. So I created a routine.

When I left my house to return to jail, I followed a step-by-step pro-cedure required by the county. I called a voice-message system and stated my name and my location, along with the current time and the precise time I would be leaving to drive back to the facility. The county's phone system tracked the time I made the call and where I'd called from. Then I drove as slowly as I could, always arriving early. I felt sick as I stood in line preparing to return to jail and repeat it all over again the next day.

However, I was amazed at how quickly my heart was softening with each passing day. My love for Kay and the kids grew exponentially each day. I really hadn't known how much I loved them. It's sad that it often takes a tragedy to open our hearts to a better life, but that experience is what opens us up to being more of our true selves.

One night in my bunk, I wrote these words: "Tomorrow is going to be a great day. I'm excited to get home and into my office to work. This is a *great* experience. Although jail is uncomfortable, there is something here for me to learn. God is simply giving me what I need. God, the universe, or some higher power is directing me to find my truth within myself. I am transforming into the man I've always wanted to be—enlightened in ways I never thought I needed or imagined could happen."

CHAPTER 27

# Andy Had Red, and I Had Burt

## July 2013

*"Greater love hath no man than this,*
*that a man lay down his life for his friends."*

— JOHN 15:13

I had been calling Kay during the weekends until I found out it cost me nine dollars per call. Talk about a true crime! As I entered Week Four in the county jail, I began to find acceptance. I thought about Gram and Gramps a lot. If they were still alive, they would have expected me to handle this situation with courage, respect, and grace, placing no blame on anyone. I bet Gram would have visited me every day.

If my grandparents were alive, I would never have been in jail. But reality is what it is, and I know they would have been calling me and providing any kind of support they could offer. Gram taught me that you must accept where you're at and either change it or make the best of it. She would say, "Dear, sometimes you have to make lemonade out of lemons—and then you build a lemonade stand." I remember that on my wedding day, Gramps told me, "A real man loves, helps, and appreciates. Don't let the world dictate your faith or how and when you love."

I had been reading about allowing, releasing, and accepting situations, and my time in jail was a great opportunity for me to do just that—to let go. I didn't have much control anyway, so why not give it over to God? I was twenty-three days down. The weekdays were going faster, and although the weekends were still crawling along, I was getting into a routine.

The month of June was filled with the same routine: get out and go to work when I could, then make sure I made it back to the cave on time. As I review my journal from that time, I notice that I wrote the same thing over and over: how much I loved Kay and the kids. Jail impacted me more each day. Surprisingly, instead of breaking my will, it was inspiring me and raising my faith. I used the words "growth," "appreciate," and "journey" in each journal entry. These words became my mantra, and as June was ending, a new friend stepped into my life.

The Fourth of July holiday weekend turned out to be my longest stint inside the pod without getting to go home. I thought I was prepared for it, but I was not. I was getting burned out on my normal weekend routine of getting up, shooting baskets, walking in a circle in the gym, showering, and reading. One Saturday morning, I wrote in my journal the line from *The Shawshank Redemption* when Red says, "That's all it takes, really. Pressure and time. That [a hammer] and a big, goddamn poster." In the movie, Andy uses a small hammer to chip out a hole in his cell and tunnels his way out of prison over nineteen years. He uses a poster of movie star Rita Hayworth to cover the hole. I wished I had a poster and hammer, so I could start slowly chiseling my way out of this place.

During the holiday weekend I felt off, strange. I had been having weird dreams at night and trouble sleeping. The entire situation was still bizarre and hard to swallow. I hadn't let go like I thought I would. The ego is a strong force, and mine did not want to subside.

The next week a new guy came into our pod, and he became a buddy of mine. His name was Burt, but he looked like The Dude in the movie *The Big Lebowski*. So, of course I started by saying, "Hey, Dude!" He looked just like Jeff Bridges in the movie. It wasn't like he'd never heard that before. He tried not to, but a grin appeared on his face, followed by a gentle chuckle. He looked sad, like someone had stolen his favorite toy or his dog had just run away. I reached out and shook his hand—which I had not done with any other inmate—and with a nod to *Shawshank*, I said, "Only guilty man in Thomas County." Burt later told me he loved the movie and got my movie reference.

He took over the bottom bunk directly across from mine. In his early fifties, Burt had been a good hockey player growing up in Minnesota and still had the accent. I would tease him when he said, "a-boot that."

"Burt, did you say 'about' or 'a boot'?"

His response was usually, "Fuck off."

On one hand, he was rough and rugged, while at the same time religious, calm, and kind. Like turning on a light switch, Burt could become bitter, pissed, and pessimistic. Having Burt to talk to during meals made it easier, and our bunk chats made the evenings fly by. At last I had a buddy to commiserate with about the humiliating experience of getting in and out of the jail every day for work release. I had someone to laugh with and make fun of some of the inmates together. We gave most of them new nicknames. One was called "Talkolate" since he only drank hot chocolate and never stopped talking. We called another guy "Numb-nuts," and we referred to a short Hispanic kid as "Doritos." I don't think he liked that name at all.

Burt's jail time was shorter than mine. A second DUI—his first in fifteen years—had put him in for sixty days. As my release-date countdown started, Burt would announce how many days I had left when I arrived at the cave. He was like an announcer on the red carpet at the Oscar Awards. He would say, "Well look, everyone. It's fucking Willie. And, Willie, what are you down to? Nineteen or twenty today?"

"Yes," I answered, smiling from ear to ear.

"You lucky fucker." Burt made those last weeks fun.

• • •

In August, I received an odd phone call at my home office on a work-release day. The caller would later help me utterly understand my mistakes and how I ended up bringing this crazy situation on myself. She would help me finally stop justifying and accept responsibility for my actions.

It was a work-release day, and I had only ten days of jail left. I was walking from the car into the house when my phone rang. I almost dropped it when I looked down and saw who was calling: my former office organizer. "Lisa! Hello!"

"Hi Will, you sound happy to hear from me."

I hadn't heard from Lisa for almost three years, and ironically I had been thinking about her earlier that very day. She'd been a wonderful office organizer when she worked for me years ago. She popped into my mind as I remembered how helpful and kind she'd been to me. I pulled up her website and thought how great it would be if I had the budget for her to help me now. I didn't think any more about the memory until my phone rang a few hours later.

"Lisa, your ears must be burning," I said.

"What does *that* mean?"

"You've never heard that expression? My Gram used to say it. Anyway, you're not going to believe this: I was just thinking about you earlier today."

Lisa laughed at the coincidence, then explained that she was reaching out to tell me about her new life-coaching business. She was part of a group that helped people with emotional issues through coaching. We scheduled a time to talk, so she could review how coaching could help one's psyche and personal development.

Later, Lisa explained that a person's situation is often a visible manifestation of their goals and intentions—an embodiment of abstract concepts. That was a lot of fancy words to say that this coaching group helped you get your mental shit straight.

At first, Lisa's words seemed odd as she explained the use of terms like "masters" and "monarchs." I never did understand the company she was with. To me it sounded like this company was in the business of dungeons, dragons, and wizards, but I was willing to dive in and learn more.

Although I avoided talking about my situation with most people, I felt good about confiding in Lisa. After I told her my current legal circumstances, she offered to do a free coaching session with me, insisting the session would help if I had any outstanding feelings about the entire legal situation. I chuckled and reluctantly agreed to do it.

The next week, we started our phone session, and it quickly became a spiritual experience. For an hour she questioned me, pushed me, and made me answer honestly. She said, "Give me the overview again in summary, but talk about the key milestones and, most importantly, the emotionally charged parts. And what about your grandparents?"

"My grandparents were incredible," I said. "They basically raised me. They sacrificed for me. They did anything for me."

"How did they cause your legal situation?"

"They didn't," I answered.

"You're sure? What about your relationship with them?" She continued diving in.

Then something occurred to me. "Oh yes, I felt like I had to be Superman for them. And I butchered the way I managed the estate. I failed them."

Lisa said, "Yes!" and then she asked me something that changed my thinking. "What did you, Will, do to cause this? No excuses. No defenses."

I sat there stunned.

"Will, you there?"

"I am, I'm wondering. Wow!"

"What do you mean? Tell me more."

The truth hit me in my chest like a bullet. "I'm wondering if the Talus business venture was part of the problem. That and the fact that I wasn't transparent on the use of my grandparents' money."

"What's Talus?" Lisa asked.

I gave her the quick summary of our Talus venture into index funding and about our meetings with all the index companies. I told her, "I kept pursuing it even though I was not getting paid. I felt I had to use the estate funds because the relatives said we could use them, but I still didn't use my head. My logic was nonexistent."

"What could you have done?"

I tried to sit down but couldn't help but stand right up. "I'm not sure."

"You *do* know. You know it inside," Lisa said. "Take a minute. Breathe deep. Your heart knows."

"Well, I could have stopped running Talus."

"Yes, that's it! But why didn't you?"

"I felt incredible guilt because I was the one who brought in most of the investors. I promised my partners I wouldn't give up. Actually, it was more like I promised myself. I promised a return."

"Kind of like how you promised your grandmother?"

"Wow, yes."

"So what does that mean, you promised them?"

I started to pace between my kitchen and the front door. "I felt I couldn't let them down. I *had* to keep going. I *had* to keep all the plates spinning."

"How would you have stopped the Talus venture? What could you have told the team members, investors, and partners?"

"I couldn't have stopped working on the Talus project. I was too far down the road in the venture."

"Are you sure?"

"How would I have explained it to them? I couldn't stop."

"Will, let your heart feel, not your head."

I took a deep breath. "No, you're right—I *could* have stopped."

"How?"

"I could have said at a board meeting, 'Hey, guys, I can't do this anymore without compensation. I'm drowning. I have to find revenue.'"

"This is good. What would they have said?"

"I don't know."

"You do."

"They would have understood."

"You got it. The reality is you knew the truth all along."

What a realization! This woman, whom I had not talked to for years, reached out to me after I just *thought* about her. Then Lisa spent an hour with me and set my soul free. She helped me with the biggest realization of my life. It sounds "woo-woo," but it's absolutely true. You can't make this stuff up. Suddenly I clearly understood the reason I was incarcerated. Because I couldn't say no. Because I thought I had to rescue or assist everyone and be the best no matter what. Maybe I really did have a messiah complex and some series mental health issues going on.

· · ·

My last week of work release included the normal routine, but with each passing day my excitement and giddiness grew. When I would come back to the jail, it was like I was floating around the room. Burt would notice, and say, "Stop that shit, you're killing me. I still have five weeks left and you're dancing around like Mary Poppins."

"I know! It's wonderful!" My usual full grin appeared. And then I'd say the number of days left like I was Ryan Seacrest on the *New Year's Rock-in Eve* show: … six … five … four …. I would show Burt six fingers, then five, and so on, just to add more fun to it. His facial reaction, along with his middle finger, told me what I could do with my countdown.

Finally, on August 13, 2013, my release day, I woke up early, got dressed, and just sat on my bunk. The night before I had packed my bag with all my personal items. Now, as I sat staring at the wall across from me, I remembered Red's words at the end of *Shawshank:* "I find I'm so excited I can barely sit still or hold a thought in my head. I think it is the excitement only a free man can feel, a free man at the start of a long journey whose conclusion is uncertain."

My three months in jail was nothing in comparison to Red's twenty-nine years, but I hoped I could rebuild my life, start again, be a better man, and grow a tremendously great family. I had a chance to start over.

When I created the three-by-five cards back in college, I thought becoming a billionaire at any cost made sense. Now I realized it wasn't the money or power I was after, it was freedom—mental and financial freedom. I realized big goals are fine, even great, but in the end the people you love and your own joy matter most. I was hoping to go from jail to joy.

Today I was also hoping the Thomas County Jail would let me go at seven-thirty. As eight o'clock approached, I realized that, like everything else about this place, my release time and the process of achieving it would be a surprise. At about eight-thirty, the guard yelled my name and those magic words: "Young, get your stuff! You're getting released."

We'd all become accustomed to hearing those words when another inmate's name was called. You had mixed emotions. On one hand, you were excited for them. On the other, you wanted to knock them down and take their place.

Today was my day. As I made my way to the cage, I realized I would be going through the release process one last time. Then I saw Neyers sitting in the chair. I thought to myself *I have to deal with him one last time.* He looked up and smiled. "Well, Young." Then he looked down at a piece of paper in front of him. "You're on the list for getting out of here today. Lucky fucking guy. It's release day for you. Go ahead and have a seat in the conference room. We'll release everyone at the same time. It will be a big, fucking party. And, you'll be released at the time *I* say it should be." Of course, I should have known. Neyers wanted to make my last moments difficult. After I took my seat, three other fellas joined me, each holding a black trash bag and a duffle bag.

About fifteen minutes passed, and I was starting to go nuts. I was almost out of there. It had been only eighty-five days, but at this moment it felt like eighty-five years. When Neyers entered the door, I almost hugged him.

He looked at all four of us. "Okay, numb-nuts. You're getting released. You'll need to leave your stuff here and go back through to be processed."

I was thinking this was a joke and that we would have to try to maneuver through some kind of obstacle course. The four of us headed back into the bowels of the facility to stop at the cashier's window. The person behind the window gave us any valuables we brought in at the beginning and then instructed us to walk around the facility and back to the release pod. It was a bizarre way to exit, but I didn't care. If they had said to run five miles and then swim across a river, I would have done it.

When the cashier pushed a button, a large brown door opened. The other guys looked at me, but I was gone like I was shot from a canon. I sprinted as fast as I could all the way around the south side, which is about a half-mile to the work-release entrance. I stopped back at the work-release front door, and Neyers pushed the button to let me in. He directed me to get my stuff in the conference room. I grabbed my bags.

"Hey Young! Good luck to you," Neyers said. And then, with a strange laugh, he shouted, "See you on the other side, ha, ha!"

I paused, turned to look at his face, and said, "Thanks. I won't be back. Have a good life. God bless you." A smile hit my face as I turned to leave, and Neyers partially smiled— I swear I saw it!—like he did not want anyone to see him smile.

I walked away as fast as I possibly could to my car. This part of my journey was officially over. Thank you, God!

Coming home from my lost summer was one of the most joyous days of my life—not that I would ever consider it an accomplishment. I thought it more like survival. I had made it. I was headed home to be with my wife and kids. No more missed weekends and evenings. I would be able to put my kids to bed again. Now the last major step was ahead of us.

# CHAPTER 28

# A New Start

## January 2014

*Never be a prisoner of your past.*
*It was just a lesson, not a life sentence.*

— UNKNOWN

It was January 22, 2014, the day I picked Kay up after she served her time in jail. It was one month shy of three years since the initial search, and her eight-day/seven-night sentence would be over.

Auntie Sis arrived at the house to watch the kids. When I opened the door to greet her, we grinned at each other with pure happiness and relief. I was giddy because this major step in our journey would finally be over. Five months had passed since I was released on that beautiful August day in 2013.

Judge Monarch had been kind to me and Kay by having me serve my time last summer and Kay serve her time in January. He had said this way one of us was always home with our kids, and we were all together for Thanksgiving, Christmas, and New Year. His foresight and compassion enabled us to properly take care of our family.

Auntie Sis hurried inside. The kids were in their uniforms, ready for school, and our youngest monster, Frankie, charged full speed at her and jumped into her arms with a loud "Hello!"

Auntie Sis turned to me. "Am I late?" I don't remember whether she was or wasn't. I was so happy knowing Kay would be home soon that her sister could have been thirty minutes early or thirty minutes late. I just smiled. I hadn't slept much in anticipation of the day. All I could muster was a quick, "It's so good to see you."

Auntie Sis and Uncle Don were the kind of people you want to be around. Good souls. Good parents. Good people. Good friends. They were God-fearing people of faith. I loved them very much, even though we didn't agree on everything. Don, with his kind heart, and Auntie Sis, with her emotional connection, both understood the power of family and supporting one another no matter the circumstances. I don't know if they ever completely understood the real facts of our situation or if they even believed our story. If they were disappointed or frustrated, it never showed. They simply were there. They supported us unconditionally. And, today was no different.

As far back as I could remember, Don and Lynn were part of almost every memory I have, whether it was high school trauma, giving up our first child for adoption as teens, our wedding, trips to Napa, Hurricane Wilma, the night Kay and I turned ourselves in to the police, and business successs and failures.

While Auntie Sis rounded up the kids to take them to school, I went to the bathroom and splashed some water on my face. I looked at the mirror and actually cracked a smile when I thought about the clarity I had now. It was almost time to go.

I wandered from the bathroom, through my office, and into the front room where I looked out the window. We had moved the couch to a different spot, but I could still see out. Sitting close to where I sat the day the police did the home search, I thought about all the time I had dedicated to driving to meet lawyers, reviewing discovery material, fulfilling court proceedings, making endless phone calls, and wasting time on this or that goddamn meeting related to the court case.

Everyone has challenges—dealing with cancer or some other disease, losing a child or mate, losing a job or income, or going through a traumatic or tragic event. As I sat there, I realized that part of the reason Kay and I survived was our ability to continue functioning day to day. Very few people in our inner circle knew the depths of the emotional roller coaster we had endured. We wanted it that way. We never acted like victims, and we only wanted to move forward.

Part of you forgets for a moment the pressure you are under and then, like a bomb going off, it's back in your face. You keep telling yourself everything will be okay. You keep bullshitting yourself like some crazy person who doesn't know they're crazy, because of course that would make them sane. Kay and I had come so far—and we had a few mountains yet to climb—but we were still a family.

As I stood up, I wondered if I could climb any more. The sun was streaming through our windows, which reminded me of the light on the day of the police search. I stared out at the beautiful blue sky. It was an ocean of blue.

It was time to go, so I jumped in my car and backed out of the garage. Our neighbor James hailed me and blathered some crazy stuff about Kay. I sped away. In my rearview mirror, I saw the kids waving goodbye. Their faces showed the same anxious feeling mine did. They missed their mom.

As I waved back, I realized Kay had been gone only a short time, but it was the first time in twenty-eight years that a day had passed without us at least talking by phone. Five days ago, she told me about her initial classification step during our only call. She went in with the regular population on Wednesday. I had chosen not to visit her during the time in order to stay with the kids, and I definitely didn't want *them* to see her there. Kay's best friend and my sister were kind enough to stop by to make sure she was still breathing.

Every morning that week, the kids ask the same question: "Where's Mom?" My answer was always the same, "She's at her women's retreat." The questions would continue, and I'd answer a few and let the rest go, pretending I didn't hear. I was being aloof, but how do you tell your kids their mom is in jail?

Kay's caregiving talents didn't just apply to the grandparents; she is the best mother God ever created. Calm yet assertive, soft yet strong, kind and confident, she has that special way of treating her kids that we all wish we had.

Our kids were number one in her life, and she made sure they knew they were number one. She would take care of their needs whether she had a slight cold, a massive illness, an awful headache, or any other temporary stress or setback.

Soon we would all be reunited. I kept one eye on the road and the other on the shine of the white-capped mountains, which looked more like sticky marshmallow than snow. I went as fast as I could, finally exiting the highway and driving into the parking lot.

After I parked, I realized I was thirty minutes early to pick her up. I was so happy when Auntie Sis had arrived, I forgot to check the time. As I sat in my car, my eyes tracked up to the top of the county jail. I remembered back to my anguish a week ago when I had dropped Kay off. Now I would be going into the place one last time.

Eight days earlier, after I had left Kay at the jail, I sat in my car for about forty-five minutes, unable to leave. I could not turn the key in the ignition. I was beyond emotional, trying to find strength, talking to God, praying for my kids, and asking for a do-over. There had been no snow on the ground then, but it was still a cold day. I was numb and paralyzed as I looked over at the building, wondering where she was inside.

When I had walked Kay into the jail's drop-off area, I noticed the remodeling the county had done since my time there. Same chairs, but the walls had been painted with a fresh coat of white. The officer's desk area was also different, and two enclosed offices with doors and glass walls were behind an open area with a raised receptionist's podium.

They had called Kay's name, and we stood there holding each other. Neither of us wanted to let go. As she handed me her wedding ring, it felt like I would never see her again. I tried to insert some levity: "This will be a nice vacation for you from the madness of little ones, business projects, school-foundation tasks, and your superwoman role. Besides, you've always joked about getting in a car accident that would put you in the hospital for a week. No major injuries—just mandatory bed rest prescribed by the doctor."

My comment was more for me than her. A slight smile unfolded on her face, but neither of us could laugh. Finally we let go, and she walked through the metal detector. My eyes welled up as I watched her disappear as the steel elevator doors closed.

Now I was back in that same parking lot, but this time to pick her up and take her home. My phone started to ring, which snapped me back to the present. I looked at the phone screen and answered, "Hi, Sharon." It was Kay's attorney.

"Is she out yet?" she asked.

"No. I just parked. I'm sitting in my car in the parking lot."

"Have you talked to her?"

"I did a few days ago, on the phone, and she seemed as good as one would expect. I'm about to go get her."

"Well, good. At least this part is over."

Sharon went on, explaining what Kay's week was probably like and what to expect moving forward. She said Kay might have weird nightmares about jail or might be anxious because of false thoughts about never getting out—or of being trapped in there. It's the same feeling as being buried alive.

After we finished talking, I started walking toward the front door of the jail. I figured even though I was early, I should get in there in case they did an early release.

As I neared the door of the front lobby, all I could think was that we should have fought harder, gone to trial, taken the risk of prison, and rolled the dice. Would we have won a trial? Whoever said, "Never have regrets" was off base and silly. If you breathe, live, and take any kind of risk, you'll have regrets. When we grow, the growth is not controlled. We evolve into something. Usually, we become a better version of ourselves, but sometimes not so good. The honest person knows regrets are inevitable.

As I sat in the lobby, I questioned myself more—thinking about why we went all the way and whether I had short-changed Kay. I should have gone down with the ship, not her. That is what captains do.

There were things we could have done differently. The truth was supposed to set us free. As my old high school coach said, "You can't live or play with 'would of, could of, should of.' Putting hope in one hand and shit in the other still means you have shit."

Sales and motivational guru Bill Gouldd had a slightly different spin on it. He said, "See which hand fills up faster if you put hope in one and shit in the other."

An hour had passed since I took my seat in the lobby. I scanned the faces of the people on each side of me. It seemed like a busy day with twenty to thirty people waiting to either turn themselves in or pick someone up. Each person had a different type of expression. Most were intense, some looked bewildered, while others seemed outraged and indifferent. There were mothers with kids in tow who waited anxiously as the kids whined. There were fathers trying to hide their concern or wearing stress like a tight pair of gloves. There were a few sets of elderly folks—maybe grandparents of inmates—looking like their patience was running thin. Several of them were holding small children, probably left behind by a parent doing time. I felt for each one.

As I looked in their eyes, I saw that same fear I'd experienced on the day I turned myself in.

Many of the people waiting looked angry, and I could tell that painful feeling was still raw. As I looked in their eyes, I saw it is a tough situation when you or someone you care about serves time. I'm sure many of our friends were pissed off at us, while others felt sorry for us. Kay and I even laughed when one of the students at our kids' school started talking about a book called *The Night Dad Went to Jail.* I smiled and giggled softly to myself, thinking back to that conversation. The guilt of having my wife go to jail mostly because of my actions was overwhelming. I was the main executor, and I had let her down, along with my grandparents. I thanked God the kids were too young to know that we both had gone to jail.

At this point, ninety minutes had passed. I leapt off the uncomfortable plastic chair and started to pace the lobby. Now I was getting upset. I swiveled my head back and forth, looking out the exterior windows and then back at the elevator. I could see all the remodeling the county had done on the jail over the last five months, but the shiny elevator doors that connected the lobby to the basement holding cells was still a gateway to another world.

I kept looking up at the deputy's desk and then at the elevator, hoping to see Kay appear. The officer behind the desk started to look like a magician, who sooner or later would say "Abracadabra!" and there she would be.

I was so eager to see Kay, but they were making me wait. Damn it. One more try with the officer on duty seemed to make sense, so I approached him. He looked at me with a bemused expression and answered with a kind, but rehearsed, half-smile. "Sir, like I said, your wife will be up soon."

As I returned to my chair, I calculated the amount of time I'd spent in this lobby each week paying my work-release fees at the machine located between the inside and outside doors. It looked like a standard ATM machine, but rather than providing cash when I punched in my PIN number, it had gobbled up my dollars like Cookie Monster. I had deposited $490 each week to cover my $70 daily-release fee. Right now I had the urge to put my hand through the outside shell of that machine and pull my money out. I kept staring at that silly machine, then I headed back to find a seat. I wanted to throw something at the officer on duty. I was about to lose my shit.

Just as I sat back in the chair and rolled my eyes upward to gaze at the ceiling, the elevator door opened. Kay was standing there. I wanted to run full speed toward her, hurdle the desk, and tackle her. I imagined her meeting me on the other side and jumping into my arms—just like the end of a romantic comedy.

As she walked toward me, our eyes met. Hers sparkled like they had never done before—as if we had not seen each other for years. It sounds like a cliché, but I fell in love all over again. I held Kay so tightly she could hardly breathe. It had only been a week, but it felt like a year. I reached into my shirt pocket, took out her wedding ring and gently placed it back on her finger. It was as if we had renewed our vows in that second. We had been through so much trauma and upheaval, yet we were still together. We were strong.

"It's really you," I said. "You're here!"

"I know babe! I'm done, thank God." Tears brimmed in her eyes.

As we headed toward the door, we felt like we were the only ones in the room. We didn't say another word but kept smiling at each other. When we got to the car, she started telling me stories from her week in the facility and describing her fellow inmates. As I started to drive away, I wanted to hit the gas, as if going faster and farther from the jail might erase the entire situation from memory.

"I thought about Gram and Gramps a lot," Kay said.

"I know what you mean."

"I just know they would be proud of us—how we've handled everything. We were put in a terrible position and, yes, we made several bad choices. But we were doing our best. We never threw any of the relatives under the bus. They would be proud of us, not angry."

I nodded. "Wherever they are, they know the truth."

As she relaxed, Kay started telling me about the other women she met in jail. One of her most interesting cellmates was Grannie, who she said was the spitting image of her own mother. "Oh, Babe, you should have seen her: white hair, about the same age as my mom when she died. Grannie even had the same Southern drawl. Every day she asked me to sit by her and draw pictures with her. They gave us sheets of paper with drawings on them. Some were strange characters or large and small shapes that looked like a kid's coloring book."

She kept going. "Then there was Terri, who got a DUI while her kid was in the back seat. The child abuse charge combined with the DUI will keep her in jail for a year. I was her therapist as she explained how she ended up in jail."

"A year?!" I was shocked that the woman would be parted from a young child for so long.

"Yes. Terri was sweet, but ruined."

"Sounds like you helped some of the women."

"I did," Kay said. "So many of them just needed attention. Someone to care for them, someone to listen. They need love."

"By the way," I said, "Cheryl caught me when I opened the garage door yesterday. She said she's happy you'll be home. She's been worried about you all week."

Kay chuckled. Cheryl was our neighbor to the south. When the police searched our house, she and her husband were new to the neighborhood. As she watched them surround our house, front and back, she worried they had bought a home next to a drug dealer. She told me she had reached for the phone to dial their realtor.

"You'll get a kick out of this, too," I continued. "As I was backing out of the driveway to come get you today, James stopped me and told me what he thought happened on the day the cops searched our house. He told me he bet his wife Linda I would come out in a body bag. He was sure you had killed me. WTF?!"

Kay looked alarmed, but she was distracted by a Starbucks sign. "How about coffee? Can we stop?"

At Starbucks, I couldn't keep my hands off her. At first I stood next to her, gently rubbing her arm. As we sat down, I reached out to clasp her hands. "I'm so glad it's over."

I started to feel something amazing as I scanned the room. A true moment of enlightenment. I was finally not denying my role in what had happened. We can all justify lots of things in our lives. The truth is we make mistakes and do dumb things. Security is a delusion.

The denial I had displayed for the last three years was melting away. I told Kay, "I think the police search was payback for my willingness to take too many risks to do whatever it took to win." I paused while the milk steamer hissed. "I remember thinking I would rather be dead than unsuccessful. I would rather die at my office desk than give up my dreams."

Kay looked me in the eyes. "You're a good man," she said. "Never forget that."

I set down my black coffee. "This whole thing was because I wanted my dreams to come true no matter what. But then, at my darkest point, the light shined in." I squeezed Kay's hand. "Now that I finally know myself, I know we can evolve. We can grow and become who we were meant to be in this life."

Some people make changes when God whispers in their ear. Others respond when He gives them a firm tap on the shoulder. In some cases, when the subject (like me) is completely stubborn, a wrecking ball must smash into your life to get your attention.

The poet David Whyte says that if you want to achieve any sort of enlightenment, you must first arrange to get really tired of yourself. I was exhausted.

When we got home, I went out in the backyard by myself, stood at the fence, and looked at the incredible Rocky Mountains. I remember Gramps teaching Kay about gardening, and I looked back on the parties when Gram would sit in a chair on the pavestone and look at me with a glowing smile. She was so proud of me. Her eyes would water, and you could see she really loved me. I think of how proud I am of our journey, our story—not because of what happened, but because of how we handled it. In more than one way it was the worst nightmare imaginable. How would *you* feel if your personal life was broadcast on the five o'clock news?

The reputation I had built over twenty years was gone in seconds. At one time, I had more friends than I could count. Now most are gone. My reputation for being hardworking and helpful was ruined. People used to come to me for business advice or for support with investment-ments or other financial matters. I will never be able to serve on a board of directors again.

Yet Kay and I are better people, better parents, better mates, better friends, and better spirits because of this journey. I love Kay and the kids more now than I could ever have fathomed. And believe it or not, I thank God every day for this experience.

Someday I hope you get the chance to live like I did. I hope you get to test your love, find out who your real friends are, examine your soul, and find the incredible God Spirit that lives in each of us. On several occasions I did nearly take my own life—what a horrible thing that would have been. They say that the few people who have survived jumping off the Golden Gate Bridge knew the minute their foot started to lift off the ledge that it was a mistake. Most people don't live to tell that part. I'm so grateful I got to tell my story.

I'm still here, and through this book I hope to help people who find themselves in a difficult caregiving situation or who are teenage single parents or who are entrepreneurs caught in their own nightmare not knowing whether to quit or continue. My story, both tragic and wonderful, could be a life preserver for someone who is emotionally drowning. They want a do-over. Like me, many people keep going, following the "never give up" or "winners never quit" mottos. Like me with my billionaire dream, they have a goal they intend to achieve "at any cost." They know it does not feel right. They know it does not work, yet they keep going.

You must listen to your gut. Maybe my story can help people stop before they land in jail. I was maybe the most unlikely felon you could ever meet. I want to help others who are bending the rules because sooner or later something—or everything—tends to break. I want to step in before others lose their family and their self-esteem. Before they commit suicide.

I'll leave you with a few lines from *The Shawshank Redemption*, when Andy and Red first met and became friends. Andy said, "You look like a man who knows how to get things." And Red answered, "I'm known to locate certain things from time to time."

I located myself. The real me was always inside but buried under ego, anxiety, and self-righteousness. The old me began to die on February 9, 2011, when the police searched our house. But the new me—the real me—is here to stay, to grow, to learn, to inspire, to lead, and, most importantly, to love.

I want to apologize to Mary, Bob, Kyle, Kay, my kids, Gram, Gramps, my sister, my parents, Auntie Sis and Uncle Don, Ricardo and Toni, and to all of our family and friends. My apologies also go to our local community and to the children's foundation, and its membership, which I still hold close to my heart. I was wrong.

These days, I laugh more, joke around more, love more, and know how blessed my life is. I can be my authentic self, and I'm so grateful. I hope you find *you*; I hope you find God's love that is inside each of us.

And so it is.

As Gram always said, "Bye for now."

Thanks, Gram.

# Acknowledgments

Thank you to my wife, Kay, for helping me tell our story. I would have never finished it without your constant love and support.

My deepest appreciation to Tenae Clyne for her outstanding guidance reading the manuscript and for advising me about the story's flow.

Thanks also to my editor, Laurel Kallenbach, for her incredible work with story structure. And to Erin, Michael, and Gretchen: you helped so much by being my early reviewers.

# Reader Resources

Please visit my web site at **www.unlikelyfelon.com** for resources
and help with caregiving, choosing assisted living facilities,
estate planning, hospice, counseling, and suicide prevention.

# About the Author

W.C. Young made his mark as an entrepreneur and civic leader, helping raise more than $25 million for companies and nonprofits in his capacity as board member (serving on ten boards), volunteer, and business owner from 2000 to 2011. He helped start several companies and raised significant funds for children's organizations throughout the Denver area through his relationship with the Denver Active 20-30 Children's Foundation (where he was the top fundraiser from 2005 to 2010).

*Denver Business Journal* named Will to its prestigious 40 Under 40 Award list in 2000 and recognized one of his companies (XploreNet) as the sixth fastest-growing privately held company in Colorado during the early 2000s. The *Journal* also included him in its 2010 edition of the *Denver Business Journal's Power Book*. He was a 2011 finalist for the *Journal's* Philanthropy Day Corporate Citizen of the Year Award.

Will has authored five books and at one time lectured and trained professionals nationwide. He considers himself a professional, creative, dynamic true storyteller and speaker, making an incredible impact architecting, writing and delivering authentic stories and keynotes. He writes and records books, podcasts, plays, keynotes, movie scripts, short stories, and blog posts from his own life experiences. Will's stories move, challenge, anger, inspire, and motivate people of all ages to listen, change, laugh, cry, and look inside themselves. He's a Colorado State University graduate with a wife and four children. He coaches volleyball, basketball, and soccer. He spends his time consulting, writing, traveling, and watching his kids play sports. He believes we all deserve a second chance.